Dr Harry Cooper graduated from Sydney University Veterinary School in 1965. Since that time he has practised in Australia and in Great Britain. Today he lives with his wife Janine and their daughter Heidi on sixty-five rolling acres at Relbia in the north of Tasmania. It is both a working farm and the set for much of 'Harry's Practice'. Many of the animals seen in the series live and breed on the farm. There are four stallions at stud, an Arabian, a Welsh Section A, a riding pony and a Paint. Seven or eight foals are born each year and there are many visiting mares as well. The cattery breeds show-quality Burmese and boards up to twenty-five cats in heated runs. Cavalier King Charles spaniels and Miniature fox terriers are regularly bred also. At the present time there are thirty-one horses and foals, twenty-nine cats and kittens, twelve dogs and six pups, thirteen coloured sheep, twelve Muscovy ducks, seven Rex rabbits, three guinea pigs, almost thirty fantail pigeons, one peacock, one cockatiel and around forty colourful goldfish. The workload is constant.

Remedies & Memories

Dr Harry Cooper

Remedies & Memories

Pan Macmillan Australia

First published 2001 in Macmillan by Pan Macmillan Australia Pty Limited
St Martins Tower, 31 Market Street, Sydney

Reprinted 2001

Copyright © Dr Harry Cooper 2001

All rights reserved. No part of this book may be reproduced or
transmitted in any form or by any means, electronic or mechanical,
including photocopying, recording or by any information storage and
retrieval system, without prior permission in writing from the publisher.

National Library of Australia
cataloguing-in-publication data:

Cooper, Harry, 1944– .
Remedies & memories.
ISBN 0 7329 1107 9.

1. Cooper, Harry, 1944– – Anecdotes.
2. Veterinarians – Australia – Biography.
I. Title.

636.089092

Illustrations by Elliot Cowan

Typeset in Sabon 12/16 by Midland Typesetters
Printed in Australia by McPherson's Printing Group

*To the wind beneath my wings,
my beautiful and patient wife Janine,
and to all my children.*

Contents

Introduction		xiii
MOVING AROUND		
1	'You Can't Miss It'	3
2	Mole Creek	29
3	Gladesville Remembered	48
4	Annangrove Revisited	61
5	Horrible Hernias at Exton	66
THE BIGGEST PRACTICE IN AUSTRALIA		
6	'Dr Harry'	75
7	The Butler	85
8	TV and More TV	93
9	Essential Viewing	107
10	Crocs and 'gators	114
11	Wasps	121
AWAY FROM HOME		
12	Good Ol' USA	127
13	America Revisited	142
14	Talking to the Animals in Europe	152
15	Second Time Around	166

DOGS AND OTHER MEMORIES

16	Gone Fishin'	183
17	Car Yards	190
18	Wyong Again	196
19	In the Good Old Days	202
20	Out of the Box	207
21	Life on the Farm	212
22	Flossie Remembered	219
23	Blondie	224
24	A Long Time with Long Tails	228
25	Steve was Special	239
26	Sally	244
27	A Fishy Story	250
28	Rosie	255
29	Ebony, 'The Light of Our Life'	259

A LITTLE INDULGENCE

Poems	269

Introduction

To be asked to write another book is a rather flattering request, especially when the marks you achieved in high school English examinations left much to be desired. So, like my first book, this is not written but rather dictated to Lisa, my very patient stenographer. I have always enjoyed telling stories, and those that follow perhaps give a deeper insight into what makes our family tick. Yes, a little of this book is autobiographical. Many people have said that memory fades with the years, and that is true . . . but it never disappears completely. For a couple of these chapters I've enlisted the help of a few friends, whose recall of some events has been better than my own. To say I've enjoyed the experience is to vastly understate it. I have loved it, for in so doing, one event has lead to another and many wonderful animals have sprung to life again, if only in my words.

In our sixteen years together, Janine and I have known a great many faithful companions. Pets have galloped, waddled, run and flown through our lives, and I would like to thank the ones that are no longer with us, those we've left behind at our previous homes. At Annangrove: our horses Coco and Amber; my cow Flossie; our dogs Shandy, Kushla, Steve and Ginge; all the dogs and birds that perished in the terrible fire; and Bush Cat and Flash. At Mole Creek: Janine's favourite cat, Lisa; and

Mitchell, the Major Mitchell cockatoo. At Moltema: Benji, the wallaby we hand raised; and Cameo, the best Burmese in the world. At Glenwood Road: Tiki, a very special Doberman. Finally, in our present home: Princess, our first Welsh pony; Matilda, a very special wombat; Pixie, Heidi's first and very precious Cavalier King Charles; Rosie, our best mate; and now the light of our life, little Ebony. We miss them all.

Thanks also to the friends, past and present, whose names I have used in some stories. And apologies to those whose names have been changed to protect them from further embarrassment. Thanks also to my colleagues in the veterinary profession for their continued support of 'Harry's Practice' and the efforts Katrina and I are making towards spreading a better understanding of and relationship with animals.

Since *Anecdotes & Antidotes* was first published we have received a steady stream of letters on an almost daily basis. We appreciate your thoughts and the many stories and pictures you've sent. Don't ever give up. The animals of this earth cannot speak for themselves. We are their voice and it must be heard—long and loud!

Finally, it's the family's turn. Being a fairly easily recognisable personality brings with it more negatives than positives. Sure, one gets good seats at the theatre and a nice table at a restaurant but, on the other hand, it becomes virtually impossible to go anywhere without being approached for an autograph or advice on an ailing or misbehaving pet. For me that's all part of the job, but for the family it can be a terrific burden. So Janine and Heidi, thanks for putting up with me and my shambolic office, at home; and with the fans when we are out. In the eyes of all those animals with whom we share our home . . . you're the best.

INTRODUCTION

As I've said elsewhere, talking with God's animals is a privilege of mine. Thank you, Lord, for allowing me that honour.

Dr Harry Cooper
Relbia, Tasmania

Moving Around

1

'You Can't Miss It'

Tasmania seemed such a long way from Annangrove but as a holiday destination it had tons of appeal, so without too much thought and very little preparation—because, let's face it, when you're a busy vet you don't have much time to prepare for anything—we headed off. To make the holiday worthwhile, and something of a tax deduction as well, we decided to include a visit to the annual veterinary conference held in May that year at the Country Club Casino in Launceston. Autumn seemed like a good season to be going to Tassie: the thought of a chill in the air was enticing, and frosty mornings but bright sunny days would be a change from the parched paddocks of Sydney's northwestern suburbs. Fly-drive was the way to go, but where to stay? We decided after wading through countless pages of travel brochures that, to really get the best out of our visit, staying in historic houses and on farms would be the best option. All this was put in place before we boarded the plane to head off on a much-needed vacation.

Everything went well until we hit the airport at Launceston. The travel agent had booked a Falcon station wagon for the five of us—Janine; little Heidi, only about twelve months old; Tiffany and Russell, my two children from my first marriage; and, of course, myself. 'Sorry, we don't have any station wagons available.' Yep, my dear old mum used to say, a bad rehearsal always makes for a good performance. She knew, because she'd spent half her life in the theatre. I got the feeling straight away that this was a bad rehearsal. We couldn't find a station wagon anywhere and with the volume of luggage we had we probably needed a pantechnicon anyhow! My family never travels light; in fact, every time Janine and I embark on an overseas trip I'm forced to issue the familiar instruction: take out at least a third of everything you've put in. At Launceston there was a suitcase for every member of the entourage, not to mention all the essential baby gear and, of course, the capsule, which offered not only safe transportation but a cot for young Heidi. The gear just wasn't going to fit in your ordinary sedan; the best the rental company could do was a Fairlane. All this mucking about and carrying on wasted well over an hour of precious travelling time.

Finally, away we went, heading westwards with suitcases piled high on the back seat, children squashed uncomfortably close beside them and the boot lid held down with a trusty occy strap. Janine always drove, and quite honestly she's much better than me. With a lot of experience on dirt track speedways she can handle a car better than most women I've met, and confidence in the driver is for my money the most important thing about motoring. We bypassed Launceston and headed vaguely towards Devonport and places further west, as our accommodation bookings meant there was a schedule to keep. First stop was Deloraine.

Now, men are very different to women and I don't mean just in the physical sense. I'm talking about every which way. From my limited experience, I believe that very few of the fairer sex can pass a supermarket without pausing to buy at least one thing. Just what is the magnetic influence that these chrome and lino barns have on our ladies? It's got me. Anyhow, we were sure to need something—at least that's what I was told—and perhaps I'd better come along as well, because that something's sure to be too big for one person to carry. On recollection, it was about five to twelve when we walked in the door. By Sydney standards the store wasn't all that big, but having a youngster in the family seemed to demand a never-ending supply of paper products, nappies, tissues, you name it. The trolley was about a quarter full, we were doing well, when suddenly a bell rang. 'It's the fire alarm,' I exclaimed, 'we'd better get out.' But no one seemed to be rushing and after thirty seconds or so the bell stopped, so we resumed our browsing, only to be confronted by this large streak of a man walking up the aisle with his arms outstretched in crucifix form.

'You'll have to go,' he said.

'There's a fire?' says me.

'No, we're closing.'

'You've got to be joking, it's only twelve o'clock.'

'Yes, we close at twelve, everything closes at twelve.'

He was right, everything closed—thank heavens the nappies were in the first aisle. Welcome to the old Tassie on a Saturday! Happily, we can report that things have changed since that first experience some thirteen years ago; in fact, in many places shops are now open seven days a week. Anyhow, on with the story.

The road out of Deloraine climbed a hill and to the left there was a turnoff to Mole Creek and a wildlife park. We were mad keen animal people, so why not sneak out and have a look? The drive out was a pretty one, through rolling hills of rich red soil and past lush green paddocks with sheep and cattle, their bellies strained to bursting, grazing happily in the midday sun. Tall leafless poplars, along with ancient blackwoods looking very much like evergreen English oaks, punctuated the skyline. A small railway line crossed the road as if to bring some sense of modernity to the whole postcard scene, but the trains only passed twice a day; well, twice a night actually. There were other turnoffs, too—to the local smokehouse for a feed of smoked eel, salmon or trout, or to Dairy Plains which sounded so picturesque—but time did not permit.

The road wound on to the top of a broad chain of hills and slid lazily down a gradual descent into Chudleigh. Behind the farmlands the majestic peaks of the Western Tiers strove to pluck lazy clouds from the crystal sky. The scene was just splendiferous. Set right on an intersection, there wasn't much to this hamlet: Loones Hardware and Farm Supplies, with a few ancient bowsers out the front, a general store, half a dozen houses and a showground, and that was about it. On that particular morning the scene outside Loones—I couldn't call it a service station, so let's call it a garage—lives with me to this day. The pumps were old, really old, the type that had glass cylinders sitting up on top, and the hoses weren't rubber, they were a sort of woven canvas. Nothing seemed to be electrical. The fuel was pumped up into the glass cylinder by hand, and then, under the influence of gravity, allowed to flow into the car's tank once the desired amount had been measured. And the cars! I don't think there were any vehicles post-1955. Strike me, even the people around them seemed to be dressed in something from a World War Two salvage store. 'Gee,' I said to Janine, 'it looks like a set from "The Sullivans". Who in God's name would ever want to live around here?' Should have kept your mouth shut, Harry. We ended up buying a place just seven k's down the road.

The wildlife park, or Trowana as it is now called, was easy

to find, with its huge concrete monolith, somewhat resembling an obese Tasmanian devil, leering out from the right-hand side of the road, its whiskers bent and twisted by would-be vandals and its paintwork in need of some restoration. We swung up the hill for a look around. It was cold, damn cold, but the chance to see a Tasmanian devil close up was worth it. There *were* devils, quite a few of them, plus wombats, wallabies and a thing I hadn't encountered before called a quoll. More about all these guys later. The park's atmosphere has changed little since then. It was laid out in a very natural way with gravel paths and stone enclosures. We felt very close to the animals we'd come to see; in fact, in years ahead I was to come very close to many of them. We spent an hour there and then got back on the road again.

The drive out of Mole Creek over the Union Bridge, an historic wooden structure spanning the Mersey River, and then up over the mountain and down into Sheffield, is a must. We passed magnificent towering gums—their tattered bark hanging in huge tresses from their blue-white trunks—dense forests, pine plantations, open grazing country and some truly breathtaking views. Little pockets of green farmland nestled between the hills, each punctuated by ancient homesteads with their barns now resembling parallelograms rather than the vertical structures they once were. But they were still standing—a monument to the engineering skills, or perhaps lack of them, that our early farmers employed. It was a pretty place, darn pretty. At the road's end was Sheffield, the town of murals, and even back in those days a visit was quite a fantastic thing. Many of the shop walls were decorated on the outside by scenes. The blacksmith toiled over his forge in one mural and around the next corner was a huge panorama of Gustav

Wiendorfer and his hut, the bush animals quiet and serene, lying peacefully around his fire. He was the man who first promoted the Cradle Mountain region in 1910. Great stuff!

Just time for a little snack, then out of town en route to our first overnight stay.

We were booked in at a place called Monateric. It was almost at the very northwestern edge of Tassie, quite an ambitious drive for our first day, when you think about it. Many of the roads were narrow and winding. The directions were very specific: It's on the right-hand side, exactly seven kilometres out of the town, and you can't miss it 'cos there's a sign on the road. Well, it was getting dark by now, we were hungry and the kids were whingeing—all those sorts of things that happen when you can't find somewhere to stop. We drove up and down the road half a dozen times and there was no way we could find a sign, a turnoff or anything. Where was the damn place? No mobile phone, so back into town and ring up. Sure enough, the directions were the same, we must be stupid, how could you miss it? Still no luck.

We called into a neighbouring farm. 'Yes,' said the farmer, 'you can't miss it. It's about a kilometre back on the left-hand side, on the old road.'

'On the what?' I said.

'On the old road,' he said.

'No one told us about the old road,' said I.

'Oh, the new road's only been open two days,' said he.

'Fair dinkum, where is the old road?'

'Oh, it's about two hundred metres north of the new road. No one drives on the old one anymore, but that's where you'll find the place.'

Sure enough, we did. It was now late, dark and very cold,

getting on for seven-thirty. We'd said we'd be there at five and everyone was anxious, particularly the people who owned the farm, as they were on their way out for dinner.

The greeting was as warm and full of genuine concern as I have come to expect on this little island. They were really worried that something had gone wrong with us, or the car, or something. 'Come in, it's cosy inside'—and it was—'have you eaten?'

No way, we've been driving up and down the road for an hour looking for your joint. It was a huge rambling house, with massive walls, high ceilings, monstrous rooms and an atmosphere that said, I've been here a long, long time and I'll be here for a lot longer, too. The kids thought it was magic.

'We're on our way out,' said the lady of the house, 'but come into the kitchen and I'll show you where everything is. There are two egg and bacon pies in the fridge, the fuel stove's behind you, bread and milk and all that sort of stuff are in the other fridge. You can heat them up easily in the oven. If you need more wood, it's just outside the door and if your husband enjoys reading, he's welcome to use my hubby's den. We're off now, see you in the morning.'

We stood there looking at each other, my wife and I, for more than a minute without exchanging one word. 'Would you believe it,' I said, 'these are people we've never met and they've gone out and left their home and all their belongings in the care of five total strangers.' I couldn't comprehend it but that's the way it was, and what fabulous people they were. My mum was right, the performance was going to be great.

The pies were heated, the tea made, children fed, washed and bedded, and we both sat down in the den in front of a roaring open fire reading from some of the huge array of ancient leatherbound volumes that crammed the shelves of the study. Boy, I thought, if this is your first experience of Tasmania, how does it get any better than this? Next morning, a typical farm breakfast—porridge, bacon and eggs. So much, you wondered whether you'd need to eat for the rest of the day. The kids spent the morning riding around in a trailer behind the farm tractor, feeding calves, milking cows and running berserk on the beach, as the property was right on the northern coastline, a great place. It was almost lunchtime when we headed off to look at Stanley and then the Nut, a most peculiar little island, if you could call it that—really just a mini-mountain perched out in the sea, which you got to by cable car. One of the locals used to graze his sheep up there. It was a novelty. Everything was terribly green, but then again it should be as they get a lot of rain in this area, well over 1500 millimetres a year. I remember the houses in Stanley as being small, brightly coloured cottages, all crammed closely together, many offering various cottage crafts and pretty little gardens already hoping that spring would soon be in the air.

A quick bite to eat, then off to Cradle Mountain.

The road into what's probably one of the most beautiful places in the world is in fact quite the opposite. To me, it is best described as an arboreal graveyard. How sad, how very, very sad. For kilometre after kilometre the road is lined by nothing but dead trees—not the whole tree, just the base with its roots now exposed because some man-made machine has seen fit to exhume them from their earthly refuge. There they lie, mostly on their sides, greying skeletal remains of former forest giants. Cut down like some young soldier in his prime. A stark reminder of just how bad forestry practices can be. I've often wished since that those responsible for desecrating such an area on so important a tourist route could be made to go and right their wrongs, clean up the mess, replant the area and make it live once again.

We'd booked a cabin in which to stay. It was part of the Cradle Mountain Lodge complex. There was a central building, the lodge proper, with dining facilities, etc. Away from this, scattered around in the nearby bushland, were any number of small cabins, some of them built side by side and each catering for up to half a dozen people. They were mainly of timber and tall, too, with high pitched roofs designed to shed the snow that often fell in the area. Inside they were warm and inviting with a glass-fronted wood heater that we soon had roaring away. There was no shortage of labour to bring the wood in from the stack just outside the front door. The kids always enjoyed doing something different and, boy, was this different. As the sun began to set, the animals started to appear outside. Little hairy paddymelons (local wallabies of the area) hopped around without any fear of man. A wombat waddled slowly past the back window of the cabin, much to the enjoyment of us all. He stopped, started grazing on what was pretty meagre-looking grass, looked up occasionally as if to say, 'I hope you guys are enjoying this', and then waddled on a bit, head down, and grazed again. By now there must have been more than a dozen animals of different species moving slowly backwards and forwards right outside our window. Fantastic stuff! A flash of black and a Tassie devil raced across the landscape. We'd seen it all.

'Make sure you keep the door closed when you get back,' said our host after dinner.

MOVING AROUND

'Why's that?' we asked.

'Oh,' he said, 'you'll get overrun with possums if you don't.'

How do you think animal people like us respond to something like that? Couldn't wait to get back and leave the door open, could we! What happened next is one of the most incredible things I think we've ever witnessed. It's bad news to feed our native animals bread, cakes and the like, but fruit is fine. We had a ready supply of apples, carrots and dried fruit—we'd been down this road before. Back in the cabin we stoked up the fire and got young Heidi ready for bed. They'd provided a big wooden cot which we set up in the middle of the floor. She was bathed and dressed and laid down for the night. The other two kids were sleeping in double-decker bunks against one wall. Janine and I were in the double bed. I guess we'd only been inside some ten minutes or so, when there was an obvious scratching on the front door. 'They're here,' shouted the kids and rushed to open the door. It's always a problem with children that they rush, and very often that's the reason why animals become frightened and also bite.

It's difficult to restrain the enthusiasm of youth, but not when you're my wife! 'Stop,' she commanded, and they did. 'Sit down, be quiet, I'll let them in.' The visitors didn't need much of an invitation. The door opened to welcome three brushtail possums, all sitting there on their bottoms, little front feet held up in front of their faces, very much like Oliver Twist with his bowl, asking for more. In they came, soon finding the apple and the carrot on the floor. Within five minutes, I think, there were nearly a dozen in there. Animals are naturally inquisitive and it didn't take them long to check out Heidi's cot. It's doubtful that she was very much bigger than they were, lying there in her bed while three possums played tag round and round the wooden rungs of her cot. We laughed, she giggled and it's a pretty fair bet that the possums giggled too. It was just the greatest animal experience you could ever hope for. By now we had a couple of wallabies as well—the word was out, tucker's on at the Coopers'. But, you know, it feels good to get so close to wild animals. That they would trust you is an even greater privilege. The whole experience lasted well over an hour. We ran out of food and, when we did, they ran out the door. It took another hour to clean up the mess, but somehow it didn't really matter.

Next morning it was the turn of the birds and the wallabies (again), who managed to find a few crumbs on the verandah before we headed off for a walk around the lake. With a youngster of Heidi's age you don't do too much walking. It was pretty nippy first thing in the morning, but beautiful too. With the mist rising off the water and that magnificent mountain behind, it was quite a place.

Next stop Strahan, and a cruise on the Gordon and Franklin Rivers. Not a lot of animal life around here except for the two crayfish we managed to consume for lunch—delicious. An overnight stay, and then through Queenstown and down to Hobart. Battery Point is a beautiful historic area set on the top of a small hill with a commanding view of the Derwent estuary. It has wonderful little English-style cottages and even its own unique 'circus'—a small circular road with a park at its centre, just like the old country had. Wonderful antique shops, good restaurants, magnificent walking and an atmosphere that transports you back in time.

It was often awkward to bath young Heidi. The place in which we stayed had a pretty ordinary sort of bathroom, but peculiarly enough it had a handbasin of fairly large proportions in the bedroom—yeah, sounds crazy, but that's the way it was. A huge mirror was positioned behind the basin. There's little doubt that Heidi enjoyed her bath here better than anywhere else, as she could see herself in the mirror while her mum got on with the job at hand. We used to joke later that she'd been bathed in every handbasin in Tasmania.

As far as animals go, the rest of the trip was pretty uneventful. We all remember the visit we made to Port Arthur before it became so infamous, and a trip up the east coast where we stayed overnight in Swansea. The stone cottages here, although built in recent times, looked ancient in their architecture. Inside ours, the decor was super. A large, open-plan living space with a bedroom on one side and over this a mezzanine with another bedroom and an ascending staircase. Stone and timber construction, a huge open fireplace and polished timber floors. They'd provided a cot for Heidi. It was stunning. It had to be an antique, with iron railings and uprights painted pristine white, polished brass knobs, and the most magnificent bed linen you would wish to see—all blue and white, hand embroidered and arranged in such a way that you'd expect to find it in some high-class magazine. It was just too good to sleep in and the trouble was that Heidi was too small for it; she'd have fallen out between the bars. We laid her on top of the sheets and took some photos, just sensational. In fact, the whole cabin was full of handmade and hand-decorated this and that. It had a magnificent country feel and to this day we are still amazed that such places seem to escape the vandalism that is now so widespread in Australia. People have lost respect and so, in turn, other people have lost trust.

Sunday afternoon saw us back in Launceston.

'Room for Cooper,' I said to the clerk behind the desk at the Country Club Casino.

'No reservation in that name,' he replied.

'You're joking.'

'No, nothing here by that name.'

'Hang on a minute, I've got a receipt in my pocket.' I fumbled through my wallet and found the receipt. 'Here you go.'

'Uh huh,' he laughed, 'you're with the veterinary conference. That's been cancelled.'

'You're joking,' I stammered again.

'Yeah, they cancelled it on Thursday.'

Total disbelief was the only feeling I could muster.

'You wouldn't believe it,' I told Janine at the car. 'The darn thing's cancelled.'

'How could it be cancelled?' she said. 'It's a damn conference, isn't it?'

'Yeah, but they cancelled it on Thursday.'

'Well, what are we going to do?'

There was nowhere else to stay, the older kids had to go back to Sydney that afternoon—and we were sort of stuck, weren't we.

They managed to organise a room for us for the night, and it was nice but a good deal more expensive than the rate negotiated for the veterinary conference. Still, the food was good and there were plenty of animals around. You see, the joint has its very own tribe of ducks. There are ducks everywhere, mostly white ones, with the odd coloured one thrown in as well, and they have pride of place as they wander all around the buildings and the golf course. Traffic gives way, golfers give way. Ducks rule, OK!

Two phone calls to the conference organiser's office finally elicited a reply. 'Oh, well, the leading speaker was sick—sorry, it was his wife—he cancelled, so we called it off.'

'Thanks for telling me! What a joke. And thanks for telling the other half dozen blokes who are in the same boat as I am.'

'Oh, we couldn't contact you because you were touring.'

'But you could have left a note in the pigeon hole, couldn't you?'

'Oh, I s'pose we could've, but we guessed you'd work it out.'

'Well, I've got news for you,' I said. 'I've worked it out. Get the President to give me a ring when he gets in.'

You know, he never did. I sent him a letter when we got back to Sydney. He rang me then, with much the same attitude that his secretary had shown a week or two earlier. I figure that if you treat people like that, you don't really need them, and I expressed that opinion to him and resigned from the association forthwith. I've never rejoined. The individual *is* important. And there were enough experienced vets registered for that conference to have carried on in the absence of the leading speaker. How sad? Too bad!

Now it was just the three of us. Too damn expensive to stay in town, so what are we going to do? No point in going home, we've paid for a fortnight. We'd better enjoy it. Time to go back to Deloraine, where the country was as pretty as any we'd seen. So we headed there after having a good look around Launceston first. I won't describe the overnight accommodation, except to say that it was as cold as the welcome, disappointing and perhaps an anti-climax after many wonderful places. The weather had turned a bit nasty and we decided to look around the town. After all, it was a workday, so there was a fair chance that Deloraine's shops would stay open till five! Just by chance, we happened to park outside a real estate agent's. Fate has a strange way of dealing a hand. What drags you to a window full of houses and farms for sale? Is it just curiosity? I don't know. But you always go and have a look, don't you. Sure enough, there in the window, down in one corner, was a farm and, boy, didn't it look a picture! It was starting to rain quite heavily, the wind was icy and, after all, it was warm and dry inside the agent's office. So why don't we have a look? It'll help pass the time.

In less than an hour, we were walking around Mt Pleasant. Situated just outside Deloraine, with a long drive leading off the highway into the property, it did look a treat in spite of the shocking weather. The big avenue of naked poplars led to two houses, one in need of some repairs but the other neat and comfortable. Wonderful facilities for horses, with stables, barns, yards and centre laneways. For a couple of animal lovers, the place was a walk-up start. But what a swine of a day, the wind lashing our faces, rain pelting down—it was straight from the Antarctic. The owner, Dick McCarthy, was intent on showing us as much as he could in the time, and the agent was waxing lyrical about this and that as we walked around.

It's funny, you know. We've bought quite a few houses over the last few years and some agents are downright stupid. Just think about it. You walk into the house and they say, straight away, this is the kitchen. Of course it's the kitchen—you don't find a refrigerator in the toilet, do you? And so it goes on: this is the bedroom, etc, etc. It's like a boring monotone learnt from some salesman's manual. If you dare to interrupt, he immediately goes back to the beginning and starts all over again. My guess is that even Dick was getting sick of our agent, because he said, 'Why don't you come back tomorrow, just you and the wife?'

'Fair dinkum?' I said.

'Yeah, have a bit of lunch with us.'

We couldn't believe this. He wants to sell us a farm and he's inviting us to lunch. Wow, things sure are different in Tassie! Anyway, the weather might be better tomorrow, we thought. But it wasn't.

The lunch was a real country roast and we were able to have a more relaxed look around the place. It's still to this day one of the most picturesque properties we've seen. The auction was in about another three weeks and we got a bit of an idea about what sort of money might buy Mt Pleasant. Back at home in Annangrove we started to think how good things might be, down south. I guess it took no more than a couple of nights for us to decide we'd put in a bid on the property. Were we really serious at the time? Hard to say, we hadn't even valued our own place and I suppose in hindsight we might have been stuck with bridging finance had we been successful. We weren't. We were about $20 000 short of the successful bid. Sometimes I'm halfway sorry. The place would have been about the right size. We would have converted the older house into a vet clinic and lived quite comfortably in the other. But, then again, it was some forty minutes from the airport and the centre of Launceston and it's doubtful whether it would have fitted into the current scheme of things. Still, it's hard to drive past without a sigh. It has changed hands at least three times since then.

When a seed is planted, if the conditions are right it will start to germinate. Ours was a slow grower, but a grower nevertheless, and as time went by we found ourselves more and more determined that we'd move.

One of the most frequently asked questions is: Why did you move to Tasmania? There were lots of reasons, I guess. It's hard to go through a divorce and live in the same area as your ex. For me it was, anyhow, and for Janine as well. Too many memories, too many problems. Then there was the pace of life. It was getting busier and busier, and somehow the velvet green of Tasmania seemed like greener pastures to us.

Over the next twelve months or so, we made numerous trips up and down, always looking around the Deloraine area—staying in Launceston, travelling out by car, viewing one or two properties. Putting in a bid on occasions or crossing them off the list. We had, after a while, such a marvellous mental map of the whole district, not to mention our numerous grid maps, that you only had to say the name of a property and we knew where it was and what it looked like. Time went by with no success for us. My workload in Sydney grew ever heavier. Then things came to a head one afternoon.

Annangrove Veterinary Clinic's consulting hours were 9.00 a.m. till 12 noon and 4.00 p.m. till 6.00 p.m., but for that read 8.00 till 1.00 and 4.00 till 8.00, because that's the way it really panned out. It was 3.45 on a Thursday when the nurse and I lifted a dog from the table and carried her out into the kennels to recover. I was just looking around the carpark, when out of nowhere it hit me. Back inside I washed my hands, for what must have been the umpteenth time that day, then walked through my X-ray room and into the house. I sat on the lounge, put my hands up to my face and began to cry. Don't know how much more of this I can take, I thought—there's another hour's surgery out there, my first two clients are waiting and each one's got an extra dog. By the time things are finished tonight it'll be close to nine o'clock. I was at the end of my rope, and Janine knew it. She put the property on the market on Friday.

It failed to sell at auction. But by February of the next year it did, and for the right sort of money. The problem now was to find a place to live in in Tasmania. Down we went again; the pressure was really on. Real estate is a funny game; sometimes you can be lucky but more often than not, you can't. Janine had found a little property that sounded ideal for a veterinary clinic. It was halfway between Deloraine and Westbury, an old house that could easily be demolished, with a surgery built on the same site. Right on the main road, it looked the goods. We even found a house nearby, really close, as a matter of fact, but only on ten acres and we were looking for something bigger than that. Hang it all, we were coming to Tasmania to go farming. We'd even spent time at the Sheep and Wool Congress in Tassie and the field days up at Nyngan. We were really prepared! But we'd have to settle for the ten acres, or so it seemed. Then out of the blue came 'The Den'. An historical six hundred acre farm on the banks of the River Mersey at Mole Creek. This was what we were looking for, this would do us. This was the place just down the road from the Chudleigh Garage that we'd joked about on our first visit.

The clients at the clinic couldn't understand why the family was so keen to go. At the beginning there were doubts, there had to be, it was a huge undertaking. As time went by, our confidence grew. A map of Tasmania replaced the calendar that hung in the corner of the consulting room. It was fun to point out the places of interest and where the various properties were. You'll be back, was the familiar retort. No, we'll never be back. The more it was said, the more determined the family became to make it work, and we were to need all this determination, as things turned out. So we started on what was to be the biggest journey of our lives, a journey that would uproot a lifetime in Sydney and half a lifetime in Annangrove, a journey that would divide a family and a journey that would send us broke.

Packing up the goods that you've collected over a lifetime is difficult enough. Moving animals from one side of the country to another is hard. But when it's over water it's really hard. There were quite a few horses. Hussar, our little Welsh Section A stallion, needed special care. Our three Welsh mares, all in foal, also needed kid-glove treatment. On top of that, there were two Australian Pony fillies and three other ponies that were just for riding. The huge horse transporter pulled up late one grey, miserable afternoon. It was to go ahead with the horses and we were to meet in Tassie in three days' time. We felt pretty sick in the stomach as, one at a time, we loaded our trusting friends into the dark bowels of that immense trailer. Animals don't really know what's ahead of them and I wondered if they had any idea that they were about to be relocated to a place so vastly different to the one they knew. Janine was in tears as the huge door on the side of the float swung closed and the semi and its load rolled slowly down the drive out of view into the night.

'Gee, I hope they'll be all right,' she said.

'They'll be fine.' The words were an automatic response. Inside I shared the same concern that she did. Some of the horses had never been in such a large vehicle, none had been on a journey like this. What about injury? What about travel sickness? What about colic? Ah . . . so many questions, but we had enough to occupy our minds because next day it was our turn to leave.

We planned to travel in convoy. Yours truly had a big blue Ford F100 with a canopy on the back, and the huge trailer we'd gone to so much trouble to have made. It was stacked full of piping, chainwire, dog kennels, portable yards, you name it. All the sort of stuff that was going to help us re-establish our animal farm in that new home. Heaven knows what the load weighed, but the trailer had a wire cage that extended almost two metres above the floor and it was chock-a-block. Janine had a trusty V8 Statesman and she had the horse float on behind as well. It, too, was crammed with all the extra bits and pieces that you need when you have as many animals as we do. I don't think we could've fitted in another thing. Add all this to the fact that for the last four days the removalists had been tearing our home apart and now they had gone, and everything we treasured in life except for our remaining animals was on its way to Tassie. Oh, boy!

That night the skies opened. It rained with a vengeance. It continued to rain all night and all the next day. The trailers were parked at the back of the property and when it came time to hitch up and pull them out they got bogged. Both of them! Up to the axles in thick pink clay. You wouldn't believe it. And still the rain came down and all the local creeks were flooding. We had to be away by ten that morning, but it was now nearly four in the afternoon. Even the neighbour with his tractor couldn't shift things. He got bogged too!

Eighty budgies in cages sat patiently in the back of the F100. Nearly fifteen cats sat waiting in the now deserted cattery for their turn to be loaded and carted off. Even the dogs seemed perplexed at what was going on. The geese and the ducks, confined to their crates since six in the morning, were now more than anxious to stretch their wings. But Noah's Ark refused to float, it couldn't get out of the clay. What do you do?

My best mate, Nev from over the road, walked down the drive. 'Hello, Harold, having a spot of bother?' Neville was a master of understatement.

'Ah, mate,' I said, 'nothing's going right.'

I think he could see that and Neville, God bless him, always seemed to have a calm head in a crisis—and this was one very wet crisis.

'You're just not gonna get out are you, old mate,' he said with a clear grasp of the obvious. 'Let's have a cup of tea.'

What good a cup of tea would do I had no idea, but we had one anyhow. It must have been a pretty forlorn sight. We three adults sat in the deserted family room. Little Heidi was sound asleep on the Spanish tiles of the near-new kitchen that we'd soon leave forever, clutching her favourite bear, those beautiful blonde locks resting on her own little blue suitcase. She, too, was totally exhausted by the sheer magnitude of the task.

Drinking from one of the cups we'd left out to use on the trip, Neville finally broke the silence. 'Let's face it,' he said, 'you're not gonna get out of here today.'

'But they're moving in tomorrow,' we groaned as one.

'And so are you,' he said. 'With us, till you get things sorted out.'

In life you meet many people. Some you call your friends, some you just get on with, and some you can't stand. I would venture to say that through my life there have been plenty of friends, but I wonder just how many good friends, honestly. Friends who would do for you what this man was doing for me—not just for me, but for my whole family. Neville remains to this day one of my few true friends.

It really only took a few phone calls to sort things out. Our buyers were happy enough to leave things pretty much as we had them. The birds went back into the aviary, the cats to the cattery, the ducks and geese to their runs and the dogs to their kennels. Life returned to normal. Each day it was just a matter of walking over the road and tending our livestock as if we still owned the place. We spent a week with Neville and his wife, while the boat crossing was rebooked and the furniture directed to our new address. Luckily there were friends in the vicinity, and also Janine's parents who had moved before us, who could be there when things arrived. So, a week to the day, we started off again. The whole assemblage really did look like a modern day Noah's Ark. The birds in their show boxes packed neatly at the front of the F100's tray, the cats behind them in their cages, and poultry in the front of the horse float where they could do less damage than anywhere else. You can imagine what ducks are like: they aren't exactly trainable when it comes to toilet habits. Each of us had two dogs sitting in the front with us. I had Rosie and a little mini foxie we called Minnie. Janine had Pixie, Heidi's Cavalier, and another mini foxie—and Heidi herself, of course.

The trip had been planned carefully, taking two days to get to Melbourne, with an overnight stop at Tarcutta. We'd been there once before on the way back from a horse-buying expedition in Victoria. It was a great place with motel accommodation and loose boxes for the horses. The boxes were great for all the poultry too and, of course, the dogs. The cats were a different proposition. We'd brought our own portable accommodation for them and the budgies; well, they just sat where they were. The next day dawned bright and sunny, there was no rush, we had plenty of time. Not a problem in the world till we got to just the other side of Albury. Suddenly, bang! One of the tyres blew on my tandem trailer. Now, the problem in all likelihood, was twofold. Firstly, the trailer was pretty overloaded and, secondly, we'd gone from a cold, wet and windy start in Sydney to a really stinking hot day in Albury and the tyre pressures may have been too high. So very slowly and very carefully, we turned around and went back to Albury. The tyre was changed. Not only that but we bought a spare rim and tyre that we could pop on if needed. Insurance, it pays to have insurance. Away we went again, got half the distance and bang! A second tyre, same wheel. No worries, we'll put on the spare. We jacked her up, went to change wheels . . . you wouldn't believe it. It was the wrong rim! We're stuck. Janine drives back into Albury in a hurry, the bloke comes flying out with a new tyre and rim. My jack collapses. He gets his jack installed and changes the wheel. No spare now, and no time either. Got to go, and go quickly.

We always reckoned the best way to get around Melbourne traffic and down to the quay to catch the boat was via Bell Street. But . . . when you get to the top of Bell Street at five o'clock, and you know the boat sails at six, you also know that you're not going to make it. And, try as we might, we didn't. It was Friday afternoon, we'd have needed a chopper to get there on time. Two vehicles and their trailers drove onto the quay only to see the boat sailing off into the distance. Janine had to be physically restrained. She wanted to jump in and swim after it. 'Why didn't they wait?' she screamed. 'Why didn't they wait?' Well, trying to explain calmly that we were just two people and that boats don't wait for you wasn't easy.

Moving Around

We must have looked a pretty sad and sorry sight, as the chill wind blew in from the sea—two people standing together arm in arm watching the ferry sail out of the bay. Ours were the only two vehicles parked on the jetty. It was a cold, lonely, miserable place and we felt the same. Heidi slept through the whole episode.

Neville wasn't here, but it was time for clear thought. OK, let's find the office and rebook for the next sailing, if we'll fit on it. Monday was Anzac Day, but thank heavens she was sailing on Sunday. We transferred our booking to then. But what do you do with a whole heap of animals that can't sleep in a motel with you and, for sure, can't sleep in a car either—all except the budgies, they'd be sweet. They were show birds and used to sitting in their little black and white, wire-fronted boxes for days at a time. So find a motel, find kennels, out with the Yellow Pages, on to the phone. Yes, we board cats but not dogs; no, we only board dogs; no, we can't help you with anything else; no, sorry, full up, it's a holiday weekend, you know. But finally, paydirt! We've always liked the area around Ferntree Gully, and sure enough the local veterinary clinic was able to board the cats. (Funnily enough I was there only recently. They had an open day at which I was the guest speaker and main attraction. There was a bit of déjà vu about the visit, though neither of the original vets now owned the place.) The dogs and the poultry ended up a long way further out of town, but they seemed happy enough when we visited them the next morning. The bloke running the joint had a great sense of humour. He thought it was hilarious that we'd missed the boat twice! Dogs are very adaptable animals, they like people rather than places and just to see us roll up the next day was all they really wanted. And what about the ducks? Well,

'You Can't Miss It'

I think all they're interested in is what ends up in their crop. So we stayed Friday, and Saturday night. Had a bit of a half-hearted look around the Dandenongs and arrived with all the animals collected again in plenty of time for the sailing on Sunday.

As we anticipated, there was in fact a bit of an altercation on the wharf over the amount of stuff we were dragging behind the two vehicles, but we'd paid on size not on weight and we were in the middle of the queue so they were not able to do anything about it anyway. When you travelled on the old ferry, the dogs and cats were offloaded and installed in huge trailers that looked like the old-fashioned sheep wagons they used on the railways. These were loaded in last thing, to be first off the next morning. I don't know whose faces were the saddest, the animals or ours, as we shut the doors behind them and prayed they'd still be OK in the morning. The good thing was that you could come and check on them once during the night, and the staff were pretty attentive and would alert you if anything went wrong. It didn't.

Sometimes you gotta be in luck, and we were! Because of the size of the vehicles and the height of the trailers, we were parked in one particular area on the bottom deck, very close to the animals. The ferry docked, the ramp came down. We got the green light and away our convoy went, out on the wharf. Good to have your feet on solid ground at last. This was our new home. The little tractor towed out the two animal transporters and parked them in the shade. We raced over to reclaim all our pets (all except the budgies and the ducks which had stayed in the vehicles) and loaded them up quickly. At that very moment there was a sudden massive groan and the creaking of metal. The ramp on the front of the ferry was going up! Horns were tooting! Everything stopped! Only six vehicles and the animals had got off. It was an industrial dispute, something to do with bringing cargo over on a public holiday, or whatever. Anyhow, we were off and on our way—the rest of them didn't get off until two o'clock that afternoon. Clearing quarantine was a breeze. I think the smell of the ducks and the horse float circumvented any further investigation by the officer in charge. Hell, they stank!

Mole Creek was only about an hour from Devonport. The welcoming committee was there in numbers: Janine's parents, the Vineys from Dairy Plains and a couple of other friends from the budgie world as well. There's so much excitement and so much anticipation that it's only when everyone goes and you sit there, husband, wife, baby daughter and your dogs, that you suddenly wonder, what have I done? Have I made the right decision? Will we really make a go of things? These were the thoughts that whirled around in my head and would continue to do so for many months. We had left a big home on a little farm in New South Wales for a little house on a big farm in Tasmania, and the adjustment was always going to be hard.

2

Mole Creek

There was just so much stuff, boxes and cartons absolutely everywhere. We had to shift things around a little to enable us to walk from one room to another. There was an overflow of cartons in the outside laundry, in the half-falling-down garage and in what doubled as a sort of shed and workroom. Where to begin, that was the question—trying to make things that fitted in a forty-five-square house fit in one that was barely eighteen squares. It took a while, but gradually everything found its place and items that didn't stayed piled in their cartons out in the shed, where the rats and the mice had a veritable feast. Our new house was a concrete block establishment, of which there were many around the area, but it wasn't the house that interested us so much, rather the land that surrounded it. The weather was good and we didn't expect things to get really cold for another month or two, so we spent time exploring every nook and cranny of the place.

'The Den' had a lot of history. Owned by the Lee family for generations, it was the hub of the major cattle drives each spring, which saw many hundreds herded slowly along well-established tracks to the mountain pastures of the central plateau. These drives were an annual event and the grazing of the lush warm pastures, with the sweet grasses that only the altitude of the mountains can produce, turned off cattle which were the envy of many a farmer. The drive started on the lower paddocks which bordered the Mersey River. The mobs moved slowly over the river at a spot where polished rounded rocks provided an easy ford. Stockmen urged them onwards up the familiar paths trodden by many thousands before them. We could imagine all of this as we stood on the hill and gazed down at the property that was now ours. The beautiful Mersey wending its way past the grassy paddocks, rolling and racing over the rocks and fallen trees. The huge swimming hole that had witnessed at least one drowning. The remnants of the first dwelling ever established on the place—still defiantly struggling against the elements, the ancient chimney was all that remained. For the early farming wives there had been no electricity, no heating and no refrigeration. And often no contact with another white woman for periods of twelve months or more.

The river flats encompassed over a hundred and fifty acres of magnificent grazing. Of interest right at one end of the rocky hill that separated our house and its surrounding land from this beautiful oasis was our very own limestone cave, complete with stalactites, stalagmites, a shawl, and a small river running through the middle. On occasions you might even catch a platypus curled up half asleep on a shelf a hundred metres or so inside. It was a truly romantic property. But romance and scenery don't pay the bills. We were farmers now and it was time to get to work. It's then you notice that a lot of things aren't quite the way they're supposed to be. The fences were falling down, the sheep yards wouldn't hold anything weighing more than five kilos. The gates, where they did exist, couldn't be closed or fell off when you tried to move them. The shearing shed looked as if it had been built around Captain Cook's time. The paddocks were infested with that wretched weed, ragwort.

In short, the place was collapsing around us and we needed to inject a lot of time, a lot of work and a lot of money to make things function.

We'll get some sheep, that'll start things rolling, we decided. Janine wanted some cattle too, so we went looking. A local stock agent turned up a mob of eight hundred Polwarths from somewhere down in the midlands, that's sort of halfway between Launceston and Hobart. The fella had a good reputation and he reckoned they were a good buy. So down we went to have a squiz. Now, I've been to conferences and conventions, read books and spoken to people and I really thought I knew what sheep and farming were all about. How could you be so wrong? From a distance the sheep looked to be in good nick. Polwarths are a breed developed from our merinos, they produce really good wool and these ewes (females to you lot) had beautiful snowy white fleeces and what I perceived to be fairly fine wool. At least I got that bit right. We changed our gumboots so that we wouldn't carry any disease onto the property, and by that I mean foot-rot, not foot and mouth.

It was all pretty impressive. The agent seemed to know what he was doing as we drafted off fifty or so and put them through a race so they could be examined close at hand. The ewes were certainly in good condition, you could tell that by feeling for the last couple of ribs, just where they leave the backbone. If you can feel a big dip between the ribs, then there's not much fat there and they're pretty poor. These guys, or should I say girls, had very little dip at all. Their feet were good and their mouths were good—if you've got a crook mouth you can't eat, so what we were looking for here was their teeth. Sheep, cattle and that sort of animal have incisor (front) teeth only on their lower jaw. On the upper jaw at the front is a hard pad. We call it the dental pad and they bite against that to graze. Of course, they also have other teeth at the back, on both jaws. But if you are a sheep and you're missing one of your incisors, you've got a broken mouth and your future's pretty grim, because you can't nip the grass off properly. There were no broken mouths here, but they were all full mouths (you age sheep by the number of permanent incisor teeth on the lower jaw, and this meant they were more than four years old). The mob was also in lamb to Suffolk rams. Suffolk rams? I'd only seen pictures of them. They were a British breed, or so I thought, big tall sheep with black faces and black feet. Experience would tell me that they were well suited to the wet conditions at Mole Creek and to many other areas on this wonderful island.

Janine and I discussed the purchase. She was for buying only half. Go on, I said, we can handle the lot. I should have listened! I didn't. The eight hundred head duly arrived. It really was exciting to see them jumping and scrambling off the huge double-decker trailers that had trucked them up from their far drier home. It didn't take them more than a minute to get their heads down and start to graze, but it took us a day or two to realise that our fence repairs were totally inadequate. The sheep would get out, get through, jump over, push past and, quite frankly, totally ignore any sort of fence. It was almost as though they wandered at will all over the entire property. Still, they did eat the grass and they appeared to do well.

Buying some cattle would have to wait—the horses needed sorting out first. All except the little Welsh stallion had arrived some ten days before us and were happily grazing away in the home paddock next to the house, totally oblivious to the fact that we had at last arrived. Not one scratch, not one problem. After all that distance. Fantastic! Hats off to Vern, the carrier, who had brought them over from Melbourne, because he was the one with a bit of a problem—what was he to do with the Welsh stallion. He couldn't just be turned out to run with the mares, he was a boy and he knew it! The little guy was safely stabled at one of the local thoroughbred training facilities in Spreyton. He had a stable all to himself and, typical of all stallions and Welsh ones in particular, he took over the joint within an hour or two of his arrival. Hussar was the major attraction of the whole establishment and after trackwork in the morning he'd be turned out in one of the day yards for an hour or two's recreation.

We went to pick him up with the horse float because by now we had at least one decent paddock which was capable of holding him. It had an electric fence.

'Geez, he's a bit hard in the mouth,' said Aunty, whose relations ran the establishment.

'What do you mean?' asked Janine.

'Well, he's a bit hard to do anything with, isn't he?'

'No,' said my darling wife, 'he's an angel, you can do anything with him.'

'I meant when I'm on him.'

'What do you mean, *on* him?' said Janine.

'Well, I rode him two or three times.'

'Congratulations,' said Janine, 'you're the first person that's ever been on his back.' Now, no offence, but Aunty isn't small.

After that amusing episode we became good friends with the family. At home on 'The Den', Hussar thought himself top of the pops once again and he'd trot round the paddock, head held high, those little legs going for all they were worth in that beautiful Welsh action. What a great sight that little grey pony made!

Buying cattle is a bit different and Janine was keen on a breed called Murray Greys. They're very much an Australian icon, derived no doubt from the Aberdeen Angus, but with a beautiful soft grey coat. We read of a clearing sale at Paradise— I kid you not, the place is called Paradise. It's just off the road between Mole Creek and Sheffield, set in a deep valley with a river winding its way through its midst. One look and you can understand how the place got its name. We had a budget, of course. The problem was that other people had bigger budgets. Nevertheless, we bid and got eight heifers (young females that haven't had a calf). Once the livestock at the property had been sold it was time for the furniture, household possessions, machinery and heaven knows what else to be sold. Clearing sales are very sad, at least I think so. When a farm has been sold, everything else is cleared from the property. It always seems so final, and so complete. Not a fullstop, rather an exclamation mark. You can always pick the owners—they're the ones with the sad expression on their faces.

Our heifers were settled on the river flats. They did well, but you don't make money out of heifers until you get them in calf. To buy a bull to service eight heifers is a little extravagant, but we were lucky enough to lease a young bull from a reputable breeder in the state. We insured the bull and he got to work and, boy, did he get to work! There's something about a bull running with a group of heifers that looks so natural and so real. Most of the time he keeps to himself, but when necessary he follows the girl around as if she's the most valuable thing in the world, snorting and bellowing, and making enough noise to put the majority of females right off the subject he has in mind.

We now set about trying to upgrade things, even employing

the services of a farm adviser. His usual advice was to stack on more, spend more and work harder. I noticed, though, that he didn't have too many calluses on his hands. We fenced, we fertilised, we worked our bottoms off. The kilos fell off too, I even got under seventy-five kilos, and that was for the first time since I was eighteen. Boy, were we fit. At the same time we started work on our surgery at Exton, demolished the old house, trucked in masses of crushed rock, poured the slab (just three of us), and built a new clinic. The aim was to have the lot completed by the end of the year. It was a simple building, six metres wide, twenty metres long, with a corridor right down the middle and a huge roller door at one end and a waiting room at the front. Everyone commented that it was much bigger than it looked. It was set well back off the road with a large parking area up front and a sign by the roadside: Exton Veterinary Clinic. It's still there today, but it sells tractors, not veterinary medicine.

Nothing quite prepares you for your first winter in Tasmania, and it was both a surprise and a burden for us. If memory serves me correctly, it was about mid-May and it was *very* cold. Walking outside the back door and looking to the south, where the mighty rocks that formed the Western Tiers rose from the fertile plains, was quite a sight. They were blanketed in snow. It ran from their tops more than two-thirds of the way down to the floor of the massive valley in which we lived. The air was sharp and crisp, diamond clear and tasted of freshness. 'Come out here,' I yelled, 'come out here. You'll never see anything more beautiful than this.' It was breathtaking. It was also bloody freezing in our pyjamas and bare feet.

Winter looks pretty, but when the snow comes the frosts follow, the grass stops growing and food gets scarce on the ground. Eight hundred sheep don't eat all that much, but eight hundred pregnant sheep do! Most of my farming experience had been on the north coast of New South Wales, where frosts and sub-zero temperatures were unheard of. It was a land where grass and pasture grew all year round. Not so down here. Come winter, everything stops. There was very little feed left on the ground, certainly not enough for eight hundred sheep, for although the property boasted nearly six hundred acres, quite a deal of it was uncleared, and very hilly and rocky. Pregnant sheep without enough food get pregnancy toxaemia. When they get that they die—and they did, quite a few of them. We bought in feed, but we couldn't manage to keep up enough to prevent the losses.

Experience is a hard teacher, inexperience is an even harder one, but we learnt. Every day saw us carting in huge round bales of hay bought from a neighbouring property, plus oats and pellets from the local agents. These big bales took a lot of handling and, really, we didn't have the equipment. To get the sheep to eat them was a matter of unrolling the bales in the opposite way to the way they'd been rolled up. You need a gentle slope. You simply undo all the string holding things together, then lever the bale to the back of the old ute and roll it off. The success of this whole adventure depends on two things. Firstly, get the bale round the right way or it just rolls down the hill and looks back up at you. Secondly, don't pick too steep a hill or the bale gets up so much pace that it fails to unroll at all and ends up in the river. It's happened to us! As well, we put up a silo to hold the oats and would feed the sheep from a special trailer with a little door on the back, leaving a long thin line as we drove along the paddock. The sheep would come from everywhere to feed on the concentrates, standing side by side or opposite one another, intent on getting every last grain. We managed to get most of them through the winter.

By early August the ewes had started lambing and, if we thought we'd worked hard before, then we were about to get our second wind. Twice a day we'd be out, first before the sun came up to try and rescue any lambs that may have been born the night before and abandoned by their mothers, or twins that may have been separated or ewes that were in trouble. Hats off to my wife, she worked like a man, pulling lambs from straining ewes, and catching and holding orphaned lambs. It was hard physical stuff and we'd be at it again in the afternoon before the cold set in. Our dog Rosie was terrific. 'Get hold of her' and she would know just which sheep you meant. Without any sort of training she would fly in and grab the sheep by the wool around the neck. Half the time she'd throw it on the ground and hold it until you had time to race in, scruff (grab hold of) it and do whatever had to be done. We'd patrol quietly around the outside of the mob in the old Toyota flat tray we'd bought at the Paradise clearing sale. It was the best investment we ever made and well worth the three thousand dollars we'd paid for it. Rosie was up on the back, Heidi between us, Janine driving and me diving in and out when necessary. Times were tough, the work was hard, but it was good to be together as a family.

By the end of lambing we had something like a dozen orphaned lambs. They lived, to start with, in the house in front of the fire, until they were strong enough to handle the cold outside. After that they initially took up residence in the house yard and were fed on a milk formula at least twice a day. We've still got the first lamb we ever hand reared. Her name is Mary, she still answers to the name and, yes, she's still got a great mouth, for all her twelve years. But lambing wasn't easy, it was bloody hard.

When we'd first moved in it took only a day or so to notice that this black, kelpie-cross male from down the road kept sauntering into our place, peeing on the garden, the back door and the dogs' kennels, and manuring wherever he deemed fit. Janine got a bit peeved by all of this and was determined to front the local neighbour about the total lack of control they had over the dog. Not only that, we were concerned about what damage the dog might do to the horses. Having made her objections known, Janine walked back home and for a time the dog seemed to stay away. I suggested that we should make a point of at least meeting our neighbours and introducing ourselves, so that we could be of help if needed—after all, there was a vet around. Gee, everyone knew who I was even in those days: I was the regular on 'Burke's Backyard'.

Dot Howe lived just over the creek. Although you could see her house from our bedroom window, you needed to walk over the bridge and go via the roadway to get there. She became our best friend, not just her but her children and their children as well, and they remain that way today. But back then . . . 'I don't like that new woman very much,' she said to her husband after Janine's visit to complain about the dog. These days we laugh, all of us, about this first encounter. It turns out that she didn't like the dog much either. Roger was his name. Dot and the kids helped us with the lambing. It was school holidays and they all enjoyed every bit of it. Without them we'd never have got through the work. They knew the area, they knew sheep, they knew what to do. Dot had her own sheep, but only about twenty; we had the best part of eight hundred.

In life you learn things not taught at university, things you only learn from practical people who have to make things work. Dot showed us how to foster lambs. Finding a ewe with a dead lamb, she would scruff the mum and the dead youngster, bring them into the shed and proceed to skin the dead baby. She'd form the skin into a type of jacket. It was incredible. Keeping two holes in front for the forelegs and two behind, she'd then simply fit the skin over the body of the orphan and, lo and behold, mum would accept the lamb straight away. I'd never seen it done before, but it worked every time. It really looked funny, this little lamb pushing under its newfound mum, waggling two tails, not one, as the ewe gently urged her pride and joy further under that woolly belly toward the milk bar. Problem was, it took time and with the number of ewes we had we just couldn't keep up with the work. Polwarth ewes were poor mothers—everyone told us that. It's a shame they hadn't told us before we bought them. A ewe would lie down to lamb, pop it out and then simply get up and walk away. It was so frustrating. All sorts of devices were invented to try and hobble the ewe so that she couldn't get away and the lamb would have a chance of bonding with her. Tying one leg to a fence post seemed to be the best solution, but even that failed on occasion. We learnt a lot during that first lambing. Too many sheep, not enough feed, not enough facilities and not enough helpers! It wouldn't happen again.

In the middle of all this I had to track off to Sydney.

I had an obligation to speak at a conference in the Hunter Valley in New South Wales. Janine said, 'Why don't you go up a day or two earlier and spend some time with your mum?' She was on her own, living next door to my brother—Dad had passed away many years earlier. So I spent a whole day with Mum talking about times past, things we'd done as a family and things she'd done in her life in theatre and at our home. Then it was time to go, up to Newcastle for the weekend. But totally out of the blue . . . bingo! The airline pilots' strike. The strike that was to cripple Australia. And how in heaven's name was I going to get home? Melbourne to Launceston is one hell of a swim and Janine, with the help of a girlfriend and Dot, was handling the lambing. Somehow, a few of us managed to scrounge a lift back to Sydney. My brother had organised both a rental car for the drive to Melbourne and a flight over Bass Strait in a Bumblebee—one of those little twin engine, putt-putt type planes.

It was to be a long drive through the night. I said my farewells, shook my brother's hand and hugged Mum. 'You know, I don't think I'll ever see you again,' she said, 'give me another hug.'

'Don't be so bloody silly,' I said, but hug her again I did, of course.

Driving away, watching them all waving furiously in my rearview mirror as the car accelerated up the hill, so often down which as a child I'd raced a billycart, my mother's words burned into me. The trip to Melbourne was pretty eventful—a great car this one, every time you put your foot on the brakes the lights went out. But we made it. I abandoned the damn thing in the carpark of the motel the next morning, caught a taxi out to the airport first thing, rang the rental company and told them what they could do with the car, and jumped on the plane. Made it home and slotted right back into things again.

Spring comes out of nowhere. The grass grows almost

overnight and suddenly the whole place is covered with so much grass it's unbelievable. The lambs grew and thrived, as did the sheep. We put wethers on the hills. The mares foaled—three filly foals. Everything did wonderfully well, everything seemed so fantastic. I can well understand why the English poets used to rave so much about the advent of springtime after the winter and the sleeping, as it were. Anything that was living springs to life once again. We felt good, we felt happy, life was great. Then my brother rang. Mum had fallen and broken her hip. When you're eighty years old and stooped like our mother was, walking is always difficult. She had tripped on a mat and the inevitable happened. 'Don't come up, mate, she's OK. We'll look after her,' my brother said. Thank heavens he was just next door to her. Ten days down the track I reckoned she was all right. It's funny when you're a vet, you know the risks involved with operations. Something like 80 per cent of people undergoing this sort of surgery at this age used to develop an embolus (a clot) which in most cases killed them. But if they survived ten days they should be all right.

Next morning the phone rang. 'Mate, Mum's got a clot. Can you get here?' A thousand thanks to the bloke who got off the plane so I could get on. I flew out of Devonport up to Sydney and took a taxi to Royal North Shore Hospital.

I was twenty minutes too late.

Grieving is something very personal to each of us; everyone deals with death in their own special way. My brother had been with her to the end, now it was my turn. I sat for two hours, did a lot of talking and listened, and imagined I heard a reply. To me those two hours and the day spent with her a few months earlier were very special. Gee, I'm glad I did it, but it was really Janine's idea. Mum was laid to rest next to Dad in the Northern Suburbs Lawn Cemetery. We buried her with a red rose, a programme from her days with J C Williamson and a bottle of 4711 cologne. It's nice to go back often and talk to them both, it's not crazy. When you love someone you never really lose them.

A couple of days were spent in the old family home, with my brother and I reminiscing about our childhood, and clearing out the possessions of eighty years. I kept very little, some jewellery for my girls, some programmes from the theatre, some coins and a thousand memories of parents who did so much for their children.

But home again with my family was where I belonged. We were really enjoying things and even decided on purchasing some Suffolks and breeding a few of our own. We just liked them, they were nice sheep. As the weather warmed it was time for shearing, weaning and haymaking. We cut thousands of bales of hay. It's hard work carting in all those bales, but the smell of fresh hay and the satisfaction at the end of a hard day is reward enough. Next year we'd be well prepared.

Prices were good, wool worth around thirteen dollars a kilo, and our lambs sold on computer to Melbourne for over thirty-five dollars a head. How good is this, we thought. The clinic was up and going and I'd spend my weeks working away there. Daylight saving made life far more livable and we couldn't have been happier.

Soon we had been farming in Tassie for almost two years. Christmas was rapidly approaching. Heidi was to participate in the nativity play at her local kindergarten, and Janine had been super-busy organising the costume for this very special occasion—the stage debut of our daughter. It was only a bit part, I know, but as her parents we were pretty excited.

Rehearsals began some weeks beforehand and by the end of the last term of the school year all was in readiness. The leading players seemed to know what was required of them, the crib was all organised and enough tame animals had been seconded to make the scene very realistic.

Heidi was not at all nervous. No first-night tension for this girl. Her mum was there putting the finishing touches to the costume. It fitted beautifully. She was a shining white little angel, her long blonde locks shimmering in the dull lights backstage. Within minutes there were, as the Bible says, 'a whole group of angels'—half a dozen little four and five year olds, all just waiting to make their debut too.

Everything was in readiness; the only items left to add were the wings. Slowly Janine strapped on her flimsy creations. By golly, our little girl looked pretty, with those beautiful angel wings and that sparkling white dress. A picture of innocence and beauty. A few anxious steps around backstage just to test things out. It all looked good to me. Mum was as proud as any mother could be. Suddenly, a frown spread across the face of our little angel as she looked over each shoulder at her mother's ornate creations, now anchored firmly to the middle of her back. Tears started to flow.

'What's up, little one?' a very anxious dad inquired.

'Daddy, I'm scared.'

'Why, sweetheart, why are you scared? There's nothing to be frightened of.'

'But Daddy, I am . . . What do I do when I get out there and I start to fly like an angel? I've never flown with wings before.'

To have the faith, the hope, the love, the trust and the beliefs of a child would be a wonderful gift for every one of us.

But good times never last long.

Within eighteen months things fell apart. Wool prices crashed to around three dollars a kilo. Lambs fell to twelve or fifteen dollars a head. All those Polwarth ewes which cost around eighteen dollars at the start were now worth twenty cents, if you could get them to the abattoirs—and it cost more than that to get them there. We shot four hundred sheep. This was the sheep cull Australia had to have, or so they said. It was, in hindsight, a dreadful mistake. The old girls had been mustered the night before. We'd drafted off the best of the flock to one side, they could have another lamb. But not this old lot, they'd done their job for us. Larry, a friend, came around to help me. Two rifles, several boxes of ammunition, a big hole dug by a front-end loader down on the riverbank. Bang! Bang! After the first dozen or so you couldn't look them in the face. If you did you'd recognise the old girl with one twisted horn—she'd had twins every year, but no more. Bang, she was gone, and with her my very will to carry on. Bang, and another went. Bang, another. One after the other they fell around us. We had to shoot them behind the head, in the back of the neck, we just couldn't look at them anymore. How do you dispose of animals that have been so good to you over the years? They don't understand; it's not their fault, it's not your fault either. It's the economy, it's the government—and most of those in authority would never have experienced for themselves what we were going through right now.

Stuff the bloody government! This was the recession Australia had to have. Only two years before, banks were knocking on your door virtually throwing money at you, now they wanted it back. Interest was 22 per cent, plus another 2 per cent if you were slow to pay. We'd lashed out, improved the farm, built sheds, fixed fences, fertilised, sprayed, cleared weeds, made it go. And what thanks for all of this? None. Governments don't care, they never do. It seems to me that politicians should spend a couple of years working, I mean physically working, doing the sort of thing we were doing, before they're even allowed to stand for election. It might very well alter the way they feel about things. The recession we had to have culled many good people from the land. It culled us too. We sold up and got out.

We couldn't go to the clearing sale, couldn't look people in the face. It was too much. We'd failed. We'd given it a go and we'd failed. There were lots of reasons, I suppose: inexperience, bad guidance, overcapitalisation. But you should never look back, though it's hard to look forward with the seat out of your pants. We left 'The Den' with our horses, our dogs, our ducks and our cats; the rest we sold. The budgies were over at a mate's place. It would be many years before time and circumstance could allow this hobby to flourish again. It hasn't happened yet. Dot still has some of our sheep, a bunch of Border Merino ewes we bought in towards the end—wonderful sheep, they'd 'twin like stink' (have lots of lambs). I've a video of the whole property, shot by one of the guys from 'Burke's Backyard'. Janine reckons it's the most expensive video ever made. That farm cost us twenty years of our life. It was a beautiful place, but beauty doesn't pay the bills. Janine used to say that Walt Disney went broke twice and eventually became a millionaire. There is absolutely no risk that her attitude over the entire thing kept the whole family going.

Renting was foreign to us, we'd always strived to own everything we had. But then, you have to make the best of the circumstances. The dogs lived in our portable yards or were chained to their kennels. The cats were housed in sheds built for the purpose or inside several rooms of our house. The ducks had a great time on the pond and the horses were agisted on a property near our friend Geoff Elmer. We lived like this for the best part of eighteen months. It wasn't ideal but it did give us some breathing space. We ventured back to Sydney and looked around the areas in which we used to live. No way could we afford to buy back in there, and anything further out was pretty disastrous as well. We had to stay where we were, at Moltema. There were no other options!

Heidi was just six years old when one day we were heading towards her local school in Deloraine. I used to make a habit of dropping her off on the way to my veterinary clinic at Exton, another ten minutes or so out of town. It was a beautiful Tasmanian spring morning. Everything around us was bursting into life. The countryside was a picture postcard. This was truly one of the prettiest spots in the world.

'Dad,' she said.

'Yes, darling.'

'Dad, do you know much about dinosaurs?'

'Oh, a little,' I replied. At the time dinosaurs were all the rage on television and every second shop was carrying some sort of promotion about these prehistoric animals. Funnily enough, kids seemed absolutely enthralled with them.

'Well, Dad . . . do you know why all the dinosaurs died?'

'No one knows for certain but there are a couple of theories. Do you know what a theory is?'

'Yes, Dad, I know what they are.' She was all attention and looking at me in a very studious fashion.

The little Magna station wagon pulled up outside her school. I switched off the ignition and turned to talk to her directly.

'Well,' I began, 'the first theory is that a huge meteor—that's a gigantic rock from outer space—collided with the earth and caused such an enormous cloud of dust to form that the light and warmth from the sun were blocked out. And the earth became very, very cold without the sun's heat. All the land became covered with ice. The dinosaurs couldn't live in the cold and they all died.'

She thought about this for quite a while, and obviously had no intention of getting out of the car till our conversation was finished.

'What's the other theory, Daddy?'

'Well, darling, some people think that all the dinosaurs were struck down with a terrible disease, and they died.'

Heidi thought long and hard about this last theory. I could see the wheels turning in the brain of my six year old.

Then, after what must have been a full minute of contemplation, she said, 'Dad, what a shame you weren't alive then, you might have been able to save them.'

Such is the faith of a child in the ability of her father. My heart sang!

3

Gladesville Remembered

Time to go back a bit. After graduation at the end of 1965, and a short sojourn on the mid-north coast of New South Wales practising with dairy cattle, the day had come to make some positive decisions about the rest of my life. Practice in Taree was all very well, but you don't need to be Einstein to realise that cattle are bigger than you are. And as the facilities there were so primitive, all the trump cards in the deck seemed to be in someone else's hands. Having been trampled, walked on, flattened, squashed, butted, licked and generally shat upon by nearly every cow in the district, it seemed obvious that something of a smaller nature would be more to my liking. So Gladesville Veterinary Clinic looked to be a pretty good bet—after all, as a young student I'd spent plenty of time cleaning out kennels and generally observing what went on in that practice. Perry and Bob offered me the job, I accepted, and joined the staff.

Back in those days the actual clinical side of things was conducted in an old house converted for the purpose, with a big waiting room tacked on the front and a very famous mural painted on its wall. (Fair dinkum, the problems that arose when we tried to paint over it or in any way deface the damn thing made life pretty miserable. The clients loved it, and when it finally did go with the advent of the new building we never heard the end of it!) Next door was a similar old house that served as a pathology laboratory and a manufacturing plant for a large number of animal-related products that Perry had on the go. All of this was overseen by Paul, a somewhat suspicious and very nervous character, we all thought. You know, the pseudo-scientific, mad professor type—that was him. He wore glasses and used to ride a pushbike!

You walked through the waiting room, past the office and the two consulting rooms, continued out the back door, down the steps, down the driveway, into what was a two car garage with a central dividing wall. This served as the surgery and the kennel block. Norm, one of our vets, lived on the premises in two or three rooms at the back of the house. These constant treks backwards and forwards were something of a worry, for there was often the risk of a dog or cat escaping while being conveyed between the two buildings. And if it was a dog then Plan A would immediately be put into action. This needed two or three runners and the mini-van, a little panel van which was used as a pet ambulance and general conveyor of anything that needed to be conveyed somewhere.

Two or three of us would pile in the back, with a nurse usually sitting in front watching for the escapee. We're off! Turn left down here. Then right. The van would race up to be almost level with the dog. The back door would fly open and one chaser would be away, 'dog catcher' in hand. Each chaser was only good for a two or three hundred metre sprint. (Over the years it's become increasingly obvious that dogs are fitter than we are, and they damn well know it.) The van would continue on as a sort of a hazer for the dog till the chaser collapsed from exhaustion, and was replaced by a fitter and fresher member of the team. The changeover took only a matter of seconds. The whole thing was down to a fine art and

I can't remember our ever not recovering an escapee. Since those days, anyone who comes to work in my clinic is told, 'The last person who lost an animal on me is still looking for it.' Yeah, it only takes about ten seconds to sink in.

With Norm living close at hand, he was on duty to handle much of the out-of-hours work—taking the strain off the rest of us, myself in particular, who lived a fair bit further afield. He had a Labrador pup and used to race greyhounds as well. An incredibly lucky bloke, always touched by good fortune. I reckon somehow his runners won in slow times at great odds, whereas ours always got beaten in a photo finish in the best time of the day. Anyhow, that's the way it goes. There were always greyhounds in and out of the practice and in the early days a lot of horse work as well. This took us to Randwick, Canterbury, Rosehill and Warwick Farm, which made getting from one end of the practice to the other on a busy day, to treat an emergency, something of an effort. Horse work was enjoyable and something that Perry had cultivated over the years. We had good clients—the Inghams, and Stan Fox when he was alive. When you're handling horses, so much depends on the guy holding the head. If you feel confidence in him then you can handle just about anything with the horse.

There were plenty of disasters, like a trotter that collided with a milk cart one day outside Harold Park. The cart sliced the horse from behind the elbow right into the groin and lifted the skin off like a doona from a bed. It look more than two hours to pull the skin back together, but trotters are tough and the thing healed pretty well. Traffic accidents were usually very nasty, and until the installation of the overpass at Rosehill, bolting horses and speeding cars made for a terrible mess—and, of course, there's the poor jockey as well. It's a risky business, thoroughbreds are accidents waiting to happen. Like high-performance cars, they're constantly wound up and can unwind with devastating consequences at just the wrong time. Even on the racetrack, collisions with running rails and with track equipment often mean unbelievable damage and, regrettably, the destruction of the horse. Many people ask why a horse has to be destroyed after injuring a leg severely. Well, with a horse standing on only three legs, the leg opposite the lame leg will simply collapse under the extra weight. It's so sad for this to happen to such a magnificent animal.

There were some highs, like the day I was about to slide a stomach tube up the left nostril of this big horse. These were the days before worm paste in easy dose syringes. It was a matter of passing the tube up the nostril, over the back of the throat and making absolutely sure that it descended the oesophagus and not the windpipe. There were lots of little tests for this. You had a careful listen and often the noise of a gurgling stomach filtered back up the drenching tube. If it was breathing you could hear, then you had to pull it out and start again. The best test of all was to simply watch it go down, and in most horses that was easy to see on the left side of the neck. 'We just knocked back well over a million for this bloke,' the nonchalant strapper beside me observed. The horse was Tulloch! God, I pulled the tube out and sat down for ten minutes. Get yourself together, Harry, I thought, it's just another darned horse.

And if you adopt that attitude you get the job done right first time.

A major part of every weekend was the Saturday afternoon stint at the races. The practice did two jobs. We were an integral part of the swab team that collected urine and saliva specimens from horses after racing, and we also provided a vet to attend the barrier for several clubs. Swabbing was something I'd been a part of ever since my student days. The team was a group of regulars and as well as doing a thorough job we were intent on having a good time. Swabbing, even back in those days, was of course undertaken to detect drugs that might be present in the horse. Everything was done in a thorough and well-documented manner. The whole process was observed and signed for by strappers and trainers. We collected saliva using a sponge soaked in acetic acid (like vinegar—you know how it makes your mouth water just thinking about it), and in those days we collected urine in a nice stainless pot rinsed out with a cleansing solution and held under the horse at the end of a long pole. Horses usually pee on cue. You just whistle. Not just any whistle, a special sort of whistle, very much like the sound of those old Swanee whistles. But some horses were stubborn. You'd turn on a tap, trickle water down over their back, run the hose over the floor, even stand in the corner and have a pee yourself. But if you didn't collect what you wanted, then it was a trip back home with the horse and a very late finish to your day.

There was the odd ale after the day's work was over, and as long as everything peed in the pot then a visit to the old Baccarat Club up at Kings Cross (the BC) was usually a must, if everyone felt inclined. As a young bloke, money was pretty precious to me. The first paycheck went on a surfboard, the second on my little black bag (the one I still use today) and the rest would be needed to register and run the car, all those sorts of things, and of course entertain my girlfriend as well. Over the years I'd always declined invitations to press on at the club, but this particular day, well, why not? Twenty dollars would do, no more than that. For the life of me, I had no idea what baccarat was all about. Sure, it was gambling, but from time to time I'd have a punt at the races anyhow, and as long as you were careful and put a limit on things, you couldn't lose too much money.

There was quite a crowd of us there, even a couple of girls from the office. Just watch, have a look and see how the whole thing works, even ask a few questions; that was the advice and it was good. After half an hour or so, things started to fall into place. Have a go, I thought to myself. Split the twenty into ten twos, when you've lost that, go home. It's not my object here to describe how the game works, but basically you bet with or against the 'bank'. Who wins or loses depends on the fall of the cards. Back then you folded the banknotes lengthwise, which was easy in the days when they weren't plastic, and you threw them across the table like gliding a paper aeroplane.

The table is busy, stacks of people standing round, money going everywhere. How do they keep track? Throw in my two dollars. Win! Put in four dollars (less the 10 per cent, not GST but for the dealer). Win! Bet again. Win! Bet again. Win! Sixteen straight winning bets; over four thousand dollars in my hand. I'm shaking. I'm terrified. Everybody at the table is following me. 'Stop now,' says Perry. 'Stop and have a break.' Wow, I've never seen so much cash in my life. It's in pockets, it's everywhere, even inside my shirt. I have a cup of coffee and take time to relax. 'Put a fair bit of it away, mate,' says a shadowy figure standing close by. Good advice, and I do—just leaving out one thousand dollars, whew! Watch a bloke come in, have two bets of two thousand dollars each, lose the lot and walk out the door. Now's the time to have one last try. Bet five hundred. Lose. Wait another couple of hands. Bet the other five. Lose. Time to go, still with well over three thousand dollars, all from one lousy little two dollar bill.

Getting home was a worry. With all this cash, how on earth was a young fella going to make it back without getting mugged?

The old EH station wagon was parked not too far down the road. I glanced up and down the street as I stepped through the dimly lit doorway, and then ran. Ran like billyo, jumped in the car, locked the doors and went like the clappers. Outside the family home there was time to count the money again by the light of the street lamp. Never told Mum or Dad. Did tell the girlfriend, but not how much—got to keep some things to yourself. The money sure did help when the old Holden finally spat the dummy! And that reminds me of another story.

Many years later, in the midst of a consultation, the tale of getting home from the club was repeated. 'Funny, ya know, I was there,' the client said. 'And you'd have got out all right and into your car. From then on, it was up to you. But we always make sure the winner gets to his car.' A comforting thought. The guy saying this was the same bloke who'd told me to hang on to my loot. He was the 'bouncer' at the club and ended up a great mate. It was sad when he passed away, and work interstate kept me from the funeral. 'That's the longest time I've ever spent on my knees,' a friend who'd gone to it related. 'But then, there was a lot of repair work to be done, I suppose.'

Down in Melbourne they had pretty good budgerigars, and one particular weekend a major breeder was having an auction sale. Well, not quite an auction, more a sale by tender. This was a chance to get some really good-quality birds, but the airfare was a little out of reach. Driving seemed the best alternative. Down on Friday (my day off), sale on Saturday, back on Sunday. The old car had a set of fog lamps fitted just above the front bumper and I thought they might be needed on the trip home, that Sunday afternoon, as the sun was already well below the horizon. A peculiar yellow glow gradually appeared on the roadway in front of the car. Didn't remember switching on the foggers, but reached down to flick them off. They were off! Looked in the rearview mirror, and there along the mountainside was a column of smoke following my damn car. Pulled up in one heck of a hurry. The orange light was flickering. Looked underneath, the universal and the back of the gearbox were on fire. Put it out. Limped into Holbrook.

Monday morning, repairs were under way; had to use a secondhand tailshaft and a reconditioned rear gearbox. Well, it *was* an old car. By Monday afternoon, after the coldest night in living memory at the local motel, on the road again. But no more than fifty kilometres up the highway—you'd better believe it—we were on fire again. It says something for the old EH that she finally made it back home to Lane Cove. Driving at no more than thirty or forty kilometres an hour made for a very long trip, and more than one driveway attendant was taken aback when the cost of the transmission fluid was more than the cost of the petrol. The 'race' at the back of the gearbox had welded itself totally to the extension shaft leading to the universal. That secondhand tailshaft was obviously bent and had thrown the whole transmission into disarray. NRMA sorted out the whole legal mess and the repair bill was refunded. But that was it. The old girl got the shove not long after. Somehow the forty or so budgies travelling happily along in their wire-fronted cage seemed totally oblivious to the whole exercise. And that's about the only time I've missed a day at work.

Sorry, I keep running off the rails. Back at Gladesville it was hard for four or five blokes not to get up to the odd trick or two. Poor old Norm. Courtship is really difficult when someone has stuffed a pound or two of rotting prawn shells under the back seat of your car. Or worse still, some stinking bandage from an unbelievably infected wound has been rolled up and shoved behind the dashboard. Even worse, a potato up the exhaust pipe or some other putrid material strapped to the exhaust manifold. All our clerical staff were female and, of an evening, part-timers would take over from the day girls. There were usually two of them and they alternated evenings so work would interfere as little as possible with their social life. One was Sally, who spoke with a lisp. She'd been everywhere, she'd done everything. There was nothing Sally hadn't seen or experienced. She was good at everything, she kept telling us. The temptation was too much.

Now, birds had always been a major focus of interest at the clinic, but not all birds recover from treatment. This particular galah, a wild one, was hit by a car. Unfortunately, it didn't survive.

'Why don't we?' said Norm, just out of devilment.
'D'you reckon?' I said.
'Yeah, mate, let's try it.'
It seemed a terrible thing to do, but by now every vet in the establishment and most of the other staff were totally sick of Sally's bragging. The bird was plucked, gutted, beheaded,

befooted and arranged on a plate—the best of Norm's crockery—with salad vegetables. Covered by a thin transparent film of Glad Wrap, it sat looking invitingly appetising on the top shelf of his refrigerator, just where Sally was bound to put the snack that she brought in each night.

'This looks good,' she said that evening. It sure did.

'Wild duck,' says Norm.

'Ever eaten wild duck?' I asked.

Of course she had, she loved it and, yes, she'd love to try a piece of this one. Producing a number twenty scalpel blade, I shaved a thin slice from the leg.

'It's the tastiest part,' she told us. The darned thing took a bit of chewing. 'I think you guys could've cooked it a little longer,' she remarked.

'Try the breast,' urged Norm. I cut a slice from there.

'Oh, this is better.'

'Really?' said Norm.

'Yes, really,' she replied.

We let her chew, we let her swallow. Now was the time. Reaching inside my left trouser pocket, I put the still feathered head on the plate.

'Congratulations,' I said, 'you're the first white woman to ever eat raw galah!'

She dashed for the loo and threw up. Oh, we were swines in those days.

After thirty-six years in practice I am now more convinced than ever that the hand of the Lord is present in so many things that happen on a day-to-day basis. And at Gladesville a helping hand from above was always welcome. Walking through the

MOVING AROUND

door of the surgery one morning, I found one of the younger vets busy administering an anaesthetic to a male cat, just prior to desexing it. Being anaesthetised, as I've said before, is as close as it's possible to come to death. This cat somehow stepped over the line. It stopped breathing, the heart stopped. 'It's dead,' my colleague whispered, pulling on his stethoscope and listening hard on the left side of the cat's chest. Nothing, nothing at all.

'It's dead, all right,' I said. I've got to tell you I was a bit angry. 'What went wrong?' I asked, thumping the table several times with my fist.

My poor young colleague just shrugged his shoulders. Poor fella, I remonstrated with him for a good minute or two, thumping the table some more to make the point. Care with anaesthetics is the number one priority in practice. Almost disgustedly, I lifted the cat from the table and slid it up on to the bench, where it came to rest with a soft but sudden thud against the rear wall. Bang went my fist again on the bench. The point was made.

The little foxie I'd come down to see in the adjoining kennels was doing just fine. Yesterday he'd been badly knocked around by a big German Shepherd. He'd probably started it anyhow, that's what little dogs do. The sutures were holding and he just needed another shot of penicillin. 'He can probably go home tomorrow,' I said. The nurse made a note on his card. As I walked back into the surgery I bumped into Brian, a regular client who had brought in a greyhound to be X-rayed.

'Excuse me, Harry,' whispered Brian, having witnessed the earlier confrontation. 'Ah, ah, is, is that cat on the bench supposed to be dead?'

'It *is* dead,' I snapped.

'Well, *I* think it's breathing,' he said.

Hell's bells, he was right! The darn thing was breathing and its ticker was going as well. To this day, the only possible explanation I can think of for the cat's reincarnation, as it were, is my thumping on the table. There seems no other logical or scientific reason why a dead animal should come back to life—but it did.

'Harry, mate,' he said, 'could you do me a favour?'

'Sure, Brian, what is it?'

'When they, umm, nail the lid on, ah, my coffin, could you just thump it a couple of times to make sure I'm really dead?'

Along the same lines . . . It was a Saturday afternoon, yours truly was the only one on duty, save for a veterinary nurse who was there to help with anything that might come in after hours. We heard a ring on the front door—a couple standing there with a helpless little black and white, and now very bloodied, kitten in their arms. It was a real mess. They could tell me nothing until a notepad was produced; they were, as we'd say in those days, deaf and dumb. From what I could understand, the cat had fallen from a balcony and landed, not safely on its feet as most cats would, but awkwardly in a rockery. One leg and probably the jaw were broken. It was a question here of stabilising the patient, warding off shock and then assessing the damage. The poor little thing was no more than six months old, and seemed to be something of a rickets case as well. Its diet had patently been deficient in calcium.

'We'll need to take some X-rays and hospitalise the cat. Could you please come back at six o'clock,' I wrote on the pad. They nodded and left the cat with me.

Without going into any detail, it suffices to say that once the cat was anaesthetised it experienced major breathing difficulties, due no doubt to a haemorrhage within the chest cavity. Unfortunately, we were unable to revive our little patient. By then the X-rays had been taken, and not only had the kitten sustained facial and leg fractures, but it had a fracture of the spine as well. Easy to say in hindsight, but the kitten would never have made it. Gee, no one would look forward to six o'clock, I thought, and it was impossible to ring them. I'd just have to wait it out.

At five-fifteen something wonderful happened. There was another ring on the front door. 'Go up and see who it is,' I said to the nurse. She was back in no more than two minutes with a basket of kittens.

'The guy wants to know how much we'll charge to put this lot to sleep,' she said.

They were drop-dead gorgeous and there, right in the middle of the five of them, was a little black and white kitten. A dead ringer for the one now sadly lying dead on the table beside me. The resemblance was uncanny; they were peas in a pod, except sizewise. This one was only half as big as our accident victim.

'Tell the bloke it won't cost him a cent,' I said to the nurse.

Six o'clock came and it was time to try and right the wrongs. Notepad in hand, I wrote, 'Your little kitten was very badly damaged . . . so many bones were broken in the fall, it was not going to live . . . it died . . . please take this one in its place.' Producing the little piebald bundle from behind me, I saw their faces change in an instant from tears to joy.

Thank you, God, for helping me on that day and on many others before and since.

4

Annangrove Revisited

'You look after birds, don't you?' inquired the somewhat continental voice on the other end of the phone. It was another Saturday afternoon; no one about except me.

'Sure I do, what's the problem?'

'Know anythin' about pheasants, do you?'

'A little,' I explained. 'What's wrong with them?'

'The buggers are dying, that's what's wrong with 'em.'

'How many are dying?'

'A hell of a lot.'

'How many is a hell of a lot?'

'Oh, ten or twelve a day.'

'How many are left?'

'Oh, a few thousand.'

A few thousand? This wasn't a backyard enterprise. This was a full-blown commercially viable pheasant farm. Being a bird vet is one thing, being a poultry vet is just that little bit different.

The only thing to do in situations like this is to go out and have a look. The property wasn't too far away from home and, sure enough, on my arrival the owner had laid out something like eight dead pheasants for closer examination. There were a lot of birds there and pheasants are very pretty birds. As far as I had learnt, the major problem with these guys was one of cannibalism; in other words, they peck one another to death.

There was no sign of that on any of the dead ones.

'What happens to them?' I asked.

'Oh, nothing really, they just sort of fly up in the air and fall down. Some of them are dead, some of them die later and some can't get up.'

Boy, this is a doozy, I thought—nothing in the textbooks about this one. 'I'll take this lot home and do some autopsies. Be back in touch on Monday,' I told the owner.

'Geez, I hope they're not all dead by then,' he said. This guy was as pessimistic as most farmers.

Post-mortem examination is the major tool of the avian veterinarian, so I opened the birds up and had a look inside. There was nothing unusual to be seen. All the internal organs—hearts, lungs, livers, kidneys, spleens, intestines, you name it—everything was normal. The birds were in lovely condition, in fact, with plenty of meat on the breast and rolls of fat. The symptoms suggested that perhaps the brain and spinal cord could be involved in the disease; after all, the birds simply fell down dead, according to the owner. That didn't sound like any disease process. Now, getting the brain out is a little tricky. Opening the bone around the skull has to be done very carefully. As I lifted the top of the first head off the brain, the organ appeared to fall out in my hand. Funny, I thought—must have slipped with the scalpel and cut the spinal cord. Popped it into some preservative for my pathologist's examination on Monday. Looked carefully at the skulls of another two or three birds and removed the brains for examination as well.

Come Monday morning, things on the farm seemed to have settled down—only one bird had died since my visit on Saturday. But by the same afternoon the man was on the phone again. 'Dem birds is still dyin', what you gonna do?'

Quite frankly, I wasn't too sure. The pathologist had the specimens and would be in touch by early the next morning. There was nothing for him to report, however; everything seemed perfectly normal.

Why in God's name were the damn things dying? Best to go out and have another look. Tuesday afternoon was bright and sunny. The owner had picked up two or three dead birds since lunch. 'You just stand 'ere and watch,' he said, 'and you'll see dem big planes come over. The birds fly up, then fall down dead.'

Richmond airforce base was not all that far away and the Hercules transports had a regular circuit around the airstrip. Just as he said, a huge Hercules hurtled overhead—down low, motors screaming, casting a massive shadow right across the top of the pens. Half a dozen birds flew up in fright, three fell down dead, one lay convulsing on the ground. He wasn't kidding.

'I'd like to shoot dem planes,' he said. And as I didn't have any answers at the present time, that was probably one alternative, but not a very viable one.

More autopsies, more looking at more brains. And once again, two fell out in my hand. I hadn't cut in the wrong place, I was certain of that. With the next bird there'd be a different approach; and as the spinal cord in the neck of the bird was slowly uncovered, lo and behold, there it was. The spine had become completely severed between the first and second vertebrae of the neck. Looking quickly at the next one, I found it was the same, so was the next and the next. These birds were dislocating their own necks as they flew in panic at the shadow of the plane.

How do you stop this problem? It's an inherited one, but you only discover this sort of thing later. Thinking caps on! The birds had another ten to fourteen days to go before slaughter and marketing. Keeping the flock alive over this period wasn't going to be easy. Pheasants are worth big money, a lot more than chickens.

We tried putting camouflage nets over the top of the pens to break up the shadow of the aircraft. It did that for sure, but didn't affect the noise, of course. We needed to take this a step further: How do you settle down a bird as nervy as a pheasant? It isn't easy. Drugs work very differently in birds, but some are reliable for all species. Valium, in my opinion, is one of these. How much Valium does it take to settle a pheasant? No one knew—it needed a guess. Working out the amount of water each pheasant would drink on a daily basis, multiplying that by the many thousands of pheasants on the farm and then adding just the right amount of Valium syrup to the header tank was probably more guesswork than calculation. But it worked. We bought up every bottle of Valium syrup in the western suburbs of Sydney. My client kept pouring the stuff in the tanks as fast as he could get hold of the pink liquid. If only we could keep them sedated long enough to get through to the following weekend, we should make it. The Hercules don't fly on Saturdays and Sundays.

'Now, make sure you take them off this stuff and just give them clean water the weekend before they're killed,' I told my client with diligent concern. To this day, I'm not sure whether he did or not; perhaps the birds went to slaughter in a semi-hypnotic state. Who knows? At least there were no reports in the local newspapers of any somnolent diners. The irony of the whole exercise was that we never got paid. But then there was nothing wrong with the pheasants I'd autopsied, no disease. They'd all died of a broken neck. And anyhow, the freezer was full and we dined on pheasant for many months thereafter.

5

Horrible Hernias at Exton

People often ask me why I became a vet, and in fact why I would still want to practise as a vet. Well, the true story is that I don't have my own practice any more. Time doesn't permit it. Over half my working days are spent enmeshed in television, and when you're often away for a fortnight or more at a time it's impossible to conduct your own practice. Nevertheless, everything I do on television is veterinary work of one kind or another and it's nice to think that in that sense mine is the biggest practice in the whole of Australia. In fact, it *is* the whole of Australia. So practice never really stops. In between filming, you spend a fair deal of time keeping up to date with recent advances in medicines and surgical and behavioural techniques. But if there is one major reason why my enjoyment of practice is so strong, it would have to be the interaction with the clients and their own interaction with the animals they love. For certain, this is what really drives 'Harry's Practice'. People like to see other people's problems that are similar to their own, so they can learn how to deal with them. I've met some great characters over the years but, of course, some stand out.

'G'day, mate, want ya to have a look at me bitch.' Hard to say how old this guy was—probably around sixty, I reckon. He was in severe need of some interaction with Mr Schick or Mr Gillette. The guy sported at least ten days' growth. The hat looked like it had been worn by people two generations before him—a sort of fawn-coloured Akubra with a big hole in the crown, the brim turned down all the way round and so stained with sweat and grease that the original colour would have been difficult to determine. His eyes were a bright sparkling blue and a cheeky grin creased his face. At full stretch, he stood no more than about 170 centimetres. A couple of blokes seemed to have tagged along with him. We later deduced that one was his son. Neither had very much to say. He did all the talking.

'Where's the dog?' I asked.

'She's out in the carpark.'

'Oh yeah, can you bring her in?'

He'd arrived totally without an appointment, but it was half an hour before the afternoon clinic was due to start. So seeing him and his dog wasn't going to be a problem. Getting up from behind the desk, I followed him out into the carpark.

Standing beside a battered Toyota Troop Carrier, he was peering in the driver's side window. The back was full of dogs, not just one but close to a dozen, jumping backwards and forwards between the rear seat and the cargo area. Every dog looked pretty much like the one next to it—all fairly big dogs, basically white with black and tan patches, but all pretty grubby.

'Strike me, which one is it?' I asked.

'I dunno,' he said. 'I'll have to get them out.'

'Will they be OK? What about the road?'

'Don't worry 'bout these mongrels. They'll be fine, they won't leave me.'

'OK,' I reluctantly agreed, 'let them out.'

Strolling round to the back door, he flung it open. It was like a 'dambusters' raid. What tumbled out of the back of that van was anyone's guess. Ten or a dozen beagle hound crosses cascaded over one another in their anxiety to get out of the van and on to solid land. There were dogs going everywhere—it was like Wirth's Circus recreated.

'Come 'ere ya mongrel,' he shouted. At a guess, they were all called mongrel. 'Come 'ere when I tell ya.' He had a voice that would wake the dead. Believe me, they could hear it in Deloraine and that was eight kilometres away. There were blokes and dogs heading all over the joint.

'Haven't you got a lead?' I asked.

'Bastards wouldn't know what it was.'

'How do you catch them?'

'Mongrels come when I tell 'em.' And he kept telling them and, one by one, they came.

'*That's* the bitch.' I was glad he knew which one it was, they all looked the same to me.

'That's the one, git 'er boy, git 'er!'

Boy took off after her. Dog and boy came to a shuddering halt in a drain that ran down the side of the carpark. Dog and boy emerged covered in mud, but at least the dog was under control.

'Better bring her in,' I said.

At this point, my nurse was really hoping that, as she'd just cleaned the floor, the father would take over and leave the dripping son outside to round up the rest of the 'mongrels'. Boy did stay outside with the other bloke (I never did determine who he was) and, for the whole of the consultation, dogs kept circling the building like some animated canine merry-go-round.

'Put her up on the table, Ken. What's the problem?'

'Have a look at this under 'ere,' he said.

'Good heavens, how long have these been here?'

The poor dog had two of the biggest inguinal hernias I've

ever seen. They're relatively common in male dogs but not so much in bitches. These were huge swellings, the size of your fist—and she was a bitch! The inguinal region is that bit between the inside of the thigh and the abdominal muscle. The hernia develops as a result of fat and, sometimes, loops of intestine making their way through the same small hole by which the testes (in the case of a male dog) passed from inside the abdomen some time in early puppyhood. In a bitch it was almost certainly a reflection of an inherited predisposition. In other words, she was born with the problem, and it was probably passed on from generation to generation. We know that is a fact in some breeds.

I endeavoured to explain all this to my whiskery client, but frankly, the dog seemed to be paying more attention.

'Don't wanna know about all that. Can ya fix the mongrel? She's me best bitch.'

'Yes, mate, I can fix her, but I'm a bit worried that if you breed from her the pups are going to have the same problem as she's got.'

'No worries. If you can fix 'er, ya can fix them, can't ya? She's a bloody good bitch, this one.'

OK, I'm not going to win. Funny how you can sense that. She was a lovely dog—gave me a lick and a wag of her tail—and pretty fit as well.

'How old is she?' I asked.
'Oh, 'bout three.'
'Had any pups?'
'No, not yet.'
'But she's in season now.'
'Don't worry, she'll be right.' I sort of hoped she would be. Next day all was done. They would have been two of the

largest hernias I've ever repaired. The surgery went well and everything would be OK as long as the after-care went without a hitch. Sure enough, spot on five o'clock, Ken turned up to get his favourite bitch.

'What's her name?' I inquired.

'What do ya wanna know that for?'

'Just for my records.'

'What do ya keep them for?'

'Well, I've got to, it's the thing to do. It keeps me in touch with what I've done, if something goes wrong.'

'Looks pretty good to me,' he said, lifting the dog up. 'Nothin'll go wrong, it's a good job.' He was even more confident than I was.

'OK, here are the instructions. You've got some antibiotics in that bottle—she gets one tablet morning and night. Don't forget. Now, you've got to keep her quiet, no jumping, just to give those stitches a chance to settle in and for the muscle to heal. And keep her away from the dogs. I don't want her getting pregnant. Oh yeah, one last thing, bring her back in a fortnight for me to take the stitches out.'

He just kept nodding. Again there was no doubt the dog knew more about what was going on than he did. 'Thanks, doc,' he said. He paid in cash and was gone.

Almost a month later, and right in the middle of a tricky bit of surgery, there was a loud bang on the front door and a familiar yell from a familiar voice. 'Are ya in there, doc, are ya?'

I sent the nurse out to see what problems might have surfaced. Ken was back. 'Get him to hang on for ten minutes if you can and I'll be with him,' I told her.

'How is she, mate?'
'Bloody terrific job, doc, the bitch is great.'
'Well, you'd better bring her in and I'll get those stitches out.'
'Come out an 'ave a look for yerself.'

It all felt like déjà vu to me. Same mob of dogs jumping around in the same battered Toyota. Only one helper this visit, and he looked a whole lot drier than the last time I'd seen him.

'Just try and get her,' I said, 'without letting all the others out.'

I might as well have spoken to a brick wall. The back door swung open, out tumbled the dogs and what followed was enough weaponry to start World War Three. Shotguns, rifles, even a pistol cascaded on to the ground, and cartridges bounced around on the gravel and threatened to discharge at any minute. You could have stocked two gun shops with the amount of artillery these two guys carried around in the back of the Toyota. 'Git all that lot back inside,' Ken yelled, and I'm sure it was the weaponry and not the dogs, who by now were beating their familiar path around the building, that he was referring to.

At last his best bitch had acquired a name. 'We've called 'er Girl,' he said, 'seein' as ya wanted to 'ave some sort of record.'

'Well, put her up on the table and let's have a look,' I said. 'Boy, she's got a bit fat!'

'Doin' well,' he agreed.

'Just roll her over on her back—that's the shot. We'll get these stitches out in no time. How's she been getting on at home?'

'Doin' just great,' he said. 'Pulled a big wallaby down about a week after ya fixed 'er, doc.'

It was no good complaining. Talk about being beaten before

you started! This was one of those cases. 'Oh, that's good,' I said in a patronising sort of way. Any other troubles?' I added as the last suture came away and the wound was swabbed with some alcohol.

'No, no problems, doc, 'cept I think Fred got to 'er.'
'Who's Fred?'
'Fred's me top dog.'
'Oh, really. Well, let's stand her up.'

Sure enough, Fred had done the job. She'd got a bun in the oven; as a matter of fact she'd probably got six to eight buns and, from what my fingers were telling me, they were about three or four weeks down the track. Yep, she was pregnant. At this stage I made a mental note that any future hernias we repaired for this bloke would be done using number eight fencing wire. No dog could have done more to undo what I'd done than Girl. But there she was, licking my face and wagging her tail, and all a bloke could do was grin.

These days, if my head's in a spin and everything seems to be whirling around me, it's good just to sit back in my chair and smile at the vision of this cavalcade of dogs tearing round and round my surgery with 'boy' weaving in hot pursuit. That's amusement enough. And I recall Ken's parting words. 'Me and the boys like a bit of huntin', ya know.' Well, good luck to you, Ken.

The Biggest Practice in Australia

6

'Dr Harry'

One day the phone rang at the clinic in Exton. 'Would you like to make a television show?' the voice said. Gee, sounds good to me, I thought. 'Good,' said the bloke, 'I'll send you a ticket. Come up to Melbourne.' I couldn't wait to get home and tell Janine the news. Strike me lucky, but three days later there's another call. He wants me to make one too, but he's coming down to Tassie.

All of this some four months after Janine and I had been down to Hobart with a proposal to do the very same thing. Between the two of us we'd knocked together an outline for a television program based around animals—domestic species and wild animals as well. There were five pages in the outline. An appointment had duly been made with the management of what was in those days Tas TV, and, proposal in hand, we sallied forth. They certainly knew who Dr Harry was, even though the name hadn't really stuck by then, for they'd employed me to make a whole series of short clips called 'Food for Thought'. But now the reception was a bit cold. The two Tas TV guys sat there, each nonchalantly turning the pages and spending more time staring out the window than concentrating on our ideas. The body language was clear even before they spoke. 'Animals,' they said, 'animals—who'd want to watch a show about animals?' Sort of shot us down in one fell swoop as they sat back in their leather chairs, feet on the desk and still looking out the window, probably planning their next fishing trip.

Now, though, offers were suddenly coming out of the woodwork. Off I went to Melbourne, but I wasn't too impressed by what I found. The bloke had this big folder. 'Sign this,' he said. It was a confidentiality agreement. In other words, don't say anything about what you're going to read. 'Might be the same as my idea,' I told him. It was nothing like it. Still, worth thinking about, things could be changed. Let's wait and see what the other bloke has to say.

We were due to meet with him at Bonney's Inn in Deloraine for lunch. He and I were on time. Janine was forty minutes late. Our cat Abi was having kittens. 'Couldn't come any earlier, she hadn't finished,' my wife explained. So there's no doubting, from the word go, FM Television knew what they were getting.

'Have a look at this,' the guy said as he handed a folder across the table.

'Have a look at mine,' I responded, 'there's some good ideas here too.'

Actually there wasn't a great deal of difference between them. Ours was the same proposal we'd put to the Hobart execs and got knocked back on. We now asked lots of questions. I hadn't heard of much the company had done, except 'That's Dancin'. Gee, I thought, if they can make ballroom dancers look good an ageing vet could be in with a show.

Then it was his turn to ask the questions. 'Have you had any experience in television?'

'Strike,' I said, 'don't you watch TV?'

'Yes,' he said, 'I watch a lot of TV.'

'Well, I've been the vet on "Burke's Backyard" for six years.'

'Never watch that show,' he said with some disdain.

'I'll let you see a video or two of some of the stuff I've done down here for the local Primary Industry Department.' These were the four- or five-minute pieces on local Tassie produce entitled 'Food for Thought', which I'd really enjoyed doing because you got to eat the product and it made a change from the pretty stodgy mutton and rabbit we were living on at Mole Creek.

'So where did you hear about me?' I asked.

'I heard you on Melbourne radio.'

'Fair dinkum?'

'Yeah,' he said, 'Neil Mitchell.'

You see, I'd been doing a talkback segment with Neil on a Monday for the last six months or so. It followed the release of my first book, *Dr Harry's Pet Care Guide*, which, with the help of Margaret Gee and her sister Christine, we'd promoted right around Australia. Talkback radio is terrific fun. A couple of sessions had been so funny that the producer thought it a good idea that we do a regular stint. As a matter of fact, on this same promotional tour, after half an hour on the air at a Perth radio station, I came off and was chatting to the production staff when the phone rang—again.

'It's the chief of the Police Traffic Authority. Wants to speak to you, Dr Harry.' I'd come in a taxi, so what had happened now?

'Dr Harry, is that you?'

'Yes, what can I do for you?'

'Have you just been on the radio?'

'Yes, as a matter of fact I've been on for the last half hour.'

'Have you finished now?'

'Yes, yes, just finished.'

'Thank God for that.'

'Why?'

'I've just had two bloody accidents reported to me where the people said they were laughing so much they couldn't see where they were going and ran into the car in front. Let me know when you're back in town again, will you, and I'll lock myself in the office.'

Well, that was that. We talked about things, the FM Television bloke made us an offer, and the rest is history. So began 'Talk To The Animals', a great television show that lasted four seasons. With newfound income and newfound confidence, we took the bit between our teeth, being horsy people, of course, and plomped a deposit on a new house—well, not quite new, but certainly much closer to Launceston. It was a nice stone home, on about twelve acres of ground at Relbia, pretty close to the Esk River. We would be happy there. The horses settled in well and the cats were ensconced in a large shed at the rear of the block, and in the portable runs we'd used at Moltema. The only problem with these was the constant criss-crossing of the backyard by electrical cables to keep the heating pads running in the depths of winter. It made lawn mowing quite a dangerous undertaking. The ducks had their own shed and we managed to purchase a couple of goats as well, heaven knows why. One day I'll ask Janine. It was the right place to be, close to the city, close to the airport and close to various facilities which, quite honestly, we missed when we lived too far from town. It's a funny thing in life that until you have to do without something you don't really miss it. The change from the big smoke of Sydney to the quiet secluded lifestyle at

'Dr Harry'

'The Den' had ended up being too much for the whole family.

Heidi travelled easily to the local school by bus, and for me the constant tracking back and forth to the mainland for filming was a lot easier. What's more, the place was fenced for horses. They bred. The ducks bred. The cats bred. We even had our own family of wedgetailed eagles. There were three, no doubt a pair and a youngster. The house was set almost at the end of a long, deep ancient riverbed that ran right into the heart of Lonnie. The wind would rush up the floor of the valley and then swing upwards and over the house. Our wedgies would ride the wind, hovering like some huge feathered masterpiece, their wings fully outstretched and those familiar tails fanned out to stabilise this avian balancing act. Right outside the kitchen window, almost weekly, the three would turn it on like tightrope walkers but without the wire. Majesty, power, defiance and grace make Australia's largest bird of prey an awesome spectacle.

They were to be 'ours' for the almost three years that we spent there. We had good neighbours and felt comfortable with our lot; for a while, anyhow. Let's face it, this place wasn't much bigger than what we'd left in Sydney, so there was always the thought that it would be for us a halfway house, something good until some place better came along.

Adrian was a great estate agent. There was something about this young bloke and his beat-up Range Rover that appealed. Of all the fellas we've dealt with over the years, and there have been plenty, this guy was a standout. With us, he was fair dinkum. He'd spent time showing the family many farms prior to Mole Creek, and now he was showing us another. A huge property with a seventy-square, solid stone house. We took a builder along. He said, 'If you've got fifty thousand a year to waste, buy this place, 'cos that's what it'll cost you in upkeep.'

Thanks, Raynor, we didn't. Sorry, Adrian, this one's not for us. No worries. He was like that.

A bit of time went by.

'Mate, I've got this great place. Looks old but it isn't.'

'Don't be bloody stupid, Adrian, the last old place you showed us was too damn expensive.'

'But, mate, this isn't old. It just looks it. Better come and see it.'

'I'm busy, I'll get Janine to.'

'All right, I'll be there in twenty.'

'Darl, Adrian's got this place he wants you to go and look at.'

'Oh, we've looked at so many.'

'No, he says it's good.'

'Why don't *you* come?'

'I'm busy.' You're always busy when you're a keen gardener.

They were gone just a little over half an hour. 'No good?' I said.

'Real good,' she said.

'You're joking.'

'No, I'm not.'

So, dirty clothes and all, we climbed into the Rangie. It was only five minutes' drive from our place. As the road turned down a steep hill, 'That's it,' Adrian exclaimed, pointing over the top of a hawthorn hedge to a big, two-storey, Tudor-style edifice.

'Well, if that's it,' I said, 'you can turn around, we looked at that place ten years ago. It was too darn pricey then and it'll be too darn pricey now!'

'Oh no it isn't, nowhere near it.'

'All right, let's have a look.'

We'd only ever viewed the house from the road. Driving in, it looked great, an American Tudor home with stone on the bottom, green timber on a cream background for the upper storey and a high-pitched grey roof—an unmistakable 'look at me, I'm different' appearance. It felt good inside. Houses are like that, you either like them or you don't, it's just a feeling.

'Where's the highest point?' I asked, and Adrian drove us to the top of the hill. 'Show me the boundaries, mate.' He did. It was about sixty-five acres, very up and down, so it drained well. A narrowish sort of property with a creek forming part of the front boundary, and a small verge that accessed the road. Hawthorn hedges outlined the fences and there weren't many of those.

We looked at each other, Janine and I. 'We'll buy it, Adrian.' His jaw fell open. We'd made the decision within twenty minutes. You either like a place or you don't, and we loved this one. 'Here's the deal,' I said. 'You tell this bloke that I'll give him X dollars more for this place than we get when you sell ours. Do you think he'll come at that?'

'I don't know, but I'll try,' said Adrian.

We put our home to auction. It didn't sell then, but one month later we had a contract.

'Tell him he's got thirty days to make up his mind,' Janine told Adrian, referring to the vendor of the new place.

'Oh, he wants X plus fifty,' he said.

'Buckleys,' I said. 'X is the limit.'

Every week the 'fifty' got smaller, and when it got to ten Janine said we should take it. 'No way,' I said, 'we'll hold our nerve and we'll get it'—and twenty-four hours before the deadline the signed contract arrived. Wow! This was what we wanted, enough room in the house for all the family and those treasured possessions still in cartons after more than six years. Outside, space for all our animals, and yet we were close to all the facilities we'd come to expect through living in Sydney. Someone once said to us, before we first moved to Tassie, 'If you stick it for the first two years, you'll never want to leave.' You know, she was right. We couldn't go back to Sydney then, we couldn't afford to go, and now there's no way we *would* go.

Funny how everything happens at once. We were due to travel to the UK for a month, filming 'Talk To The Animals'. It was a great chance for the two of us to have a working holiday together. This sort of thing doesn't come along too often, and when it does you grab it. So we organised for fencing and a cattery and the dog yards to be constructed while we were away. Everyone worked like demons, apparently, and we came back to a ready-made farm with central laneways, electric fences, paddocks with water, everything! It was fantastic. There was still plenty to do, though. All the manual stuff, like wiring up the cat runs, gravelling the laneways, setting out the garden—all that sort of thing that you wish could just happen with a click of your fingers. Regrettably it all takes time, a lot of energy and a lot of expense as well.

Today it's very much the way you see it in magazines around the country. There's a verandah on the house, the fencing's all done, the dams are dug, pastures sown and the garden would do Gertrude Jekyll proud. With over six hundred roses, daffodils and perennials, it's our pride and joy and my passionate diversion. We've added a huge watergarden, and, of course, there's our special garden for all those who are no longer with us. It lies very close to the house. We like to be near our friends; that way they are, in a sense, still a part of the family. 'Arcadian Downs' is our little piece of peace.

'Dr Harry'

These days it's also home to 'Harry's Practice'. We make a good many of the links between the various stories right here and, of course, the opening and closing of the show are filmed on the property too. Most of the animals I use are our own. It's so much easier to work with livestock you've reared yourself. They tend to behave better and respect what you want to do. The animals have grown a bit in number. We now stand four stallions at stud. Hussar is still here and he produces one or two foals every year. We've added Sniffer, our chestnut Arabian stallion from Forest Hill in New South Wales; George, our black riding-pony stallion, also from New South Wales; and Shadow, our black and white Paint stallion from the mainland. The boys are kept pretty busy during the mating season, from September through to about the end of February, but the facilities that have been developed make their job easy. We learnt our lesson the hard way! Each year we produce half a dozen foals of our own, and sell on a regular basis at open days or, by arrangement, to studs and riders right around Australia.

In addition, the cats continue to do well on the show bench and their number has stabilised at about twenty. Even with regular litters of kittens coming through, there are still back orders for Burmese. This ensures that we will continue breeding. But these days half our cattery is given over to boarding, as the demand for good facilities is so great. The dog numbers have increased to eleven . . . oops, twelve. There are five Cavalier King Charles spaniels, two mini foxies, a Papillon and a Dandi Dinmont; Isabel, our Italian greyhound; her new little friend Tabbatha; and Scarlet, our wonderful Border collie, who's now top dog on the farm. Regrettably, Rosie and Pixie are no longer with us. Well, in a way they are, I suppose. The ducks are happy, they've got their own dam and they are really enjoying life. The only problem is that it's very hard to breed ducklings—the marauding crows make life very difficult for them. What did I say about facilities? Don't worry, we'll cover that whole area over, that'll fix it. That's *after* we upgrade the driveway . . . aaah. There is still plenty to do. And I haven't bred a budgie since we've lived here. It wouldn't be fair to leave all that to the family. One day, when my television work finally finishes and Dr Harry goes back to being just a vet again, I'll get on with it. We've added guinea pigs, Rex rabbits and fantail pigeons where the budgies were supposed to go. Says something for the priorities of television, doesn't it.

In one way we've reverted to life as it was in Annangrove. At least, what it was like when we first met each other. All my life, as a vet, I've spent time looking after greyhounds. No risk, I like them; better still, Janine does too. For the first time in nearly twenty years, we've got a litter of greyhound pups running round at the back of the property. They look great. They're out of Dashing Rainbow and she was very quick, so with luck we might have another winner or two. Funny how things turn full circle, but that's life, isn't it. We only get out what we put in. Well, we've put in plenty and now might be the time when we start to get a little bit back. In truth, we both look forward to the future when there will be time, as I've said before, to enjoy the things that have taken so much thought and effort to achieve. 'In time, there will be time,' and hopefully plenty of it.

7

The Butler

'Talk To The Animals' went into production towards the end of 1992 and began screening in early 1993. We remember the launch very well. It was in a park on the banks of the Yarra in Melbourne. They had television sets strung up in the trees around the perimeter, and the whole event was magnificently catered for by a very upmarket Melbourne restaurateur. There was no shortage of tucker and none of grog either. It was a sensational night. Standing alongside Janine as the familiar music burst through the speakers, I looked up stupidly at the screen and said to my image in some ridiculous form of admonishment, 'Don't make a mistake, will ya.' Make a mistake!? I'd seen the darn thing six times; no way were we going to make a mistake.

The show was a hit from the word go, screening all over Australia on the Seven Network at 6.30 Sunday night, the old Walt Disney time slot. The critics loved it and were unstinting in their praise for the show; all except one. This one, Robert, said he'd liked it—you know, in a very condescending sort of way—but at the end of the hour he'd simply felt 'animaled out'. Well, good on you, Rob, I got the message across; this is just what we'd planned. Funnily enough, we've become really good friends since and we often laugh at the 'animaled out' saga when we're having a yak or he's conducting an interview.

The show enjoyed success right through 1993, and deservedly so. It was well produced and had at that stage a cast of some five presenters. There was Pam Graham, who'd already worked on television with Derryn Hinch; Mike Lester from up the bush, a tried and true journalist who'd cut his teeth on the Lindy Chamberlain case; and there were the youngsters, Richard Fitzgerald, always the joker; and Kelly Pomeroy, our beautiful blonde (who's now a regular on 'The Today Show').

Each one of them would contribute a segment on a weekly basis. They were animal stories. Unusual animals, ratbag animals, people's relationships with their animals, sad tales—but all true and all entertaining. My job was to host the show and link the whole lot together in little bits throughout the hour, and occasionally contribute a segment or two myself, usually with a veterinary flavour. The Seven Network wanted to capitalise on the success of the show and so we were invited to our very first Logies night. That's really something, you know, because there's no way we could qualify for an award—the program only started screening some eight weeks before the event and most of the judging had already been completed. Nevertheless, it was a chance for us to get out there and wave the flag!

Janine was super-excited; it was going to be a great time. The gold invitation arrived and was answered immediately: Yes, Dr Harry and Mrs Cooper would love to attend. What to do with Heidi? Don't worry, they'd fix that. Janine bought a special gown for the evening. It always amuses me that we poor old blokes are sent out in the same tired old dinner suit year after year after year, but if you should even meekly suggest that a dress worn on some previous occasion should grace the female form for such an auspicious event as this, you find yourself in danger of severe vilification. Which is a nice way of saying she tells you where to go. So there it was. We only had to wait a month or so for the evening.

'Aaaah, my back! Oooh, I can't move.' Janine had done in her back lifting a bag of horse feed out of the boot of the car. She found herself in bed, flat on her back. The doctor, busy prescribing painkillers and suggesting referrals to surgeons for major undertakings, seemed to be calling on a daily basis. There's no risk she was in pain, but we weren't ones to go down the surgical road. Things got worse. She lost feeling in her left leg, and pins and needles developed in the right. This is not good: a dog with a problem like this has a dodgy prognosis. As we had always been into alternative medicine— and by that I mean things like acupuncture and chiropractic —hospital treatment at an early stage was not on. The local chiropractor came to pay a visit. He and, at first grudgingly, the GP worked together to aid her recovery. And recover she did, but slowly. That wife of mine was shakily on her feet after three weeks, just five days prior to the Logies.

'There's no way she's going,' said the chiro to me. I wish he'd said it more quietly, as Janine overheard. 'Too bloody right I am, you just fix me,' she told him. So, loaded with Janine's painkillers and back brace, Heidi and we scrambled—and I use that word in a very literal sense—on to a plane and headed for Melbourne. We arrived on the Friday night and were ushered into the Sheraton Towers Hotel. Everything was simply amazing. We'd been picked up at the airport by a chauffeur-driven Mercedes Benz limousine. It had all-leather seats, a deep-pile carpet, a built-in bar, you name it. Boy, we certainly

The Biggest Practice in Australia

felt important after riding around in an old Magna wagon. This was really upmarket. The hotel, well, this was something special too. What a difference! If this was the television life, bring it on. The opulence of the hotel foyer, with running fountains, wide staircases and marble floors, was something to behold. Up to the second floor from the top—'Your bags will follow directly, sir'—and they did. The 'room' was just amazing. It was actually a suite with its own lounge room, two bedrooms and a huge bathroom, all decorated like something out of *Vogue* magazine. The suitcases arrived and Janine lay down to rest her aching back.

This was certainly a long way from the days at Mole Creek. At last, it seemed, we'd arrived, in a metaphorical sense, and people actually appreciated what we were doing on television. Back in the early days, we had purchased an answering machine. You see, so much of our working day was spent out on the farm that it was impossible to be in the house taking calls. Mobile phones remained out of our financial reach as well. Coming in of a night, we'd play back the messages and we were always bemused by the number of seemingly blank spaces on the tape. One day the reason became obvious. 'Come here and listen to this, will ya,' the voice on the tape exclaimed, amidst a heap of giggling and laughing. People were ringing up just to listen to the recorded message. Things back then were pretty tough, and everybody deals with hard times in their own way. (I remember once having such a pile of bills that just looking at them made my blood run cold. So one day I carefully carried the whole lot outside and burnt them. Didn't solve anything, but it made me feel a lot better.) Anyhow, my wife was always the joker and she took her frustration out on the answering machine. Her greeting would go something like this: 'Good morning, you've rung the residence of Janine and Harry Cooper. Unfortunately, the butler cannot attend to your wants at the present time as he is far too busy crutching sheep and drenching the lambs to be able to be of assistance right at this instant. Should you wish to speak to our butler you will need to leave your name, address, telephone number and the nature of your problem, and we will ensure that his good self will attend upon you at his earliest convenience.' Other little gems included: 'We are looking for a butler who is well endowed . . . with money, of course.' All this was her lighthearted way of making the best of a pretty bad situation.

Children are funny. I really doubt that Heidi knew the depth of our problems in those days, and her memories are totally different. Memories of feeding thirty-five orphaned lambs one year, of tobogganing down the front lawn in a baby's bath with twenty centimetres of snow on the ground, of fishing in the creek, of collecting blackberries and squashing them through a strainer with a teaspoon to make juice, of talking to Dot, and of water fights with the kids next door. Perhaps we never let her know what we kept bottled up inside. But she longed for the day when this mysterious butler that Mummy spoke about so often would finally appear. Even though we'd left all that behind and now lived in Relbia, those telephone messages must have made a real impression.

Heidi was exploring everything in the suite, turning on the taps, climbing on the chairs, bouncing on her bed, looking out the window, when suddenly there was a knock on the door. 'I'll get it,' she shouted as she ran to the door and flung it open. She was suddenly silent. There in the doorway, resplendent in his black and white penguin suit, stood a tall, dark gentleman.

'Good afternoon, madam, I'm your butler,' he announced.

'Mummy, we've got a *butler*!!' Heidi screamed.

All her dreams had at last come true. There he was, all six foot of him, smiling down at her, holding out his hand. She took it and shook it and brought him into the room. I'd never seen a child look so proud. She had her butler after all these years, her very own butler and, 'yes', he was happy to do whatever she wanted. He would press clothes, polish shoes, remove stains, turn down the bed—probably even kiss her goodnight if he had the chance. You've never seen a child with a smile as broad. Oh boy, we've talked about this many times since and we still manage a smile ourselves.

Our butler walked round the room explaining how everything worked, the TV, the remote control, the video player and, 'yes', of course she could have a video. A video . . . 'Daddy, I want a video!' And she got one. But the tour of the bathroom I found a little perplexing. It's often of great concern to me that some architects never get to live in the rooms they design. I don't know who was responsible for the bathroom; it looked good, but functionwise it was just not there.

'Be very careful getting into the bath, sir, someone slipped and broke their leg only last week.' And now this knob on the floor. 'Be careful of that too, sir, someone tripped over that recently and broke their wrist on the basin.'

By now I was beginning to wonder whether our insurance policy was up to date. All this and we were only one floor below the penthouse.

'Yes,' I observed, 'you're right, and if you happened to be sitting on the throne and someone burst in, flinging the door open, you could fracture both kneecaps as well.'

'You're quite correct, sir,' he said in an acquiescent fashion. 'But thank heavens, it hasn't happened recently.'

The next morning we spent enjoying a sightseeing tour of Melbourne, including a visit to the local markets. It was a bit embarrassing, actually. They picked us up from the hotel in a sparkling white Rolls Royce. It even had its own bar in the back seat. 'Gee,' I said to my darling wife, 'this is a bit over the top, isn't it?' She just smiled and continued to enjoy our dramatic change of fortune. It must have looked quite amusing, in fact, at the markets: one Rolls Royce surrounded by all these beat-up VWs, clapped-out Holdens and rusting Falcons. Everyone was looking at it, and at us too, when we got out. Back in those days nobody knew who we were, and we mingled with the crowd just like anyone else. Sometimes I long for those days.

The Logies night was fabulous. All the glitz and glamour of the walk in, mingling with celebrities that you only ever saw on the small screen. Tom Jones and John Farnham were the major stage act. We were seated at a table with Channel Seven executives. Heidi watched the whole thing on TV back in her room with the babysitters! A couple of liquid anaesthetics seemed to dull Janine's pain. Suddenly this family had been transported from the life of your everyday vet and broken-down farmer to that of a television personality. Believe you me, that's one big step. The night was a great one, certainly one to remember, as your first always is. Rhonda Birchmore was dancing with Hot Shoe Shuffle. She slipped over in the middle of the act but was back on her feet without anyone really noticing—what a great performer!

The night was over far too soon, especially as we were meeting people who, in the years ahead, would dictate the way in which we lived our lives. One conversation stands out in my memory. A particular group of people were discussing our show and one of them seemed to doubt whether 'Talk To The Animals' would in fact last the distance and whether my good self would be able to 'cut the mustard'.

'Don't you worry about Harry,' said my darling, as she gently patted the man on the top of his head. 'He'll manage and so will the show.'

'Do you realise who that executive was?' her poor husband inquired later.

'Doesn't matter, does it?' Janine said. 'Always say what you mean.' That was her attitude then and it hasn't changed since.

There have been lots more Logie nights and hopefully there'll be more ahead. We've never managed to win one, although we've come close twice. 'Does it really matter?', people often ask me. I don't know, but it would be nice to have one on the shelf, just as an acknowledgement of the fact that I've spent some fifteen years in the industry. Then again, it probably doesn't put one more dollar in your pocket. For the girls, though, it would be the icing on the cake.

8

TV and More TV

Back at the very beginning, everyone had a lot to learn about working with and filming animals. 'Talk To The Animals' was the beginning of a very steep learning curve, not only for me but for the camera crews as well. Cats are not the easiest animals to work with; sure, they're happy to sit contentedly on your lap at the end of the day, but most of the time they are very independent beasts. Finally, a cat named Otis settled down on my knee. 'Just face him a little bit more camera left,' asked the producer. OK, which way's camera left? I went the wrong way, it's actually my right. Everything sorted? No. Noel wasn't happy.

The back of a cameraman's Tarago contains about as much equipment as you'd need to make a low budget movie. Back Noel came, carrying a little circular frame, walked behind the bench on which the cat and I were now so uncomfortably poised, and then, *floop*. Bloody hell! Otis flew vertically off my lap, shot twenty feet into the stratosphere, hit the ground with all four legs going like the spinning wheels of a freight train, and was gone. 'What happened?' said Noel.

'What the hell do you think happened?' I said. 'What was that goddamn thing?'

'Sorry, mate, just the flecky.'

Flecky is the colloquial name for a reflector. They fold in a most difficult fashion, being made from shiny fabric held together with a spring steel loop. Once released, they literally floop to their full size (about three times their previous diameter). One side is white, the other silver.

'Got any other cats?' inquired the producer somewhat sheepishly. Otis was gone for the day and Milo, the chocolate-coloured Burmese, got her chance at stardom. Noel's a lot more careful these days when working around cats, but he's taught better people than myself plenty of very useful lessons.

'Noel, I'd like to stand over there to do my little bit to camera. Will under the tree be OK?'

In each episode there were little bits and pieces used to link stories together which we filmed, or shot, as the saying goes, out in the field. Usually only fifteen to twenty seconds were needed, but the setting up was what took the time.

'I'd rather you stood over here on this mound.'

'Why can't I stand over here? I like standing under this tree.'

'If you stand under the tree you will look like a pile of vomit'—his favourite expression—'but if you stand over here you will look good.'

I've never argued with a cameraman since; it's their job to make me look good and in some situations that's not real easy.

Rosie was another of the original cameramen on 'Talk To The Animals', also known as TTTA. Noel and he between them probably produced most of the material in those first two years. One day near Perth in Western Australia, in the middle of a very hot autumn, we were out shooting ducks (in the television sense, of course) on a beautiful property landscaped with lakes and lagoons, waterways and creeks. All in all, it was very spectacular. The ducks were, too; some of the rarest individuals I'd ever encountered. But to Rosie they were just bloody ducks. 'Harry, I can't see what you see in them,' he said. The day was long and the day was arduous and at the end there was a distinct feeling that dummy spitting might occur at any moment. 'You drive, Rog,' Rosie said to the soundman. It is usually the cameraman who drives to and from location, while the soundo provides directions and encouragement where necessary. The producer is charged with supplying snacks and lollies to all and sundry in an effort to keep energy levels high and spirits almost as elevated. Rosie was tired, really tired. Carrying a heavy camera around on your shoulder for hours at a time is plain hard work. Taking beautiful pictures in between is even harder.

Roger had an unpronounceable last name. For certain it was Dutch, Van Windersveen or something like that. But to us it was Windscreen. He climbed behind the wheel of the rented Commodore wagon. (TTTA didn't have a real good rapport with Commodores. A previous soundo had destroyed one in Tasmania on a mountain road—rolled it three times. 'I was only doin' fifty k's,' he claimed. In fact, he never did less!) No more than three hundred metres down the dusty track that served as the driveway out of the property a group of huge grey kangaroos charged out of the scrub. We were getting along a bit, Rog hit the anchors, the Commodore slid sideways, Rosie ducked under the dash. One roo, two roos, just barely scraped past the bonnet. Three, *bang*! We slammed into the big fella and he rolled ever so slowly, almost like a gymnast practising his repertoire. Right up the bonnet, onto and over the windscreen, continuing right along the top of the vehicle and disappearing from sight. By the time the car ground to a halt, the windscreen was an opaque obstruction. The roo was gone, no sign of the big animal. He'd probably sustained very little in the way of injuries, but by golly the Commodore looked sick.

'Geez, Rog, I give you the bloody wheel for five minutes and look what happens.' Rosie was only joking—they were the best of mates—but somehow, ever since that day, the name Windscreen has really stuck.

Rocket Rod was another to join the fray on TTTA. He'd spent a good deal of time working in studio television and his first day of freelancing was with yours truly. We were to film an operation.

'Don't want to see any blood at all,' said the producer.

'Would you like me to kill it first?' I asked. 'That way nothing will bleed.'

'Don't be smart, Harry, you know what I mean.'

Yeah, I knew what she meant. One drop of blood and she'd be the one crashing to the floor.

Young Rocket was a pretty cluey operator. He shot the whole scene from below, looking up, as it were, from floor level past the patient on the operating table at my face. Not one drop of blood graced the screen. Don't get me wrong, there was a bit but you couldn't see it, and the patient finished up just fine. Hats off to Rocket, on that, his first day.

The next time out wasn't quite as good. 'Harry, be a bit careful, mate, with that big kangaroo. He can be a bit aggro, and if he comes at you just keep going backwards, that way you'll be sweet.' It's always handy when the keeper provides this sort of warning. The roo sure was a big red and so many of these males that become pets, as it were, develop really nasty dominant, aggressive sort of behaviour. They can open you up with the toes on their big hind legs.

Everything was set, the camera sat on the tripod, light was

right, sound was right, I had some tucker and the roo seemed pretty co-operative. Cameras rolling, and away we went. Couple of takes in the can. 'Can I just get another?' called the producer. They always want another. (Heard the old joke? How do you know you're talking to a producer at a party? Don't worry, he'll tell you.) Suddenly the attention of the roo was more on the camera and the producer standing behind it than on me. Three or four slow bounds saw the macropod staring intently into the lens of the camera. Many animals do this, although some become quite frightened by the camera, looking on it, I suppose, as a giant eye. Others see their reflection and are intrigued. This roo was fascinated and got real 'up close and personal' with the camera. Cameramen are very protective of their investment, and so would you be of something worth well over $100 000. Rocket grabbed the camera. The roo jumped back in fright, dislodging the mat box which landed squarely over his head (the mat box is a square, flat, black-painted protruberance that extends over the lens and reduces flare from the sun). It fitted magnificently, but the roo didn't think so and was off. Really off, going for the lick of his life with Rocket in hot pursuit—mat boxes aren't cheap. Picture a big red kangaroo with a big black picture frame locked firmly around his head and a rapidly more annoyed cameraman and soundo in hot pursuit. Twenty minutes it took to calm the animal down and finally retrieve the box.

Soundmen run into plenty of problems as well. Trying to record sound when the wind is blowing a gale is more than a little difficult. Most of the time I'd wear a small microphone taped just inside my shirt, with a radio transmitter clipped to the trouser belt. These days the boys secrete it in the brim of my cap. When recording other people for interviews it's often a lot easier to use a boom. This is a large pole with a microphone suspended from the end. In windy weather, a fluffy is applied over the microphone holder to reduce the wind noise. These fluffies are simply what they sound like, large hairy-looking devices that, believe it or not, soundos spend hours combing!

Now, the Falconry Centre at Mooroduc in Victoria had a magnificent display of raptors. There were hawks and falcons, harriers and even wedgetailed eagles. They agreed to fly one of the wedgies even though the day was windy and wet. This bird was being reprogrammed for release into the wild and had to be taught to hunt for its food. There is something about a large bird of prey that is quite spectacular. They are nature's airforce: they hunt and they kill with consummate ease. The very size of a wedgetail is overpowering. There he was, sitting on my heavily gloved fist, becoming weightier by the moment, looking me squarely in the eye as if to say, 'Old fella, I'm so much better than you. You can run, you can walk, but I can fly.' The beak is big and powerful but it's the talons, those huge nails on tungsten-like toes, that do the damage.

The bird would work to a food reward held in the hand. He would drop from a fairly low height directly onto a gloved fist held at shoulder level, to get the tender morsel. Three or four times he did this and then came the best demonstration of all. A rabbit skin was dragged along the ground by a thin line and, out of nowhere, this bird crashed onto his make-believe prey, to be rewarded once again as he hopped around his would-be meal.

'Could we do that one more time?' No need to ask who said that. The trainer looked a bit concerned; the weather was worsening and it was pretty obvious that he wasn't too happy about working the bird much longer.

'Harry, could you talk to this bloke while the bird's doing his thing?' asked the producer.

'OK, I'll give it a try,' I said.

Marty, the soundo, got out the boom and the hairiest fluffy he could find. The trainer tossed the bird in the air and away he went in a slow, deliberate circle right around the perimeter of his training field, those massive wings working like two huge blades beating the air into submission. God, what a sight, how could anyone have shot these birds? Thank God they don't anymore. The skin went out and began to move along the ground, Marty hoisted the fluffy above the bird's trainer, and so began the explanation of what was happening. The eagle made another leisurely circuit and then appeared to pause, almost confused for a moment. He circled and then folded those wings and came to earth at frightening speed for such a huge bird. But it wasn't the skin he was after. Hell, it was Marty's fluffy! Panic ensued. The fluffy was rescued, Marty was pacified and the bird was rewarded.

'Did you get that, did you get that?' the producer asked the other crew member excitedly.

'Of course I bloody got it. I'm a cameraman, aren't I?'

All up, there were four main cameramen with whom I worked back in those days: Noel, Rosie, Rod and Brendan. This last fella was the ultimate in laidback attitude. The car, the equipment, everything was just so relaxed. Many, many times I've turned to say, 'Are you rolling, mate?', only to find he's been rolling for at least twenty seconds. Such was the man. As far as equipment goes, Warner Bros probably don't carry as much as he did. Over the years he had collected all the little tricky bits, so when it came time to do a bit of underwater stuff, Brendan got the job. We were to shoot an opening for TTTA up on the Barrier Reef.

'Harry, I want you to swim around underwater with the snorkel on, come up from under the boat, grab the side, get rid of the snorkel and welcome us to the show,' the producer told me. Sounds easy? How do you keep your cap on under water? 'Harry, we'll tape it on.' And they did. Somehow Brendan managed to get enough gaffer tape on me and on the cap to hold the darn thing in position. Then Brendan and Rog, with their scuba gear on, went down below to film me in the water, coming up. Take after take, after take. It wasn't a good day, the water was a bit cloudy and the current was really racing. A TV vet needs to be in training for this lot, I thought. In the end it came out all right, but the cap is now two sizes too small.

Sound recordists seem to align themselves with one or two cameramen in particular. Roger and Marty were the last to join us, Peter and Andy were the first. Pete managed to distinguish himself by collapsing in Thailand. We were shooting just outside the Royal Palace. It was stinking hot and very humid. We'd been at it for nearly ten days, starting early in the morning and trying to finish well before lunch to avoid the heat of the day. Things were catching up with everybody.

'Here comes the Princess, get a shot of her,' yelled the producer.

Even prior to this, Pete was looking pretty seedy. In the middle of all the fuss and kerfuffle he did his little horizontal trick and collapsed on the ground. It was no fake, the guy was crook, really crook.

'Did you get it? Did you get her?'

'Damn the Princess,' said Noel. 'My mate's lying flat out on the ground and he's more valuable than any princess.'

It was a day or two in hospital for Pete before we saw him again. He had a domestic pilot's licence and from time to time this came in very handy if we needed to zip off to somewhere beyond the beaten track.

Andy was a real ladies' man—never thought he'd ever get married. A first-class soundo, a good friend and a top class skier, and as he delighted to tell us on more than one occasion, a member of the ski patrol. These days he's happily married to a beautiful wife and has two lovely children. His main claim to fame was the ability to sleep anywhere at any time. Five minutes down the road and Andy would be snoring his head off, the ultimate in a relaxed individual. Except for one particular day in Africa. Rosie and Andy were out in the jungles of Botswana with an experienced local guide. The object was to get some really close footage of a rhino mum and her baby calf.

'Just stick with me and try to remember a few things. Rhinos have very poor eyesight; if you stand still they can't see you. But they have a good sense of smell and hearing,' the guide said, as they approached the family pair.

Rosie is closing for a really tight shot, creeping ever nearer to the baby. Suddenly a funny 'clink' noise develops. Eyes glued to the viewfinder, he presses on. The shots must have been amazing, but then the clink becomes a very loud clunk. There's a yell from the guide and the sound of crashing bushes. 'Watch out, Rosie!' And from nowhere this female rhino is charging. He was so intent on getting the pictures, he'd not seen her out to one side. There are no trees to run behind, just grass. She closes in. It's only twenty metres. Suddenly the guide runs straight in front of her and off to the side. She turns in her charge and careers after him. Rosie beats a retreat.

Andy could see it all coming. He'd disconnected from the camera, but left the sound lead banging against the metal sides. Mum had heard this and was alerted. Where was Andy? Not just behind a tree but halfway up the darn thing. All he could muster was: 'Sorry, mate.'

When TTTA finished and 'Harry's Practice' began it was a case of getting used to a whole new set of film crews. There was Andre, who worked mostly with Steve as his soundo, and Craig, who enjoyed the enviable reputation of being one of the best in the business and was later to become known as FBW, as you will discover. Craig worked mainly with Spartacus, whose name would imply the persona of a quietly handsome classical hero. He was all of this and a good soundo as well. There were others who filled in on the odd day, but to all intents and purposes most of my work was with these guys. Travelling, particularly when it's for a long period of time, brings you all much closer together. These boys and the in field producers have been my real friends in the industry.

Andre takes lovely pictures. He's quick, he's efficient and by cripes, when we're making surprise house calls you've got to think on your feet, and he's very good at that. Believe it or not, he is actually quite an emotional sort of character. He's cried over rats and shed a tear or two over the odd dog as well. When you own an animal yourself, it's far easier to understand what other people are going through when their pet is in trouble. His dog, Scully, is a little Jack Russell. Andre talks about her all the time. Hate to tell you this, but in his wallet is a picture of the dog, not his wife! How does she feel about this, Andre?

'She knows her place.'

And I know straight away he's talking about the *dog*. How their first child is going to fit into such a situation is a question that perhaps I'll need to solve some way down the track. Could make an interesting house call.

Andre's offsider, Steve, is a huge lump of a bloke—just the sort of individual you'd like to have on your side in a blue. Standing by, Steve's always ready. We've been in some pretty hairy situations soundwise. Roaring gales; being right alongside building sites, main roads and airports. He handles the lot with no worries at all. It was he who invented the cap mike. In the surgery it's very difficult to stay on mike, which is technical talk for the fact that I bob up and down as the consultation progresses, turning the old noggin this way and that. These little microphones are very directional and only pick up the sound in a certain area. Turn away from that and you're off mike. But once it's in your cap the darn thing turns with you. There are three caps which get used regularly for filming, they all look much the same and all of them are modified to accept the tiny little pickup which sits just on the edge of the brim. You can't see it. No one knows it's there. The cord is taped to the back of my neck and hidden in what little hair manages to grow thereabouts. The transmitter sits in a pocket in the 'corset', an elastic belt running around the waist under my shirt.

A word or two about FBW. Craig has shot most of the opening titles that you see at the start of the show. He is inventive and he's thorough, and brings with him all the bells and whistles that manage to fit into his garage. If there's anything new out there, Craig's sure to have it. On location, he spends any spare minute experimenting with new pieces of equipment. Now, I love shooting in Hobart—the breakfasts at the Grand Chancellor are sensational. The thing that really got to Craig was the made-to-order omelette. Every morning before filming, he'd order his very own special omelette delivered to the table by a chef complete with chequerboard trousers, pristine white top and similarly virginal headgear.

Six months have elapsed. It's breakfast time once again. Seated at the table are Craig, Steve, the producer and myself. Craig's getting stuck into a bowl of cereal, then a little toast and jam.

'Where's the omelette?' asks Steve.

'Oh, FBW,' Craig replies, gently patting his abdomen.

'FBW?' I ask.

'Yes, Fat Boy Watkins,' comes the reply.

What a shame, the omelettes used to look so good. Perhaps one day the chef will twist his arm again. The name FBW, of course, has stuck.

Spartacus, or Alex as he should properly be called, offered to drive the whole crew to the Blue Mountains for a week or so of filming. He had a big four-wheel-drive which he was anxious to sell and one of our cameramen may have been interested. It was a wretched few days, it rained and it blew—cold, miserable weather and pretty difficult to take nice pictures in. But we managed. When things are slow you eat, and with all their travelling around, the crews soon know where the best tucker is. Everyone seemed to have tomato soup on the menu. Good stuff too, homemade, plenty of seeds, plenty of pulp, plenty of flavour and, in the case of the last lot, plenty of chilli as well!

TV and More TV

Chilli sits well with some people and not so well with others. It burns on the way in and, unfortunately, on the way out too. There's something about the stuff that really irritates the colon to such a degree that some poor souls are subjected to bouts of what could best be described as hyper-motility of the lower abdominal contents. I don't have to put it any more plainly, surely.

Making filmed house calls out in the scrub sometimes necessitates a little time in setting up, particularly when they are surprise visits. This particular afternoon we are two kilometres down this gravel road, nothing but rocks and scrub, and several of us suddenly feel the effects of last night's soup! A hasty trip into the mulga. Aah, that's better.

'Where have you been?' asks Alex.

'Don't ask,' we reply.

'Shouldn't have had the chilli,' he advises. Too late now.

The surprise was a bummer. The people were home but they moved with all the speed of a tranquillised three-toed sloth. The dog had about as much personality as a museum specimen in formalin. We weren't going to get anything out of this one. A polite explanation of what was wrong with the dog and a simple solution took no more than ten minutes of my time. Even if the whole thing falls flat on its face, we always fulfil our obligation to solve the problem.

'You're not going to film us?'

'No,' said the producer, 'the dog doesn't really do what you said it would do in the letter.'

'Of course it doesn't. What do you expect it to do with all you people here?'

True, this does happen occasionally. We're a little bit of a distraction for some animals, and in assessing what calls we'll make, one of the major criteria is: Will it do it when we get there? We're in the business of making television, and it relies on pictures, not words. If the animal doesn't do whatever it's supposed to we don't have a story. I can understand people being disappointed, but this couple started to get a bit stroppy. We tried to be polite as we made an exit. The couple were still mumbling and grumbling as we retreated up the driveway.

'Looks like it's gonna rain again,' observed the cameraman.

'Let's hope it rains buckets,' quipped Alex, obviously annoyed by their attitude.

'Haven't we had enough, mate?' I asked somewhat stupidly.

'Let's put it this way,' Alex went on. 'If it rains heavily enough, the remnants of all that tomato soup you guys left up in the bush should wash right down their driveway, the damn seeds will grow two metres tall, and they'll never find the road!'

Yeah, they were funny people, we all agreed with that sentiment.

9

Essential Viewing

When 'Harry's Practice' first started, there were certain things that just had to be done. Our home had to be established as the focus of the program and the real hub around which the episodes could be built. It's funny that a vet has an entirely different perception from a producer about what makes good television, but then it's the producer who writes the story and makes the whole thing into something you find entertaining. We utilise a small animal clinic in Mowbray, just on the outskirts of Launceston proper. It's a busy little place and Peter, who owns it, is kept pretty flat out himself. Spending some twelve months giving him a hand one night a week turned out to be a stroke of luck. Back in the beginning he was on his own and never got home in time to see the kids, they were always tucked up in bed. For me, it was a chance to pick up where I'd left off when 'Talk To The Animals' started. You see, battling to keep going with a practice, when you're away for long periods of time, just doesn't work. So we made a sensible decision and sold the building at Exton. From then on it was just a question of working out of the back of my station wagon. The small bits and pieces of the clinic became part of the mobile equipment, while the X-ray plant, operating table and the like went into storage.

It's easy to remember when 'Talk To The Animals' finally finished in December—suddenly life seemed to stop. Gone was the weekly routine of scanning video tapes, picking out the best shots from the list that had taken all day to compile, and then putting it all together into a story of about three and a half to four minutes. It took around four to six hours of my time for every minute on the screen. Gone, too, were the weekly trips to Melbourne and the recording booth, where time after time the same lines would be recorded until the sound editor was happy. A man was lost! Mooching around the place with nothing to do, well, relatively nothing after the fencing and spraying and all that sort of stuff had been done, boredom began to set in. Janine reckoned that that husband of hers was getting under a woman's feet.

'Why don't you go back to work?' she asked.

'What sort of work?'

'You're a vet, aren't you?'

Yeah, I hadn't thought of that! After nigh on four years of television, suddenly there was a huge hole in the working week. So that's what happened. The gear was dusted off and practice started all over again. Just a couple of days a week as a mobile clinic, and Thursday nights at Mowbray. That's why we ended up using that surgery for 'Harry's Practice'. The people were so genuine and their love for their pets was all too apparent.

Television is a bit like an addiction. It gets right into your blood, and even though my practice was going well, somehow the urge to get back in front of a camera was ever present. The contract that had kept me employed making 'Talk To The Animals' also kept me off the TV scene for another six months. Pretty soon after that, things started to get interesting.

'How would you like to make a television show?' Sound

familiar? This time it was Channel Seven asking the question. The answer was pretty obvious.

'Come up to Sydney and we'll talk about the show.'

'No. You guys come down to Tassie and we'll talk down here, because this is where it should be made.'

Tim came down. We met at the airport. 'Have to get you out of that suit,' I said. 'What size shoe are you?'

In no time at all we were walking around the river flat paddock, him in my spare gumboots and old windcheater, and me in the usual farming clobber. 'This is a good place to think,' I confided as we started on our second lap. There was a fair element of country in the man. He liked horses. He could talk about pasture. He was fair dinkum. In a little over two hours, 'the animal show' format was decided. In those days there was no name for the program.

'The pilot should be made in Sydney.' Here we go again.

'No way, Tasmania is the place to do it. The show won't have the same feel if it's done up there.'

Tim agreed and convinced the rest of the management. Brad came down and spent a Thursday night in the consulting room at Mowbray. The first client was a lady in a wheelchair with a dog on her lap. The boyfriend rolled her in and the dog was soon on the table. Nasty little skin rash that had become infected as well. Antibacterial wash, antibiotics by mouth and a shot of cortisone to stop the scratching would do the job nicely. All the while I could sense that my mainland executive had his eyes on the lady's slippers. They were huge fluffy ones that looked like a pair of long-haired pussy cats. 'How come you've got cat slippers on your feet, but you own a dog?' he finally asked.

'Oh,' she replied, 'I really love cats but I'm allergic to them, so I just wear the cat slippers. It's the next best thing.'

It broke him up. He was sold. The network was convinced. Finally, a name was chosen. A contract was signed. Katrina came on board to join me. 'Harry's Practice' was born.

This particular consulting room got a bit of a facelift. Some stained glass windows, new cupboards, a paint job and a variety of animal pictures and ornaments were added. All this was designed to give it a very 'country vet' feel. The clients and the staff were great as well. It was and always will be a wonderful place to make television. These days, other TV surgeries exist in Melbourne and Sydney, but Mowbray in good old Tassie was the first!

Once we started filming it seemed there was one major procedure that everybody wanted to be a part of. 'Harry, can you geld a horse?'

'Sure I can.'

'Righto, can you set one up?'

'Yeah, I reckon I can do that.'

It's hard to imagine why this was so important. But they went on and on about the damn thing, and as there weren't any young foals at home that needed this sort of surgery (they were fillies) it was a matter of finding one that did.

'Why do you want to do it?' I asked.

'Oh well, it's important that people see you with other animals, not just dogs and cats,' said Simon the director.

'Well, I can do lots of other things with horses, there are plenty that we own.'

'No, no, we really want to see this.'

'OK then.' They would all witness a gelding!

Geoff Elmer, our good friend from Wegena, had a couple of

young Welsh-cross ponies. I'd gelded the eldest some twelve months before but now his mate was approaching ten or eleven months and was probably old enough for me to do the job.

'Mate, have you had a good look at him?' I inquired over the phone.

'Yeah, Harry, I have. They're both down.' (We were, of course, referring to the testes in the scrotum.)

'Goodoh, what day will suit you?' The time was fixed.

Talk about an entourage, everybody was there. It would have to be the biggest film crew that had been carted anywhere in the whole four years to date. Even the top brass came along for the ride—well, so to speak. Two cameramen, two sound recordists, a field producer, Hilary the producer proper, Simon the director, and a couple of hangers-on as well. Boy, talk about performing in front of an audience!

'Better not get this one wrong, eh Geoff?' I said.

First up, there's a need to explain to everybody what goes on. Working with horses can be dangerous. 'OK, guys, this is how it works. I'll give the pony a little injection which will sedate him. He'll get a bit wobbly on his legs but still stand up. After another ten minutes or so he'll get another injection of an anaesthetic agent and the little fella will sink to the ground, hind legs first. Then it's just a matter of pulling the top hind leg up out of the way and tying it there for safety while the vet leans over and does the job. The pony will get up in about twenty minutes. Now, don't get too close, and watch all those ropes just in case something goes wrong. Horses are a lot bigger than we are and accidents can happen, so look after yourselves because I'll be looking after myself.' Lecture over. Some of the audience are already sorry they came.

You could feel the anticipation in the air. He was a great

little pony, light grey in colour, though stained a bit red by the fertile soils of the area. Geoff already had a halter on him and we led him, closely followed by his mate, out towards the centre of the paddock. It looked a nice flat grassy area which would be ideal for the surgery. A dose of pre-med and he relaxed almost instantly. There was enough time to organise all my instruments and ropes while the drugs took their full effect. Cameramen were running in all directions, getting shots here and shots there, from every angle. Lots of excitement. It was like being front row at a local Aussie Rules final, not a simple gelding. I checked underneath to make sure both testes were there and were relaxed. No problem.

'You ready, Geoff?' I said. He nodded. Geoff was a man who said little and did plenty, and had a great way with animals.

The pentothal hit the pony like a sledge hammer. Almost as the needle left the vein he rocked back on his haunches, and rolled slowly away to the left and on to the ground. There was no time to waste. The hind leg was pulled upwards and forwards, and tied out of the way. Safety is a priority when you work with horses. The surgical area was washed and scrubbed and disinfected. With instruments laid out and scalpel in hand, it was time to begin. A look up at the crowd. 'Here we go,' I advised them, and that was probably the right turn of phrase to use. Because the moment the scalpel flashed across the skin and the blood began to well up through the initial cut, go is what they did. In every direction. Clutching their mouths and their stomachs. Ah, but the finale was yet to come—that terrible sound of the emasculators crushing the cord. A sound which Andre, my head cameraman, still remembers and imitates to this very day. A soldier in the trenches of World War

One could not have been more traumatised than the audience fast disappearing into the shrubbery. 'That's the first one gone,' I said. But there was no one to talk to. Couldn't see a soul, they were all behind me. They couldn't look, even the sound was too much as the second squeeze was applied. 'It's all over now,' I said as we cleaned up. I noticed that two of my previously avid audience were back sitting in the van, looking pale and still holding their abdomens. Just thirty minutes later the little fella was on his feet and walking perhaps a bit shakily around the paddock with his mate. It was all over, all right!

Funnily enough, I've never ever been asked to geld another horse on television. There are still plenty to do for ourselves, because we breed half a dozen foals each year and, as a necessary part of managing any horse stud, most males are desexed. If left entire, males, or colts if you like, go on to be stallions and can be a problem, whereas geldings tend to be much better behaved. The little fella recovered without any problem. He was sold later and these days is a great kid's pony. It's nice to wonder if he knows that his big experience in life was recorded and that somewhere it's filed away. You know, it's a pretty fair bet that it'll never grace our television screens.

10

Crocs and 'gators

Some time back a young reporter asked, 'What's the most unusual animal you've ever had to treat?'

'Have you ever read any of my articles in newspapers or magazines?' I asked casually.

'No,' he replied, 'I haven't.'

'Don't you guys do any research before you come out on the job?' Don't get me wrong, I wasn't in a bad mood, I was just a bit stunned. I was thinking, as this was the hundredth time I'd been asked this question, that perhaps journalists might come up with something a little more original. 'Fair enough,' I said, 'I'll tell you. It was a dolphin.' And I left it at that. Well, can you believe it, the young bloke wrote the most scathing article suggesting that I'd got out of bed on the wrong side, and making a few other derogatory remarks. I'll never do that again. Always be polite to journalists . . . even if this one was a bit simple!

So do you like all animals? That's the second most popular question, to which there is a standard reply: Yeah, everything except crocodiles.

Now, there are at least a hundred reasons why I don't like crocodiles. Let me list a couple.

The venue was a wildlife park near Ballarat. Kevin was the producer. A man who up until that day I would have trusted with my life. 'Harry, I want you to walk out on that bridge,' he told me. The bridge was a narrow wooden structure no more than a metre wide, spanning maybe two and a half metres over the narrowest part of a pond shaped like a figure eight. On one side lived a large male crocodile; for 'large', read approximately three to four metres. On the other side was a female, twice as nasty but half the length. 'Now, when you get out there, mate, just hang on to that little fish and hold it carefully in those tongs so he comes right out of the water and grabs the morsel. Rod will get the pictures.'

Yes, OK. Nerves of steel, all that sort of stuff, out I go, holding a fish about the size of a sardine in a pair of tongs that are little more than thirty centimetres long. Grab hold of the rail with one hand, hold out the bait. Whoosh! The bludger leapt from the water and grabbed the thing out of the tongs before I had time to even get balanced. 'Great,' says Kev. 'Missed it,' said Rod. 'Again,' says Kev. This time I'd be ready—balanced, in position, holding the tongs out well away from the bridge. 'Lean out.' Lean out much further and I'll be in there with the croc! 'OK, hold out the tongs.' Hell's bloody bells, here he comes again. And the huge reptile propels the upper part of his torso right out of the water to grab the microscopic offering from the tongs.

'Mate, mate,' says Kevin. He always uses the word 'mate' when he's gonna get you to do something really difficult. 'Look, that was great, but I want to see him sort of come up right underneath you.'

'You're kidding,' I tell him.

'No, mate, you'll be right, just hold the fish sort of under your face while you're leaning out.' Even the guy who ran the place had reservations about this trick.

'Don't you damn well miss this, Rod,' I gasp, 'I'm only doing it once!'

Lean over, look into the murky water, you can't even see him. He can see you, though. Grab the fish by the tongs and hold it out tentatively half a metre below your face (that way he won't have to jump too far). In an instant he's there. Your reflexes take over. You pull the fish away. It's now only centimetres from your face and so are his jaws as he grabs the damn thing. You're looking fair down the swine's gullet and his breath smells pretty rotten from where you are. Sensational!

'Got it, mate . . . OK, now I want a POV,' says Kev. POV means point of view—that's simply the camera taking my place.

'Rog, when Rod cops an eyeful of this in his viewfinder the brown corduroys will be the order of the day.' At least I could just glimpse the croc in my peripheral vision before he lunged, but when you're looking down the viewfinder of a camera the animal will just explode on to the scene.

Rod's out on the bridge, camera on shoulder, looking at the water. Roger and I are on each side, with our arms linked behind him. If he goes backwards he'll join the female in the next pool. I hold out the fish in the tongs, just below the lens. 'Up a bit, up a bit,' calls Rod. 'Good' . . . but the 'good' sort of turns into another word that rhymes with 'sit' as the water erupts in a reptilian detonation. To this day Rog and I are certain that without physical restraint Rod would not be with us today.

Kakadu boasts some of the liveliest crocs in the world. In fact, Australia has the most aggressive of any of them. I don't know that that's anything to be proud of. The Yellow Waters Cruise of an evening is extremely picturesque. There was the host of 'Talk To The Animals' sitting right on the very stern of the little boat we'd rented for the day. Rosie had the shot pretty well lined up. 'Rolling, Harry.' That was my cue to start talking in about three seconds. 'G'day, welcome to the . . .' Whack! The wooden oar crashed into the water right alongside where I was sitting with my big bum hanging right over the stern (it was one of Rosie's long-lens shots).

'He was coming for you, mate,' said our guide with consummate hilarity.

Actually, the whole trip was quite an experience. 'Harry, just walk along this ledge here . . . Yeah, I know there's a bit of a gap there in the middle. But if you measure out your paces you'll just step over that. Don't look down, mate, just keep looking at the camera.'

The Jet Ranger helicopter owned by Rosie's dad had plonked us fair on the top of Jim Jim Falls with about a two hundred and fifty metre plunge to the pool below.

'You'll be right, mate, you'll be right,' piped up Andy.

Right? Terrified would be closer to it! Two tourists had plunged off a spot not far away a fortnight earlier. They'd had to scrape them up with a spatula.

Deep breath, and measure it out. Once. Twice. OK. The gap's half a metre—probably couldn't fall down through that anyhow. We'll give it a go. 'G'day, welcome to the show,' etc., etc. Delivered in as cheery a manner as I could possibly manage, considering that my life hung in the balance.

'Again, mate, please.' Rosie also used the term 'mate' when your life was in danger. 'Again.'

But this time, a better delivery. 'Lovely, mate, great stuff,' calls Andy. I'm shaking like a leaf on a tree. 'You look a bit white, H,' jokes Rosie. Andy walks up, puts his arms around my torso and gives it a squeeze. 'Don't know too many people who would've done what you've just done,' he says. You bastards!

'Mate, we need you to do one more thing,' Rosie said. 'Just stand on the cliff top over there and look at the falls. We'll fly over the top and get some great shots with you in the foreground.'

The motor springs to life, the rotors start to turn and the chopper lifts slowly from the clearing. In the background, the roar of the machine is growing louder. The scrub around you starts to erupt in some wild willy willy. Suddenly the air spins with the force of a massive blast. You find yourself clinging to the rock, face down, struggling for a grasp of anything that might prevent a fatal fall to the valley floor. The downdraught moves on. You stop sliding. The edge is forty centimetres away. The Jet Ranger is gone, hovering somewhere near the top of the falls.

They are back in another ten minutes. 'Thanks, H. Great pictures, mate.'

'Yeah, thanks, Rosie.' What else do you say?

'Don't worry, Dr Harry, they had a big feed of chickens yesterday. You'll be fine. Just walk slowly and don't touch them, step over each one as you go. Truly, you'll be OK.' Our African guide was more confident of the whole exercise than the show's vet was. 'African crocodiles are nowhere near as aggressive as your own in Australia.' Some reassurance, when you're disappearing down their gullet.

Crocs and 'gators

But we did the sequence, three times in all. Imagine how hard it is to step over twenty-two sleeping crocodiles all laid out in a row without touching them, smiling and looking at the camera and delivering some equally drivellish lines of dialogue at the same time. Still, that's what they pay you for. These crocs lived round a waterhole; the whole enclosure was fenced to a height of a couple of metres. Believe it or not, this was on a golf course and the idea was to drive from the tee, over the obstacle, if you could call it that, and land your ball on the green about thirty metres beyond it. It was hardly a sand trap, more a booby trap.

Everyone will tell you—that is, everyone who knows or is supposed to know—that alligators don't really eat people. Crocodiles yes, but with alligators you're pretty right. (Never mind all those people that get eaten by 'gators in the swamps of the Florida Everglades.) Rather encouraged by this information, the crew ventured into the alligator enclosure at an Aussie wildlife park. The five reptiles we were interested in were basking in the morning sun around a small concrete pond. They were all facing the water and arranged like the spokes of a wheel. Nearest to the camera were two females, then a fair gap to a large male and another two ladies.

'Harry, just go over there, mate. Ah, you'll need to squat down between all of those 'gators. Yeah, that's right, get in the middle. Yeah, go back a bit, back a bit—right, that's it. Squat down there, right next to the male.'

Like a fool, I did. How could you come to any harm? Alligators don't eat people and the keeper was there, a small slip of a girl with a controlling device in her right hand.

'Is that an electric prod?' asked the soundo, worried it would interfere with my radio mike.

'No,' she said, 'it's just a bit of bamboo.' A bit of bamboo? A bit of bamboo! And a pretty skinny bit anyhow. What was that gonna do?

'You're there now, mate, just squat down and get on with it,' the producer called.

OK. 'Coming up after the break we'll be catching up with Kelly, who's visiting,' etc., etc.

'Good, Harry, lovely.' The producer was clicking his fingers, as was his constant habit. 'Could we just have a safety?' That's in case there's a little fault on the tape.

Right. 'Coming up after the brrreaa . . . I'm going to stand up very, very slowly and I'm just going to walk backwards, away from all of this.' By now I'm at the rear end of the nearest female. But he's still coming. This huge animal with his jaws wide open had spun himself almost totally around before the word 'break' had left my lips. He was there, no more than half a metre from my outstretched hand, and hissing for all he was worth. If he'd opened his mouth any wider I reckon you'd have seen daylight at the other end. He stopped. I stopped talking, but kept going backwards slowly and deliberately out of the pen. 'Where's the bloody keeper?' I demanded. Poor girl, she'd gone to water, standing immobilised against the back wall of the enclosure. So much for the 'electric prod'—and how much good would one little bit of bamboo have been if he'd kept coming?

We don't encourage crocs or 'gators on 'Harry's Practice'.

11

Wasps

When filming 'Talk To The Animals', I often spent long periods of time away from home, overseas. Trips to the US and to Africa could last well over a month. These were great times, but they left a lot of work for Janine to do back home. Mind you, she was a pretty busy lady in any case. Horse shows, cat shows and, of course, Heidi's school all took up a lot of her time, and in those days there was no help whatsoever. She did it all, but there weren't the numbers of today. The property was very much smaller.

I've always done my own packing and for the last eight years it's been pretty much a routine. Same suitcase—you know where everything goes. It's just a matter of working out how long you're going to be away and what sort of climate you're going to. The rest's easy.

This was to be a short trip over to Melbourne for outdoor filming and some studio work, a little 'voice over' and not much else. The whole thing should be over in a matter of five days or so. In most cases, the first flight in the morning, leaving around 6.30, or the last plane of the afternoon, around 4.30, were the best bet. Today it was the afternoon flight. Leaving on a Friday meant that the weekend was going to be a busy one for me. Suitcase lying on the bed, all the essentials packed. Now it's time for the shirts—they're the last. They sit on top. That's the routine. That way nothing gets forgotten.

The door of the wardrobe opened easily. It was a built-in. My right hand grabbed the first three shirts on their hangers and shut the door. It was hinged, not sliding. It just so happened that, while the door was open, a couple of European wasps flew out. Gee, I thought, that's a bit peculiar, where'd they come from? Didn't think much more about it until it was time to get my shoes. As the door opened again, suddenly four or five more insects flew out. The door slammed shut in a hurry, believe me. There were now almost a dozen wasps buzzing around the window, looking for a way out. They're easy to kill—just a quick squirt with any sort of insecticide and they turn up their toes. So half a can of insecticide got emptied inside the wardrobe, and the door slammed again. After I loaded the case into the Magna, it was time to go back for another look.

Hell's bells, the cupboard was full of them! Couldn't get my wife on the phone, no way of contacting her, so I left notes all over the house. 'Don't open the wardrobe. Taped it closed just to make sure. Call the pest controller.'

The sequel to the story is simply this. The wasps had entered the house through a small hole in the stonework, for the home was made from field stone, and the walls were some thirty centimetres thick. The rotten little insects had then tunnelled into the bathroom and made their way under the bath. The side wall of the bathroom and the back of the built-in wardrobe were the same structure. The wasps had eaten through the timbers of the wall and escaped into the wardrobe. It took two visits from the pest company to shift them completely, and half a day from the stonemason to make sure they didn't pull the same stunt again!

The story doesn't end there. It seems that every time Janine is left on her own, some disaster strikes. We hadn't been in our present home all that long when a similar thing happened. Filming was taking place up in Brisbane. We were in the middle of making a surprise house call and there's my darling on the other end of the phone, yelling something about 'bees in the house'. B was probably the right letter of the alphabet at that particular time—things 'on set' weren't exactly going too smoothly.

What's a man supposed to do? I'm up here in Brisbane and haven't got a clue what's going on. 'You'll have to call somebody,' I said to Janine.

'Who will I call? It's Sunday.'

'I know it's Sunday. Call the builder, he'll be home.'

And so it was that the trusty builder would sally forth on that Sunday afternoon to solve the problem. Well, half solve it anyhow.

When we bought the place there was a swarm of wild bees in one of the large elm trees about fifty metres from the front of the house. There were a couple of avenues of these magnificent trees on the farm. The locals reckoned their age at around a hundred and thirty years. 'Arcadian Downs' was part of what was once a huge farm covering more than twelve thousand acres. We had asked the previous owners if they could eliminate the bee problem before settlement, but nothing had been done. And being super-busy, as we always were, nothing got done later. Now the colony had swarmed and they'd lodged right in the chimney and were happily descending through the fireplace to explore the rest of our house. The lounge room was full of angry little buzzers, the kitchen and hallway were filling up as well.

'What about the cats?' Janine said on the phone. Her priority will always be the animals.

'Open the doors to let them out.'

'Let the cats out?'

'No, not the cats . . . the bees!' What other advice can a man give?

A hasty screen was fitted to the fireplace that at least kept them buzzing in the one area. Thanks again, Raynor. The bee man arrived on Monday to remove the offenders. So much for the wasps and bees. And you often wonder, as you climb aboard a plane, what disaster the insect kingdom can rain upon your house when next you travel away.

Away From Home

12

Good Ol' USA

I've been to the States several times, but Janine and I went to a world veterinary conference in Montreal before we ever moved to Tasmania. It was a great trip, starting with a week in Hong Kong, then on to Vancouver, eastern Canada, Cheyenne (Wyoming), Florida, Hawaii, and finally home. It was our first big trip away together and the excitement was fantastic. Hong Kong was a familiar destination, as I'd been there at least three or four times previously. For Janine it was the first time and for us both it proved to be a real experience. The approach to the old airport was exciting enough. The huge jumbo would aim for the chequerboard, a massive arrangement of black and white squares painted on the side of a mountain, then bank around sharply and begin a shallow dive toward the runway. It seemed to be flying almost between the tall apartment buildings, even the washing hung out on the network of clothes lines appeared so close that you could pluck it off as the plane roared past. In those days every hotel was top class, with a chauffeured car to meet, greet and deliver you right to the door. The place was and is alive. Shops are open till ten at night—a real bargain hunter's paradise.

It was always best to make an early start to a shopping expedition. The locals believe that if they make a good sale early in the day, the rest of it will go well for them. With that in mind we set off to spend some of my darling's well-saved money. 'I've been recommended to try this jewellery store,' she said, showing me a crumpled business card that a friend had given her months ago. That sounded OK to me, but experienced shoppers had suggested that you didn't let the shopkeeper know it was the case, otherwise you became a captive audience and were less likely to end up in front in a bargaining duel.

A massive necklace hung in the window. Diamonds and sapphires danced and sparkled under the electric neon lights. 'Wow, I'd love to have something like that,' Janine said, and to this day I'm grateful that she used the word 'something'. In we went. Out of the window came the necklace. It became the basis of a design which, thank the Lord, was only half the size. It took nearly three hours, looking at sapphires, matching the stones, checking for shape and colour. Then the diamonds—same procedure. Finally, all were assembled. Now the fun started. Another half an hour haggling over the cost. In the end, a price somewhere about half of what was first suggested was decided upon, and a deposit paid. It would be ready in forty-eight hours!

Plenty more to do. Clothes to have made, shoes as well. And the food. Aaah, how good was the food. We used to get on a bus, make a note of the number and travel for some twenty minutes, right out of town. We'd get out and walk around and look for a restaurant that was interesting. We were the only non-Chinese for miles and the yum cha was sensational. You could make yourself understood just by grabbing hold of the waiter, carting him along and showing him what someone else was eating.

That's the way to do things. It's the way to enjoy the real feel of the country. When it's time to go, simply cross the road, jump on the bus with the same number and you were on your way home. No worries.

Flying out to Canada was an experience. After a week's shopping in Hong Kong there was just so much stuff! We must have been overloaded by ten or fifteen kilos and were only booked on tourist class! Janine stayed hidden behind a pillar with all the stuff we were going to carry on board as hand luggage. There I was, standing in a queue, the only white man for miles around, when this very good-looking uniformed lady says, 'Excuse me, Dr Cooper, would you come with me please?' Gee, I thought, we're sprung, and we're not even on the plane.

'What's the problem?' I said.

'Oh, I've got some bad news,' she said. 'Please come this way.'

Crazy thoughts ran through my mind. Perhaps the cases had been stashed with contraband! She summoned a porter to carry the bags and I was ushered into a fairly plush office.

'Dr Cooper, please sit down. I have to apologise. You and your wife's seats have been double booked.' (Gulp!) 'We will have to move you to first class. Would you mind?'

Mind? I thought it was a bloody sensational idea, but you never want to appear to be too enthusiastic. 'I'll have to ask my wife,' I said.

'Very well.'

'What's wrong, what's wrong?' Janine stammered as she saw her suitcaseless husband hurrying across the vestibule.

'They've double booked our seats.'

'What does that mean?' she asked anxiously.

'It means we'll have to travel first class.'

'You're joking.'

'No, I'm not.'

'Will that be OK?'

'What do you reckon? Now, don't look too keen about things. Come with me.'

'This is my wife.'

'Good evening, Mrs Cooper. Has Dr Cooper explained everything to you?'

'Yes,' I said, 'I have, and we're happy to make the move.'

'Thanks very much,' she said. 'Leave everything to us.'

Her English was perfect. Only one thing bothered me. 'How did you know my name?'

'It's written on your suitcase, sir, and you weren't difficult to find in the queue.'

What a great trip! We wandered down to cattle class occasionally to have a look. It's the only way to fly. Thanks, Cathay.

Arriving in Vancouver, after a fourteen hour flight, we were thoroughly jet-lagged. Standing outside the airport terminal in the half light of morning, with a chilly wind blowing lazily right through you, is a lonely feeling. Where are the cabs? How do we get to the hotel? Thank heavens, everyone spoke English. We caught our first limo in to the hotel. It was just like the one you see in *Crocodile Dundee*. Remember when he ripped the antenna (shaped like a boomerang) off the boot and hurled it? There was a cocktail bar, television—strike me lucky, if this was the car, how good was the hotel? We were tired and all we wanted was a shower. Washed and refreshed, a stroll around the town was the go. Now the shops were starting to open. 'We've got to keep going,' I said to my poor weary wife. 'Got to adjust to their time. If we go to sleep now it just won't work.' OK, walking was the best way to stay awake, but first we booked a tour of the city for the afternoon. It was only ten, which left us a few hours to look around. Camera in hand, we were off.

Later, only a few hundred metres from our hotel, we came across a car rental company. Out the front was a stunning red Mustang convertible. Boy, what a car! 'Take my picture,' Janine said as she dashed across the road and jumped in. Up to the eye with the Pentax, a great chance to grab a few snaps before the salesman appeared out the door. 'C'mon, we haven't got time for that,' I said. 'Let's have a bit of tucker and get organised for the tour.'

If you've been to Canada and the States you'll know that food is something they specialise in. They're world leaders at getting more food on the plate than any other country I've known. We ordered something from the three page menu that sounded like crudités. In other words, fresh vegetables that you dip in various concoctions. That's what arrived. Broccoli, cauliflower, beans, radishes, tomatoes, spring onions, all fresh, and all delicious with simple guacamole and hummus dips 'on the side'. The serve was a plate for one and between us we could eat only a quarter of what arrived. The food! They certainly pile it on.

The tour was great. It included visits to see Indian relics, like brightly decorated totems, then a huge swingbridge suspended seventy metres above a ravine, salmon ladders in the river up which these mighty fish literally climb to get to their spawning grounds, and the magnificent gardens of Vancouver.

Our next destination lay some hours away on the eastern side of Canada, and that's like going to the other side of Australia. Canada is a big place.

Things are always different overseas and here we are queuing up for our flight the next morning and half the people are speaking French. Boy, that's a change! I get to be third in the queue at the check-in window and the attendant closes it. The flight leaves in twenty minutes. We've been here for two hours. It's the craziest system I've ever seen. All the airlines check in passengers together. How does that work? That's the problem. It doesn't! So we're just about to start a bit of good old Australian ranting and raving when an announcement comes up. 'Anyone holding tickets on Air Canada's flight to Montreal should proceed to window seventeen.' That's us. The plane's now gone, according to my calculations. It left ten minutes ago. When we finally get to the front of the queue: 'Oh, yes, Dr Cooper and Mrs Cooper, well, we've had some problems with your seats.' Not again, I thought, why do we always get the problems?

'What sort of problems are they?' I inquired in a rather patronising voice.

'Well, Dr Cooper,' she explained, 'quite simply, you don't have any.'

'What do you mean, we don't have any? I've been here nearly three hours trying to get some.'

'What I mean, Dr Cooper, is that we don't have any seats left in economy.'

'Well, what happens now?' I'm beginning to get a bit hot under the collar, and am probably still jet-lagged as well.

'We *can* get you on the plane, though.'

'How can you do that?'

'Well, we can give you other seats.'

'What sort of seats?'

'We can seat you in first class, sir.' Oh, I loved the 'sir'!

Good Ol' USA

'We'll take them,' I said, without even asking Janine.

Two of the longest legs on our whole trip—and we've got first class seats again. How good is this?

Montreal we didn't care much for; Quebec, Ottawa and Toronto we enjoyed. Montreal was the venue for an international veterinary conference. On most days the sessions were either lacklustre or over fairly early, and that gave us a chance to explore the other three cities. In them was preserved a lot of older architecture and the buildings had true character. The cities had an overall ambience that made the visitor welcome as the people seemed so much friendlier than in Montreal. As for the conference; well, there were some good papers presented on pancreatic and malabsorption problems (all to do with intestinal malfunctions that are a very common syndrome in veterinary practice). It was a very worthwhile experience and the knowledge I gained has certainly helped a lot in practice at home.

From here we'd planned a week's touring around the Rockies, and if you ever get a chance to do the same it's quite spectacular. The Buchart Gardens and their stunning begonias planted in row after glorious row along every path, with their vivid red, yellow and orange blooms, were just the start. Then came the beavers of Lac le Jeune, and the joy of sneaking out after dinner to catch a silvery glimpse of these amazing builders at work on their dam. The view from your window at Lake Louise is stunning. Standing in the darkened room, with the curtains drawn back by the hotel porter, the vision fills the window and saturates your very soul. It is awesome. There is a sapphire blue lake with a huge shimmering glacier at the far end, its reflection covering almost the entire surface of the water. Sheer, tree-dotted mountains enshrine the whole scene. Canoeing on the lake, whose water temperature is about 3°C, makes any paddler doubly careful they don't tip over. A climb up the mountain—'it's only two kilometres, we'll do it in half an hour'—takes well over twice this time. The ascent verges on the vertical. A sensational end to a very full day.

Finally, after unending miles of shimmering snowfields almost blinding in the autumn sunshine, and pine-clad precipices cradling truly wild rivers fed by still melting snows, you arrive in Banff for a bit of horseriding and some really close encounters with nature.

Now, we can't go anywhere there are horses without my wife having to go for a ride. Janine had teed it all up the night before. Not long after sunrise, with the mist still hanging heavy around the stables, we were mounted and on our way. The trip took us out around a beautiful lake and all we could talk about was the fact that it so resembled the lake in *On Golden Pond*. It was uncanny. We hit a clearing and out of nowhere three or four loons swam into view. I reached for the camera to take a shot of the birds.

'Don't take a picture on that horse, he'll buck,' our guide called.

'What?' I said.

'Yeah, he'll buck, he's spooked by cameras. Just get off and you'll be right.'

As far as riding goes, Janine will tell you that her husband is not the most elegant rider in the world. Riding for me is staying on and not falling off. Obeying instructions, I dismounted, snapped on the telephoto lens and blazed away.

'I've lost my ring, I've lost my ring!'

'What?'

'I've lost the stone out of my ring.' Tears welled up in my wife's eyes. Here we were, having such a wonderful time and suddenly, crash, back to earth again. 'Show me,' I said. Sure enough, the sapphire from the middle of her engagement ring was missing. It was a big stone, her pride and joy, teardrop in shape.

Men always say the strangest things, don't they, or so women tell us. 'It'll be right, it's insured,' I went on.

'That's not the point,' she said, with such a desolate tone in her voice. And of course it wasn't the point. The stone was something special, she'd chosen it and designed the ring herself.

The rest of the ride was an anti-climax. Back in the mounting yard we started to search, but two more rides had gone out since we'd left—that's more than a dozen horses shuffling around in the dirt and sand of the mounting area.

'This is where you had to have lost it,' I said. 'It's the only time you really used your hands for anything. Probably happened while you were adjusting the stirrups.'

We looked and we looked. For over an hour the two of us crawled around in the dust and dirt of the yard. Nothing, absolutely nothing. Janine was in tears. What a swine of a thing to happen!

This unfortunate episode was to put quite a dent in the holiday. We bought another ring, set with some semi-precious stones, for her to wear, but deep down we knew that it wouldn't solve the problem.

There were more horse rides and finally an encounter with a bear. The luggage was on the tour bus and the driver was calling 'All on board', when a ruckus broke out in the hotel grounds. Raiding the garbage bins was a huge black bear. No one was allowed too close while the park rangers fired a tranquillising dart that immobilised the big guy. They bundled the now snoring animal into a huge trailer-mounted bin for relocation back in the wild.

Every morning we had been up looking for moose or any other form of the wildlife that was supposed to frequent the hotel golf course. No luck at all. Yet no more than a kilometre down the road, we're tooting the horn to get a moose off the bitumen!

Finally, after tripping through Calgary, so famous for its rodeos, we ended up in Cheyenne, Wyoming, south of the border. Struggling up to our room on the first floor of the motel seemed to me a monstrous effort. A terrible pain began to develop in my chest, like someone tightening a vice around my ribs. Breathing was an effort. 'I'm going to have a heart attack,' I gasped. The bags were heavy, no risk about that, but with every step they felt heavier and the pain became worse. At the room, stumbling through the door, my exhausted form, as white as the sheets, collapsed on the bed. After the episode with the ring this was all we needed and, besides, medical treatment is just so expensive in the States! Janine went to get help. Someone came from three doors down. 'Hea'll be just faine,' drawled a large American lady. 'Hea'll be OK, it's the altitoode.'

'What are you talking about, the altitude?' I gasped from my deathbed. 'The joint outside is as flat as can be.'

'Ya,' she replied. 'But youse awl are one helluva long way above the sea. This is a beeg plateau and y'awl get used to it.'

Good Ol' USA

Gee, let's hope so, we thought. Fancy being buried here!

She was right, in time the patient did recover. We spent the next two days with our American friends at an enormous cat show. Janine was in her element and there was plenty to keep me interested as well. You know the belt buckle that you see holding my moleskins up on television—the one made from deer horn and hand painted. Well, that's where it came from. The guy even kept this huge western outfitters store open for an hour after closing, just to look after his 'Orzzie mates'.

From there it was down to our friends' home in Florida. Talk about hot and sticky, we were nearly asphyxiated by the humidity. Another plane flight back across to the west coast and—for any animal lover—a visit to San Diego's famous zoo. In just two days we'd be on our way home via Hawaii. There was yet one more veterinary conference, but this one was really special. This one was about my favourite subject . . . birds.

Stepping off the plane at Hawaii airport, we found no one on hand to meet us. It was pretty lonely standing in the airport terminal, the rest of the passengers having departed long ago. We were it. The conference schedule was quite clear about transport arrangements: a bus will meet all incoming flights. So where's the bus? A phone call soon sorted things out.

'Waal, it's like this,' droned the voice, 'you are the only guys on thaat plaane. Y'awl 'ave to wait till another plaane curms along.'

'How long do you think that will be?' I inquired.

'Oh, four, maybe five hours.'

'You're bloody joking.'

'Waal, you could get the island buuss or you could get a caar or you could wait.'

Damn the bus, we thought. We're not sitting on some rattly

old thing that takes an hour to get to the other side of the island. We'll rent a car. They're cheap as chips in America, and they were cheap in Hawaii too. Of course they were, you fool, it's part of America!

We thumbed through the brochure. The cars were displayed in a sort of a photo album, each leaf with a full-page shot of a vehicle. It was hard to recognise any of them, really, but finally there was one that looked something like a Commodore.

'Reckon you can handle left-hand drive?' I said.

No problem. I should have known. She can drive anything except a nail and she's getting better at that too, 'cos she keeps hanging more and more pictures. Out with her licence and my credit card. 'There we go, sort that lot out.'

Meanwhile, yours truly keeps thumbing through the book. 'No . . . hold it! Hell's bells, have you got one of these?'

'Yes,' he said, 'I have.'

'Is it red? It's got to be red!'

'They're all red.'

'We'll have one.'

'What are you talking about?' Janine asked. She'd been busy with the paperwork.

'This,' I said. 'Look at this.' There on the page was a beautiful shiny Mustang convertible—exactly the same as the one in which she'd sat for a picture that first day in Vancouver.

Yahoo!! We must've looked a couple of idiots tearing round the island, our suitcases teetering on the back seat, held down by a rope and occy straps. We were like a couple of big kids, the wind in our hair and the Beach Boys on the radio—re-living a long-forgotten adolescence and loving every minute of it!

The entrance to the Turtle Bay Hilton hotel is a long gravel drive forming a very narrow U-shape. Mountains of tropical greenery are all around. 'Take it slow on the gravel,' I cautioned, then said, 'No, no, give it the gun, darl! See those guys out the front? Slide past them and give them a thrill.' Now, if you can drive dirt track speedways, spewing gravel is kids' stuff, even if it is on the wrong side of the road. That wife of mine dropped it down a cog, floored the go pedal and executed a perfect handbrake turn right in front of the three men.

'What the hell? Harry, you mongrel!' cried one of my best birdie-vet mates as the gravel ricocheted around the place. The three of them were all pretty stunned. Frankly, we didn't expect to see them either. Got shot of the luggage. Hang everything, check in later. Let's go for a spin. And spin we did.

They were five fantastic days. Mind you, the conference started every morning at eight o'clock and ran to well after six. We still managed a swim each afternoon at famous beaches like Sunset and Makaha. There was no surf to speak of—the big stuff only rolls in over winter. Of any conference I've ever been to, this was the greatest learning experience of my life. There were so many experts with so much knowledge that each of us felt brimming over with information and equipment, and keen to get back home and put our newfound skills to work. This meeting of so many avian specialists was to lay the foundation for the formation of a group of vets in Australia who specialise in the care and treatment of birds.

After nearly five weeks away, Annangrove sure looked good, even in the dark! There's nothing like your own bed, and we hadn't been in it more than four hours when the phone rang. It was six o'clock in the morning.

'Haallo,' drawled a voice, 'is thaat Mrs Cooper?' Janine barely mumbled an answer. 'Iii've fouund yaw stone.' There was a deathly silence. 'I beg your pardon,' said Janine, fighting sleep from her brain. 'Iii've fouund yaw stone,' the caller said again.

It's hard to talk when you're crying. What a fantastic thing to happen! To go from one extreme to another. A wonderful holiday capped off by the best ending anyone could have prayed for. It had rained in Canada early on the morning she rang. Our friend had walked outside to catch a horse and there, glistening under the hazy stilted sun, right in the centre of the yard, was Janine's sapphire. She just picked it up. Good as gold, not a mark on it. Fantastic, eh? How many horses and how many people had been through there in the last two weeks? Miracles do happen!

The sapphire came home, wrapped in cotton wool, in an empty plastic film container. We sent her back a Drizabone coat and a pair of Blundstone boots. These days the sapphire sits in a somewhat firmer setting.

What about that Hong Kong necklace? Well, we'd just got over the sapphire shock when I got another. Rushing down to her local jeweller, Janine was keen to get her precious choker valued. He looked at the item carefully, studied it with a glass for over five minutes. 'I think it's a fake,' he told her.

'Didn't you tell him how long we took to match all the stones?' I asked.

'Yes I did, but he said it would be impossible to get the stones matched so perfectly, so they would have to be copies.'

What rubbish! Thank heavens, he elected to send the whole thing off to a gemsmith for appraisal.

Two days later, there's a very different expression on the

face of that wife of mine. 'He says they're real, for sure, and because they are so perfectly matched the whole thing is worth over three times what I paid for it!' All stories should have such a happy ending.

13

America Revisited

'Talk To The Animals' was a great television show, and one of the best things about it was the fact that we, as the presenters, got to travel all over the world—places I'd never been to and may never have gone to had it not been for television. On top of all of this, we were paid to go. One of the longest and most memorable trips took me back to the good ol' USA. The show had been going about a year and a half when we took off and flew directly to Los Angeles, travelled up the coast to Seattle, and from there trekked our way back down the coast by car till we reached San Diego and then flew home. The trip started fairly uneventfully. There were nice little stories about beavers in the wild and another about squirrels in a park. The problem with these little fellows is that they carry one or two nasty diseases which are quite contagious to man, so you need to be just a little bit careful when getting up close and personal with a squirrel. They have a very good set of teeth and know how to use them. Yeah, they bite!

San Francisco was a standout. It's a beautiful city and has some great stories too. We see plenty of it on television, it's the home of so many police dramas. With its trams, its steep hills, its waterfront, the Golden Gate Bridge and wonderful, friendly people, it is a very welcoming city. The 'but' in a job like mine is that you don't have much time to enjoy all the niceties of life, it's a matter of getting on with making a show. Then, if time permits, you can soak up a bit of local atmosphere at the end of the day. The usual shots are the first things to get in the can. A walk under the bridge. Then it's on and off a tram—sorry, trolley car—riding it down a hill, and later strolling on the jetties of Fisherman's Wharf. That done, now it's down to the real work. But for me this was going to be all pleasure.

The California Academy of Sciences is a huge complex dedicated to all things scientific, and a visit to this establishment was without a doubt the highlight of our American trip. Louis Baptista, who I met there, is quite a man, one of the most interesting human beings it's ever been my pleasure to meet. He's a scientist, a researcher, a comedian, a whistler, a joker, an entertainer and a super-intelligent human being. Just to be in this man's company for a day was electric. His particular interest at this stage in his very full life was the voice of the song sparrow. There had been many research projects before and no doubt there would be many in the future, but for Louis, at that moment, the call of the song sparrow was pre-eminent. This man was intent on studying different groups of this rather colourless little bird. They look very much like our own sparrows but have a little yellow patch on their head. They do a lot more than just tweet, they sing! Louis was convinced that different groups of birds had their own dialects and that birds from certain areas spoke, or rather sang, with contrasting accents and in musically separate ways. He experimented by taking orphaned chicks, bringing them up in isolation and then teaching them to sing, using tape recordings from various locations within the huge park that lay adjacent to the academy buildings. Most of his work was done in the park, as it stretched over some twenty acres. He recognised at least seven families, or rather dialects, within this one park. By teaching the orphaned youngsters the songs of three or four different dialects, he could make them multilingual.

Now, all of this sounds very high-tech and indeed it was. He used the very best in recording apparatus. Oscilloscopes recorded the sound waves, and printouts of the melodies were made, enabling him to 'read' the music of the song. Then he could compare one with another. But Louis was one step ahead of all these machines. He had the most amazing ear. The man could identify, without the use of any machine, individual dialects by listening to the sound of the recording. (I couldn't.) Not only that, he could exactly mimic them!

Louis is only a little guy. About 170 centimetres, with olive skin and black hair, and fairly bubbling with enthusiasm, he would sit there tracing his finger along the oscilloscope. Contorting his lips into the most unusual configurations, he exactly reproduced the sounds the waves conveyed. Talk about talking to the animals—this bloke did it. He was so good that the birds talked back to him. A walk round the park with Louis was an invitation to every song sparrow in the neighbourhood to come down and say g'day. This man was the pied piper of the sparrows. To walk with him and have the birds literally fly down to join you was unbelievable. They flew past you, around you, and perched right alongside you if you sat. It was just incredible. He took it all as just a matter of course. Changing the dialect only a bit would cause that group to fly away, then we'd walk on a bit further and a new bunch would fly down.

He'd done similar work with other birds but over a much wider area. This was really high-tech stuff, as the differences between individual groups were fairly minute. But Louis could pick them in an instant. Back in the office we were surrounded by monitors, computers, recorders, stuffed birds, and drawers full of skins and feathers. Bouncing around in all this dusty atmosphere was Louis, whistling as he went. Out on the roof were his aviaries, where he kept quite a big collection of his little friends. The idea behind this breeding was to attempt to produce birds that he could train to sing whatever song he wished. His energy and enthusiasm were contagious.

One major attraction of the academy is a huge aquarium situated right in the very centre of the building. It spans something like three floors, is circular in outline and has water that revolves continuously. The fish are enormous and you can view them from each floor and also from the top. From there, if you're lucky enough, you can get to feed them as well.

Next day, the crew were back again. Surely we couldn't have half the fun today that we enjoyed before. Well, perhaps we did. Jackass penguins are native to South Africa. They're rather cute little guys and stand about sixty centimetres tall with the usual sort of penguin configuration and markings. They were being studied up on the top floor of the building. There was a whole group of them, about ten in number, and they would waddle around the corridors, line astern behind Karen, their carer. She was investigating the various behaviour patterns of these birds and, of course, there had to be one that became a favourite.

Prue was a female, and she was in love with Karen. You see, birds are like this. They 'imprint', as we call it. It means they bond very closely to something or someone that they grew up with and they regard that particular object or person as their soulmate. Yeah, they're virtually in love. So this little penguin followed Karen around as if she, that is, Karen, was her mate. She'd gather nesting material, picking up little sticks and bits of paper, carrying them in her beak. She would try and build a crude nest in or around wherever Karen stood. With the nest arranged to her liking, she'd go into this crooning sort of gesture where she'd bend at an angle of 45 degrees, lift her head in the air and, with a 'ka ka ka' call, implore Karen to come and give her a bit of a scratch.

Sure, all these guys had a pool and all that sort of stuff, but can you really imagine a gaggle of penguins walking around the floor of your office block? No one even noticed they were there. It's almost as though the penguins were there first and we moved in later. Well, I'm sure that's how the penguins felt about it, anyhow. Strangely enough, that's the thing about people who live and work with animals. We accept situations like this as being the norm—and why shouldn't we? But it took quite a while to wipe the smile off my face.

And if you ever visit the place, you can have a smile on yours too, even if you don't get to see the penguins or visit Louis. Downstairs there is a huge vestibule devoted entirely to the works of Gary Larson—you know, the cartoonist—with his very satirical outlook on man's relationships with the animal kingdom. There are hundreds of his cartoons, enlarged and framed, hanging on the wall. We ran an hour overtime just walking around looking at these.

There's something about the area around Los Angeles that reminds me of a bushfire. The sky has this almost permanent brownish orange tinge. It's not due to any fire, just to the sun struggling to find a way through the horrific air pollution that enshrouds the whole area and stretches out as far as Disneyland. You can see it when you fly in. It looks that thick, out the window, you could cut it with a chainsaw. The air is so still it's hard to breathe. The heat is dry, or it was when we were there. It adds to the feeling of claustrophobia. It was here that my normal disease resistance suddenly deserted me. Boy, did a bloke get sick. Every member of the party came down with a dose of some sort of respiratory virus, but yours truly copped a double double dose. The memories are fairly vague but one thing remains: the vision of driving a car, a red-hot car. In fact, everything was hot. The car was driving on a white-hot road, heading into an orange sunset through flames, at an incredible speed. You name it, if it was hot it was in the nightmare. After I'd had three days of this sort of carry on, lying on a bed that was constantly wet with sweat, the doctor duly diagnosed a virus infection. He supplied antibiotics and a bill for US$350.

'Got any other calls today?' I asked.

'Naa,' he replied, 'you're eet for the morning.'

'Yeah,' I said, 'two or three patients a day with a bill like mine and you could retire in a year.' Cripes, these guys know how to charge.

Though my body as a whole began to feel better the voice began to crumble. Finally, it just packed up and went. It's very hard to make television when your voice goes completely. But, as my dear old mum would have said, the show must go on. There were several days when that physical part of me called the body was literally carried into the spot, propped against a fence or a pole, and left there balancing with what little strength it had while mouthing the words of whatever it was that the producer wanted said. 'Don't worry about it, we'll fix it all when we get back. Just speak naturally and we'll be right,' I'd be told. My voice came out in a whisper. We'd do two or three takes and I'd often just fall over, still sweating profusely.

People walking into Disneyland must have wondered what we were up to—the sound recordist standing me up every time I'd hit the ground like a bag of dirty spuds. If that's being really sick, there's no going down that road again. It's probably as close to death as you'd ever want to be. Maybe all this red fiery stuff is what hell is really like. Don't think so. With a temperature well over the 100 degree mark most of the time, you never stop sweating. But you have to keep going. That's the way it is. There's a time limit. The work has to be done. A schedule has to be kept up with and the show has to be made. And you thought television was easy? No way!

The trip down to San Diego, lying stretched out in the back of a Chrysler Voyager, did seem to bring a little life to those aching bones and muscles. By the next day, the antibiotics had started to kick in and the old torso was feeling a little better, but the voice was on holidays still and the coughing had started. So here we are again, standing on the cliffs overlooking the beachfront, carefully choosing the words and whispering my lines to the soundo, while the cameraman blazes away. 'Don't worry mate, we'll fix it'—and sure enough we did. When we got back.

San Diego is a place that anyone interested in animals really has to visit. The zoo is world renowned and justly so. With a huge range of exhibits, splendidly laid out in a great habitat, it draws visitors from all over the world. The birds were of particular interest to me, though sadly a lot of the exhibits weren't up to it. The housing was a little disappointing and the condition of most of the inmates showed evidence of boredom and frustration. There were a lot of feather-plucking birds! Spending time with exotic animals like the kinkajou and an American o'possum was a rarely experienced privilege. Not too far away is the San Diego Wildlife Park. It boasts a huge open area and is built in a shallow valley with a railway line circumnavigating the whole park. As the train travels round, you look down into the valley floor where the wild animals, mostly African natives, wander at will. It's one of the first wildlife parks I'd seen outside Australia and, no risk, it creates quite an impact.

At last my old voice had returned. 'Gee, you've got a lot of gumtrees planted around here,' I observed to the manager of the establishment, who was a fairly young and rather dogmatic individual. 'Yeah,' he said, 'they grow pretty well around here.' He was correct. Right throughout California we had passed stacks of Australian native vegetation—enough to make you homesick. Since the climate of California is very much like the eastern seaboard of Australia, and there are none of their natural predators, the gumtrees had grown at an alarming rate.

'If you ever get a fire through here, the whole joint will go up in smoke,' I commented.

'No way,' he said.

'Don't be too certain,' I replied. When you've fought a lot of fires in and around Sydney over a period of twelve years you can see problems. 'There's enough rubbish lying on the ground to start a pretty good fire,' I added.

Not only did he laugh it off but he was quite offended and offensive about my suggestion that the grounds should perhaps be cleared of the debris. You know what eucalypts are like. After five or six years, a fair amount of bark and dead branches have built up underneath them. A wind, a hot dry day, a careless spark, and away it goes. Our own brigade had seen enough of it back home. Given the right circumstances, this joint would go up in no time at all. And how would the hippos and rhinos, giraffes and zebras cope with such a blaze? All land animals are terrified of fire. It's one of the few things they can't escape.

Back home in good ol' Oz, not much time for lazing about when there are stories to write and get to air. Then there's that problem of the voiceless presenter. You solve it with a thing called lip sync. It goes something like this. Firstly, standing in a recording booth, all insulated, quiet and dark too on most occasions, you finger the script in front of you. Putting the headphones on both ears you listen for the whispered tones of the stilted delivery and watch the pictures on the monitor in front of you; staring time after time at the video screen, looking for some clue as to where you should begin your delivery. It's sort of like miming in reverse. The clifftop shot outside San Diego was perhaps the hardest of the half dozen or so that had to be done. Twenty minutes of watching the same footage over and over (waves rolling on to a beach), looking for a point at which to start and knowing the pace at which to speak. Finally, there it was, a little surfboard way out in the shadows at the base of the rocks, with its pointy end just showing over the tip of the third wave. That's where to start. We play it a couple more times to be sure. Practise it, practise it again, so that when the camera swings to you the words match your lips. It took half a day to get the lot right, but you'd never pick it then or now.

Spring rolled on into summer and Christmas as the year drew steadily to a close. It had been a busy one and the ratings had continued to be good. There was even a chance we might pick up a Logie in April, but then again it's one of those fickle things. It surely depends on who reads which particular magazine and just what people's tastes really are. Even though, ratings-wise, we were giving the opposition a thorough thrashing, we would miss out yet again. Always the bridesmaid.

On the news some time later there was the terrible sight of the fires burning through California. They burned with a fury through the mighty pine forests that surrounded the palatial homes of San Francisco and San Diego. The cameras showed vivid pictures of gumtrees exploding in flames as the volatile oils sealed within those dull green leaves fed the combusting catastrophe. There in the middle of it all was a wildlife park. The same park through which our crew had wandered not all that long ago, kicking as we went the dry and crackling debris that now fuelled the inferno.

A letter arrived a month or so later. An interesting letter from a man trying to be apologetic and yet still claiming to be right, but wishing all the same that he'd taken the time to listen and to clean away the leaf litter from around the park. Too many animals lost unnecessarily. You felt for them, not for him.

14

Talking to the Animals in Europe

Australia has literally grown up on the sheep's back, and quite honestly they're an animal I don't mind at all. Mind you, our present-day sheep are by a long way different to their forebears that first made the long journey from Europe and South Africa to establish the flocks that we know today as Merinos, Corriedales, Polwarths and the like. The history of the world's sheep population would suggest that they emanated from two different sources. One of those was a group of coloured sheep, and some distant relatives of these guys, Jacobs sheep, still remain.

Jacobs sheep had always intrigued me. They are just so different to anything in this country. Sure, we have coloured sheep—Janine and I breed a few every year. But these are very different. Not only are they coloured black, brown and white in patches; they've got four horns, not two. One pair curve forward towards the eyes and the nose and the other pair stick straight out to the sides. A chance to do a story in Ireland on these very famous and very ancient sheep was not to be missed.

'Stop the car, Noel, stop the car.'
'What's wrong now, Harry?'
'Back it up, back it up.'
'What in the hell for?'
'There's something in that paddock I need to look at.'

'Not bloody sheep, are they?'

'Sorry, mate, they are.'

I should warn you at this juncture that Noel Jones, one of my favourite cameramen, has a certain thing about sheep. You wouldn't say he doesn't like them, you'd have to say he can't stand them. Over the years we'd filmed together, poor old Noel seemed to get all the sheep stories. So much so, that by the end of the first year on 'Talk To The Animals' he'd fair dinkum had 'em. Believe it or not, the very first 'wild animals' he filmed in Africa were sheep. We'd done sheep in Tasmania, sheep in Goulburn and even sheep on the Isle of Man. Pet sheep and sheep by the thousands. Noel was 'sheeped out'!

'Nothing to recommend them, mate. No personality, damn stupid animals,' he'd said more than once.

Yeah, he didn't like them, but good lad that he is, we're now backing up in the van. What a great sight! Thirty or forty of them dotted around this huge emerald green meadow, right out in front of a wonderful grey stone Irish tower. Picture postcard setting if ever there was one.

Ireland is chock-full of castles, mostly falling down, and these other things called towers. They are basically just that. No walls or ramparts, moats or drawbridges. Simple structures, with the odd small window. Huge stone cylinders projecting vertically from the face of the planet, presumably used as some sort of watchkeeping device. We rattled into the driveway and up to the front door. I'm out in a flash.

'Good morning, my name's Dr Harry Cooper and I come from Australia.' That was stating the obvious.

'Mornin',' the woman says, in that wonderfully smiling Irish brogue.

'I was wondering if I could spend a little time with your

sheep? We'd love to film them for my television show.'

'It'd be a pleasure,' she responded. 'But I'll just be on me way out at the present.'

Oh, bad luck, I thought. 'What about tomorrow, or the next day?'

'Oh, sure, Thursday will be fine.'

'Ten o'clock OK?'

'I'll be lookin' forward to that.'

Wow, this was going to be good. No risk, she'd know all about them and we'd get a really good story. It'd fit in OK because we were due to come back past the place that day.

Right on the knocker, ten o'clock, we're there. Noel, Peter the soundo, Suzanne the producer, and Steve, another presenter on the show. No reply to the knock on the door, not a soul around anywhere. We waited and we waited. Finally, after forty minutes, it was time to take matters into our own hands. Problem was, you couldn't get near them. As the only member of the party who'd had any experience at all with sheep (with the exception of Noel, whose every experience had been bad), it was time for me to give some orders.

'OK Suzanne, you and Steve make a little bit of a human fence across here, and I'm going to gently move them around the boundary until we get them in this corner. Then we'll all close in really slowly and I'll dive in and grab one. Sound OK?' There was no reply.

The field the sheep were in—and as I've said before, the Poms and the Irish don't have paddocks, they have fields—was a fairly big one of about five acres, and the corner I'd hoped to catch them in was under a huge pine tree. Now, sheep are pretty good at reading body language, and this lot knew from the word go exactly what we had in mind. Sure enough, they would move calmly and contentedly along the fence as I cajoled them into a false sense of security. But on approaching my two colleagues they would charge, right at them. 'Stop! Just stand still—they're only sheep, they won't hurt you,' I finally called out, as Suzanne and Steve beat a rapid retreat. 'But they're chasing us,' gasped my intrepid producer.

The poor lady had to gasp. She was, to put it bluntly, just a little bit heavy, a bit overcompensated in the avoirdupois department. Yes, folks, she was a fatty! But she was jolly, just like her ancestors. She'd brought with her to Ireland, the country of her birth, a pair of bright red rubber gumboots, the like of which I've never seen before or since . . . beautiful, shiny, glistening footwear, suddenly splattered with Irish mud as she ran headlong from this monstrous herd of assuredly rabid sheep. The gumboots were of the mid-calf design, the sort of thing that comes halfway up to the knee, though in Suzanne's case they barely got above the ankle. Poor girl, her legs were like tree trunks. These boots had more corrugations than the average Australian tin roof and they were all horizontal. The only practical solution would have been amputation at ankle level, converting the footwear to galoshes.

Heaving and puffing, she leant against the fence. 'Do we have to do that again?' she panted.

'Of course we do, if you want a story,' I angrily retorted. 'And Steve, mate, all you've got to do is stand there and just wave your arms about a bit. They really don't hurt.' Steve wasn't amused.

Next verse, same as the first. Noel's getting hotter and it wasn't a warm day. 'Let's pack this in,' he said.

'No way. We've come for a story and we're gonna get one. Anyone know where the bread is?'

'Back in the van,' said Noel.

So was the producer, stretched out on the back seat gasping and wheezing like some out-of-condition octogenarian who'd just completed the Sydney to Surf marathon. 'I feel terrible,' she moaned.

You'll get over it, I thought. 'Where's the bread?' I found it anyway, under the seat. On the very first day we'd stopped to get a few supplies; you know, drinks and the like, a packet of biscuits and some nibbles to consume on the trip. Something had told me I should buy a few loaves of bread too.

'Gunna make some sambos?' Noel had asked.

'Just might come in handy. You never know, you might need a shot of a donkey over a fence or something.' Animals love bread.

Well, it was worth trying on sheep.

Talk about body language! Walking out on to the lush Irish pasture and fumbling with the wrappings of the bread bag was temptation enough. No joking, three sheep walked straight out of the mob, came directly up to me and started to eat the bread. 'Jackpot, boys! We've got ourselves some pet sheep!' The rest was easy. These three would do anything for bread and even Noel got a kick out of some of their antics. Pet sheep can be a problem sometimes, but a real help at others.

And what of our wheezing producer? Well, we heard later that she was congratulating herself on what a marvellous story she had done on the Jacobs sheep. Sadly, though, like so many of her species before her, Suzantasaurus, as we'd affectionately named her, eventually became extinct.

Glasgow in Scotland was for us a pretty depressing sort of place, probably not helped much by the weather, which seemed to be perennially wet and cold. The grass grew, the moss grew, and Janine and I both got a good dose of the flu.

'If we put our washing in this morning, we'll get it back tonight OK, won't we?' I asked the desk clerk at our hotel.

'No problem, sir,' he replied.

'That's good, because we're off to Ireland this time tomorrow.' Quite frankly, when I'm on holidays washing is about the last thing I want to do, and if it can be done elsewhere, hang the cost, let's do it.

Janine had joined us for our last day. We were filming in and around the city and spending a lot of time on a magnificent property right in the very heart of the town. It was a couple of hundred acres of park-like farmland with a whole collection of purely Scottish animals—Clydesdales, Highland cattle and Border collies, just to name a few—all set in the grounds of an ancient and historic house. All in all, it was a fitting finale to a good month spent in the British Isles. Ireland was to be a short break as, once we were home again, it would be go, go, go.

'Where's our washing?' I asked the desk clerk that evening.

'I've no idea, sir.'

'Well, would you mind finding out?' He obviously did mind, because it took ten minutes.

'Oh, sir, the laundry's had a bit of a problem. They broke down and everything had to be sent elsewhere.'

'Well, when will it be back?'

'I'm assured it's later tonight, sir.'

We have our last evening meal with the crew, a leisurely stroll around the city—and three hours later, still no washing!

Six-thirty the next morning. We've got to be out of here by seven-thirty at the latest. Our patience is just about at an end.

Where is the washing? Same response as before: shaking of head, staring at floor, looking anywhere but at me.

'I've no idea, sir.'

'What are we going to do?' asked Janine.

'I guess we'll just have to give them some sort of forwarding address and get them to parcel it up and post it to us when the darn stuff arrives.'

'We're in contact with the laundry right now, sir. Your washing is on a truck somewhere. We'll get it to you if we can. What are your flight details?'

Sitting at the airport, we'd given up. 'Do you think we'll ever get it?' asked my rather distressed wife.

We've been round the world twice and the only thing we've ever lost is a facecloth. You sort of hope, don't you. You wait right till the end. You keep looking towards the door where someone might finally appear with your washing. But it's too late, it's time to go. Final call, no more stalling. This is it. Slowly walking out on the tarmac, following the painted white lines from the terminal to the aircraft. Standing at the foot of the steps, looking forlornly back towards the building. Nothing.

Then, out of nowhere, a green-capped Irish lady is yelling, 'Dr Cooper, Dr Cooper, your washing!'

And there it was, folks, all on hangers, all shrouded in clear plastic, and everybody in the Glasgow airport terminal that Monday morning knew that the Aerlingus hostess was carrying our washing. She never stopped calling out. There has never been a more public display of my wife's smalls. And I'm sure every passenger knew what colour undies we both wore, what size they were and what Australian company manufactured them. The aisles on these aircraft are fairly narrow and the washing only added to the effort of finding our seats, since we were up to the limit with carry-on stuff anyhow. Excuse me, thank you, thanks very much. And finally we're there. Yes, folks, right down in the back row!

Remember that my mother once said a bad rehearsal always makes for a good performance? Well, we had a terrific performance coming up.

The town of Kildare is only a short drive out of Dublin. They call it the 'Home of the Horses', for that is exactly what it is— the very centre of Irish-thoroughbred breeding and training. It's the home of Dermot Weld and of course our Melbourne Cup winner Vintage Crop.

For the previous two months I'd heard nothing from Janine but: 'Why do we have to go to Ireland, what's so special about Ireland?'

'Never you mind,' I used to say. 'You'll like it when you see it.'

And now we were there.

'Would Helen be in?'

'I'll just see for you, sir,' said the receptionist at the entrance to the Irish National Stud.

Helen was the assistant to the manager, and she'd been kind enough to look after things when 'Talk To The Animals' visited some two years earlier. A Canadian by birth, she had, like so many other young students in this field, come to improve her knowledge and expertise with horses. Apart from being a major tourist attraction, the stud functions as a breeding facility specially designed to help less financially able owners to access the services of most of the leading stallions on offer in the country. It is a magnificently designed establishment;

everything is just so. The staff consist mainly of young horse-orientated trainees who spend anything up to two years working through an apprenticeship-like curriculum. The graduates are recognised throughout the world.

The setting is picturesque: a huge lake with ancient pines and brilliantly coloured maples cascading down the grassy banks to the water's edge. There are swans and ducks, and heaps of tourists. There's even a Japanese garden located right alongside the restaurant, with a pathway mimicking a journey through life. Bonsai, artistic rocks, neatly raked gravel and running water make it a really pretty picture. Never mind the gardens, though, it was the horses we'd come to see, and see them we did.

Overlooking all of this were the stallions' stables—a huge long row of magnificent timber boxes with massive stained and polished wooden doors adorned with solid brass fittings. Hinges, bolts, locks, everything was polished brass and it shone. In front fanned out a generous parade lawn and gravelled ring. Behind were day yards and a sand roll. What a setup! There must have been a minimum of twelve stallions standing the season, each with his own huge box, beds carefully laid, not a scrap of manure or waste feed anywhere to be seen. Every horse was paraded out, walked around, trotted up and down, examined, talked about and put back in again.

Off to the side were the foaling boxes, all beautifully arranged around a central lawned area with bronze statuary and colourful beds of annuals. It is here that the valuable mares come to give birth to their offspring under the constant surveillance of at least two experienced members of staff. And there are vets as well. Everything is on hand to make sure that the foaling process goes without a hitch. It's just so clean and so nice that even the farrier's shop is neat and tidy. There are special areas for problem mares and facilities for orphaned foals. Nothing is forgotten. Out beyond the buildings, brood mares and foals were racing and wheeling around white-fenced fields with grass so green that it just had to be Irish. Nowhere else in the world have I seen grass as green as in the Emerald Isle.

There's a museum tracing the history of the modern thoroughbred, a huge display of riding equipment, farriery and all sorts of paraphernalia associated with breeding and racing horses. It's such a leisurely, wonderful place, with so much history and so much atmosphere. Five hours was enough to digest the whole. There was even an ancient abbey, now nothing more than a pile of crumbling stones in an equally ancient graveyard. Boy, we don't know how old things can get. Australia is such a young country that two hundred years seems forever to us; to the Irish it's merely a paragraph in the history book of life.

We were saying goodbye to Helen.

'Where do you reckon we should eat tonight?' I asked.

'I'd try the Curragh Hotel.'

'What about somewhere to stay?' asked Janine.

'Oh, there's plenty of places just along the road. Pick anything you like.'

No more than a kilometre or so outside the town was the sign that would become so familiar over the next week. Green writing on a white finger post, 'Accommodation', and a shamrock—certain endorsement by the Irish Tourist Board that this was a good place to spend the night. The farmhouse was reasonably modern and certainly looked clean from the outside. 'You go in and check,' said Janine. 'OK'. A wonderful Irish lady answered the door. Heaven knows how many tourists she'd seen before me, but wreathed in smiles she invited me in to view either of the two rooms that were on offer. Bed and breakfast is big business in Ireland. There are books, lashings of them, dealing with just that, and literally thousands of individual houses in both the city and the country.

When your wife approves of your choice, things must be on the right track. In no time at all we were made to feel totally at home, with a cup of tea and some homemade Irish cakes. And where would *she* suggest for dinner? The Curragh, of course, and after that, well, just a short walk up the main street to Nolans. 'It used to be a hardware store but now it's a pub ... there's drinkin' in the front bar, music in the middle and out the back there'll be dancin' tonight.' Sounded like an offer too good to refuse. I don't mind Irish tucker. A good stew, some soda bread to mop up the gravy, and a pint or two of Harp Lager makes for a great meal.

The night was mild and the walk bracing. From the outside, Nolans looked like so many other Irish pubs—pretty bland exterior, perhaps a few slightly frosted windows, the mandatory sign over the door and a few ads for Guinness, Jamieson and the like. Inside, the joint was jumping. You literally fought and wrestled your way to the back bar where something like seven or eight couples were busy dancing traditional set dances under the instruction of a rather tall lady who seemed to know exactly what had to be done.

'Sit down here, darling, and I'll just slip over and get a couple of pints of Guinness.' Easier said than done. There was a fair crowd at the bar and a good five minutes elapsed before I got back with the black stuff.

'You'll be puttin' those down here,' says the tall lady. No time for a reply. 'You'll be dancin' with us.'

'I can't dance to save me life.'

'Don't you worry, this lady here will teach you everything.'

And she did, well, dancing anyhow. No kidding, it was the greatest three hours ever spent on a dance floor. Whirling and twirling, kicking and twisting. Talk about a workout, it would've taken half a day in a gym to get the same results. The music was infectious, wonderful melodies, much like many of our own folksongs—tunes we'd heard on CDs or cassettes purchased over the years but never really listened to with any great intent. And at the end of the evening there was time for some song. How the Irish can sing! Have you ever heard 'Raglan Road' sung *a cappella* (without music)? It's beautiful. The local schoolteacher sang it with a voice that only an Irish upbringing can deliver. Words like 'lilt' and 'brogue' roll easily off our tongues, but to be there and to hear the angels sing was just magic. Janine sang too, she has a lovely voice. Then out to the middle bar, more singing, the atmosphere heavy with cigarette smoke and fiddler's tunes.

You suddenly feel you've lived there forever, and if you haven't then perhaps you should. If you ever ask me I'll tell you quite honestly it's the second-best place on earth.

Two o'clock in the morning and we're finally rolling into bed. 'Enjoy it?' I asked.

'What d'you think?'

The Irish experience all packaged up in one day: horses, music, singing, dancing and, on the side, a little drinking too. Ah, you don't forget a day like this, and Janine never has.

Over black pudding, bacon and eggs the next morning our hostess was bubbling over with information on what to do and where to go.

'But isn't there anything close by?' asked Janine.

'Faith,' she said, 'there's the old church next door.'
'Oh,' said Janine, 'how old is it?'
'Around six hundred years,' came the casual reply.

The wheels were ticking over; my wife was doing mental arithmetic. Six hundred years, that means around 1400 . . . good heavens, that's before they discovered America.

Sure enough, there the church was, a bit overgrown with vines and the like, but with enough plaques and engravings to authenticate its age. They're everywhere in Ireland, incredibly enough. It's just a matter of going and looking.

For the next week or so the little Vauxhall clocked up plenty of miles. Westward, down to Cork and then Killarney and most of the southwestern tip of Ireland. The weather was anything but good. 'You'll be better just lookin' at a little bit, that way you'll be wantin' to come back and see us again,' we were told. Too right we would, good advice. Yeah, and wouldn't you know it, the very day you go to leave, the sun starts to shine.

A day at the Irish races was probably the best way for us to bid farewell. The Curragh is a huge expanse of reasonably flat but slightly undulating land on the outskirts of Kildare. The local racehorse trainers use the ground—which is owned, incidentally, by the military—to exercise their horses. It's incredible to watch. The trainers don't measure out a course with a tape, they simply start at the bottom of a hill, walk up counting their footsteps, jab a pole in the ground, give the jockey a wave and get him to gallop the horse up the hill. Then they clock it! Don't know how they get accurate times, but the results speak for themselves.

Every so often the Curragh Racecourse hosts its very own meeting. Today was one of those days. It's a huge track with a massive layout but a fairly modest sort of grandstand—then again there's probably never a huge number of people in attendance. Our timing was spot on and we viewed nearly the whole programme. The race we'd come to see was a staying event— and guess who was racing? You're right, Vintage Crop! To get to the starting point would've exhausted most horses, so instead of going around the track they simply cut right across the middle of it. The barrier was so far away, the crowd needed binoculars just to pick up the horses, never mind the jockeys. The straight was so long that most of *our* thoroughbreds would've been looking for a taxi halfway down.

They're off . . . and thank heavens for the course commentary, so much slower and more deliberate than our race callers. Mind you, if he'd been calling a sprint he'd have been lucky to get through the whole field before the race was over. They turned into the straight and to my way of thinking probably still had a kilometre to run; it seemed to go forever. The jockey took Vintage Crop to the lead. To this day, I believe his regular rider doesn't set the world on fire—well, let's face it, he won one out of three Melbourne Cups but in the other two the poor sod probably needed some GPS apparatus just to find the racetrack, let alone the rail. Fancy taking a noted stayer to the front with a kilometre to go. He finished fourth. Another dreadful ride! This was before his last Melbourne Cup appearance.

15

Second Time Around

When the time came to make the overseas pilgrimage that many Australians seem to make with their children when the kids reach their early teenage years, Ireland was to figure very prominently in our schedule. Planning a trip is half the fun and the Irish Tourist Board seem to run neck and neck with their Singaporean counterparts in providing more information for the intended visitor than any other country. Poring over countless books and brochures on bed and breakfast places, country accommodation, luxury hotels and resorts, if you could call them that, was for Janine, in particular, an exciting experience.

'Do you think we could afford just one night in this place?' she said, thrusting a copy of a little blue book under my nose at the dinner table.

'Looks OK. How much is it?'

'Doesn't matter how much it costs, it'll be great.'

Women have a different way of thinking about money, yet there was certainly no tree on which it was growing in our backyard. The trip was going to cost a pretty penny anyhow, what with Disneyland then London, followed by ten days in Ireland and a week in Singapore. These days, a man feels exhausted just thinking about it.

A fax was sent, a booking confirmed. 'What about this place too? It looks nice. It's a great big house in the country and they've got fishing and . . .' At the very sound of the word fishing Heidi was all ears. 'Fishing, Dad, did Mum say fishing?' Unfortunately, she had said fishing. So how dear is this place? Send a fax and find out. Talk about the thin end of the wedge! By the time the whole trip had been planned one night in luxury accommodation had suddenly grown to four! This little blue book had cost me a fortune. By golly, the rest of the trip would need to be pretty cheap.

No point in dwelling on Disneyland. It's really for the kids, but then we were all kids once and quite honestly everyone should spend a couple of days there and be a kid again. London followed too closely behind. We were tired and even a tour of the city from the open top deck of a London bus was not enough to keep my two girls awake.

While London has some saving graces, certain hotels are not among them. 'Book us a pub a bit out of town—we don't want anything in the centre of the city and don't mind if we have to catch a train into town,' I'd instructed the travel agent. And where did we end up? Kings Cross, just near the station! What a dump, and what a dump the pub was as well. (I'm always in trouble for calling hotels pubs, sorry about that.) The Royal Scot was undergoing restoration; it was difficult to see where. And trust us to arrive on the hottest day they'd experienced for nearly two years. Nothing worked in the room—the airconditioner, the fridge, you name it, it was broken. The beds were so close together that moving between them was an exercise in tightrope walking. In the oppressive atmosphere, sleep was damn near impossible, and after sleep came breakfast. The meal was delivered on a tray, wrapped in Glad Wrap. Three miserable glasses of orange juice, served in plastic cups, and two sticky Danish pastries for each of us. And the tea . . . enough to make you throw up. Even the milk was made from powder. Heaven knows how they cleaned the room, but the staff washed up the breakfast things in our handbasin. The place was the pits and the cost would get you a suite in most mainland motels in Australia. A check under the beds before departure produced a hairbrush, a box of Smarties, a deodorant stick and a secondhand condom. None of them ours! So much for the cleaning. (When we complained, half the cost of the room was refunded.)

London says *theatre*. A night or two at some live show would make up for all the inconvenience. 'Beauty and the Beast' was just stunning. The costumes, scenery, music, lighting and the whole exhilarating atmosphere of the performance had Heidi on the edge of her seat—it was in the fourth row—for the whole performance. You walked out from the theatre with a wonderfully buoyant feeling. Live theatre is value for money.

Next night, 'Starlight Express'. We paid for good seats. 'These are Row N,' said Janine to the usherette.

'Show me the tickets, please . . . N9, 10 and 11. I don't think you'll be disappointed, madam.'

We weren't. The stage extended out into and above the audience. It was a rollerskating track; the whole show was done on rollerskates because it was about a locomotive. And guess where seat 11 was. Right next to the track. Heidi could have touched each one of the cast as they skated past. Action from start to finish, great story line and memorable songs.

Two top nights. You forget the bad and remember the good. Ireland, here we come!

Another tour of the Irish National Stud. Vintage Crop was now part of the show, as many Aussies wanted to see him. This time, with Heidi in tow, we pushed out further into the countryside, heading towards Tipperary before turning west and north through Limerick and beautiful County Clare on the way to Galway and the Connemara region. From there, further north to Donegal—I needed some more caps and that's where they come from. Donegal Town in County Donegal is a seaside tourist area with narrow streets, plenty of double yellow lines painted endlessly along the gutters, and very little parking anywhere else besides. All the shops are pretty grey and unimpressive. You need to get inside to really get a feel of things. Just about everyone sells caps, but a visit to the factory is what my heart was set on.

It takes a bit of finding, tucked away in a back street and with no big signs. You just need to know it's there. The management was kind enough to actually allow yours truly into the showroom. Imagine a room the size of a four-car garage stacked from floor to ceiling with caps: caps of every colour and every size. And hats as well. In another room, they were being made right in front of my eyes. If time had permitted, colours and patterns could've been made to order. Janine was beginning to get just a trifle restless after an hour. We'd narrowed the selection from about sixty down to twelve and that's what we brought away, with a promise that I only had to request this or that pattern and colour, and they could be made and shipped right home to me in Australia.

It always paid to book ahead and make sure there'd be a room available. Even at this time, there were stacks of tourists around and to get the best it paid to get in early. Bed and breakfasts are scarce in some areas. The town was Leith and the place sounded really nice. The owners were keen gardeners and that's something that we had in common with them. The radio was playing and the day was somewhat overcast and a trifle misty as our little rent-a-car made its way slowly and steadily towards its northern destination. Radio is something that's often in the background and to which, quite honestly, a lot of us don't pay much attention.

'There's been an explosion in Omagh and someone has been killed,' a quiet voice mumbled through the speakers.

'What did he say?' Janine asked.

'Something about a bomb going off,' I said.

As time passed, the death toll grew and one by one every news bulletin seemed to add numbers to the carnage.

'Oh my God, do you know how close we are?'

'No,' she said.

'Probably no more than half an hour away.'

We'd decided to avoid going into Northern Ireland and were simply scouting around its western border. It took another forty minutes to arrive at our overnight accommodation. They were there waiting at the door as we pulled up. Getting out of the car, we walked over to introduce ourselves. The lady of the house burst into tears, flung her arms around us both and just sobbed. We'd never had a greeting like this before. She was shaking, really shaking, as white as a sheet.

'Are you all right?' asked Janine.

'Yes, yes,' she said in a stumbling voice. 'I'm so glad you've come. Thank you for ringing.'

'Oh, that's OK,' says me, trying to be light about the whole thing. It took her husband to explain the reason for the outburst.

'You see, every Saturday afternoon she goes shopping in

Omagh. It's just across the border, only twenty minutes away, and she didn't go today because she knew you were coming early and thought you might like some afternoon tea.'

Did we save her life? I don't know, but she thought so. To us it seemed such a terrible tragedy. In a country with so much beauty, all of which is natural, how can mankind wreak so much destruction and desolation on his fellow man? No one there could tell us, no one really knew why and perhaps that will be the perennial question—why?

Some seven days later, we were to find ourselves in Limerick on a very similar Saturday afternoon, standing in silence watching the memorial service on a small television screen propped up on the counter of a clothing store. It all came flooding back. Let's hope that that will be the last outrage because for sure and for certain it was the worst. I remember thinking—as we walked back along the road lined by parked cars and totally devoid of people—golly, any one of these cars could have a bomb planted inside them!

Of all the places we'd picked to stay at from that little blue book, one in particular stands out. The one with the fishing. Funnily enough, it was called 'Cooper's Hill'.

'Let's get there early, that way we can do all the things they talk about in the brochure,' I said. But ten o'clock in the morning was probably a fraction too early. They definitely weren't prepared for us. The greeting at the front door was one of mild surprise. I think the lady of the house was somewhat taken aback—apparently most people arrive around mid-afternoon. Not us, we wanted to get our money's worth.

The fishing was easier said than done. The boat had a hole

in it and no one could find the oars anyhow, but there were a couple of rods and if we slogged through all the stinging nettles and thistles we could eventually get to the water's edge, where with luck we might snag a trout. Well, we snagged everything else, lost the lures and came home a bit disgruntled. What about some tennis? We all had a bash on the court, but thirteen-year-old kids get bored pretty quickly and that was the end of that. Croquet? Isn't there anything this child likes? Videos! Thank heavens, they had videos. A light lunch, beautifully presented in a magnificent old sitting room, really filled the bill. Relaxing in leather chairs, whose age surely meant they could tell many a tale from previous centuries, we made a decision. We'd go for a walk while the good lady of the house set the videos up for young Heidi. On the way we met their African Grey parrot. She was a very smart little bird, as most of her species are, with a good vocabulary and a real attraction to shoelaces. You didn't dare leave footwear anywhere around or the laces became confetti. Strangely enough, although this was Ireland, the owners were very distinctly English!

Walking is good for the legs, the heart and the soul, particularly when you're walking through the sort of countryside and woodlands that we were enjoying. It even gives you a chance to talk to one another, which is exactly what we were doing when confronted by this defiant gentleman in corduroy trousers, tweed jacket, collar and tie. 'Would you be quiet, please,' he said in a commanding sort of fashion. Gee, we were a bit taken aback.

'What have we got to be quiet for?' I asked. You never want to die wondering, do you?

'I just want you to be quiet!' This had a somewhat mysterious ring to it.

'Yeah, but why do you want us to be quiet?'

'I've got some deer in there, if you really want to know.'

They had quite a large deer farm and the path that we'd followed meandered around many of the enclosures. In the background was a large shed. 'They're in there, and if you make too much noise you'll frighten them.'

'What've you got them in there for?'

'I'm trying to catch them so we can remove their antlers.' He did seem just a trifle jittery about the whole experience.

'Mind if I have a look?' Although I think he did mind, we had a look anyhow. 'What's the problem?'

'Keep your voice down!'

'Yes, keep your voice down, darling.'

A man can't help it if he's got a loud voice. It comes from living on twenty-five acres and trying to summon wayward children from the back of the property. As things turned out, what the gentleman basically wanted to do was to cut off the antlers of two stags so that the lads could be returned to the rest of the herd and not do the females any damage.

'I can't get a vet,' he said.

'Well, you've got one,' Janine replied. 'My husband's a vet' ... volunteering my services without a second thought.

'Now, hang on a minute, I'm on holidays, I haven't got me black bag and I've only handled deer once before.'

He lit up like a neon sign, and well he might. A vet and he's right on the scene! It was agreed that the deer would need some sort of tranquillisation. A phone call to the local drug company had some Xylazine ordered and delivered within the next couple of hours. Dose rate was a bit of a problem, but a friendly colleague from down the way was able to provide the right sort of information; the rest was up to Dr Harry. The handling facilities were first class. A long, narrow race leading to a semi-circular yard all padded in thick rubber, and a pivoting gate in the middle, allowed the stag to be squeezed into the appropriate corner. Then, by lifting a flap in the rubber, enough of the animal's anatomy would be exposed to let me give a quick jab. Everything went in textbook fashion and, with the help of a couple of hefty Irish lads, the job was accomplished. How? Once the stags got a little bit dopey and started to rock from side to side, it was just a matter of opening the gate enough for one of the blokes to wrestle the deer's head around in my direction—and with a wire saw each antler came off in a flash. It was funny to watch the stags swaying along the laneway as they hurried to join their girlfriends up on the hill. They both looked so unbalanced now, without those magnificent trophies crowning their craniums. Janine was fascinated, she wouldn't have missed it for quids.

Well, talk about being grateful! We were the guests of honour at dinner that evening, drinks were on the house and the meal was just fantastic.

From the outside, 'Cooper's Hill' was just a big grey square box, looking to be about three storeys high but actually only two. Inside, there were polished timber floors with that beautiful deep mahogany-red toning on them. The windows, the staircase and anything else that was exposed had the same stain and polish. The staircase to the upstairs bedrooms was huge, fully three metres across, with a landing halfway up. The vaulted ceilings were decorated with ornate plaster designs and on the walls hung every instrument of warfare imaginable. Spears, staves, pickaxes, cudgels, they were all there, and shields, longbows and crossbows. Suits of armour stood against any spare slab of wall. All were polished to a metallic sheen. The dining room was something else—massive wooden beams across the ceiling, huge tables with tops at least ten centimetres thick, all solid timber! And the crockery, and the cutlery, like something out of the best hotels in the world. Thank heavens Heidi didn't break anything. The service, as you'd expect from the Irish staff, was warm, friendly and extremely knowledgeable. And the wine waiter, well, he was our friend the deerkeeper and was, in fact, the man of the house. While his wife looked after the inside and the food, he looked after the farm and the grog!

Breakfast the next morning was a leisurely affair, a chance to talk with our hosts about the history of the place. It was originally owned by the Cooper family, but apparently, as an heir was not forthcoming, the property was finally sold into other hands. Strange to remark, an ancient painting on one of the walls, and there were plenty, bore a stunning resemblance to my late father's brother. He's been gone some thirty years, but the fellow in the painting departed this mortal coil about three hundred years ago.

We've remained good friends with the owners and one day we'll be back, and this time I'll know a lot more about deer.

The Connemara region held for us a very different attraction. It is here every year that the best ponies bearing that famous name come to compete. En route we'd spent a night at the Cashel House Hotel, a really famous establishment, and certainly a little bit ritzy for the likes of us. (Even three years ago the exchange rate for the poor old Aussie dollar made holidays in the northern hemisphere amazingly costly.) The hotel was like a 1940s time warp. Huge, glassed-in verandahs looked out to the sea. Reading rooms with luxuriant leather sofas and roaring open fires claimed an ambience that belongs to another era. Dining was an experience, with almost as many starched and ironed staff as patrons. The food was truly excellent. No wonder it was a favourite holiday spot for many of the upper class. (That doesn't mean us!) The rooms were decorated in a charming country fashion and the beds were big, deep and embracing. Our room looked not out to sea but over the hills behind and the stable area. They had horses. This place was starting to seem even better.

A ride in Ireland. Mother and daughter were off, Heidi on a pony and Mum on an Irish draught cross. They rode out along the seashore, over the roads and up into the hills beyond, on steady mounts already sporting thick, hairy coats in advance of the chill of winter. It rained. They got soaked, but it takes more than a drop of water to dampen such enthusiasm. A huge Irish wolfhound lounged on the front lawn, resting his enormous frame in the watery afternoon sunshine. Photography was limited—there just wasn't enough sunshine, though even through the dampening mists there was something special about the place.

Clifden, where the ponies were, was brimming over with people. The showgrounds were packed. Stallholders had set up on both sides of the main street. The Garda controlled traffic. Parking at the other end of town meant a long walk in the rain. Once inside, you were up to your ankles in mud! When it rains, it just keeps raining. The ponies were competing in the main arena, which now resembled a ploughed paddock rather than a grassy patch. Competitors and their exhibits sank up to their knees in the mire. 'How on earth can they judge anything in this?' Janine enquired, programme in hand. Answers came from everywhere, all saying much the same sort of thing: this is what they had to work and perform in most of the year, so this was no different. Strike, back home we'd have called it off.

Apart from the horses there was saddlery to inspect, and food and entertainment—an Irish folk dancing competition. Up on an elevated stage sat a fiddler and an accordionist. Time after time they played the same dancing tune, while each young contestant kicked and strutted her way through a set routine. There at the other end sat the judges, a very stern-looking Irish lady and, of course, the parish priest. The dancers' costumes were traditional and the whole scene looked like something out of a tourism magazine.

Sometimes you're lucky, most times you're not. Our trip was coming to an end. The last couple of days would be spent in the southeast corner around Waterford and Wicklow. The former is famous for its crystal and naturally enough, if the opportunity presents, why not have a look over the factory and watch the craftsmen at work? Sitting there all day cutting crystal is skilful, for sure, but pretty mind numbing. In the vestibule is a notice: 'Waterford Show.' What's the date? That's today. A good old-fashioned agricultural show, not held in a traditional showground but right in the middle of a paddock. Plenty of cattle on show—Friesians with their enormous udders and polished black and white exteriors, huge Belgian Blue cattle with their rumps obscenely shaved to reveal the double muscling for which they are so famous, and a few other beef cattle as well. All just simply standing, out in the open, tethered to long rope lines. Large semi-trailers with drop-down sides selling all sorts of agricultural equipment. Tents housing displays of fertilizer and feed. A pack of hounds charge into the main arena with the Master, resplendent in red jacket, riding hard at heel. A blast on the horn and he summons the pack. His grey gelding wheels round on a hind leg and they're all gone.

On the far side are the horses, enough quality livestock to start any stud. It's a mare and foal class we are watching. There are twenty-two entries. Every one of them we would gladly take back home—from the first to the last they are all superb. The winner is an electric bay mare with a foal at foot you would die for. The pair have won nearly everything this show season. With a simple grey tweed cap pulled down firmly over his head, and sporting at least five days' growth on his face, the proud owner shoves the cheque in the pocket of a sagging tweed jacket and talks quietly to the local press about the success. Simple, sincere and thoroughly absorbing. Most of these horses are thoroughbred crosses, with a sniff of Irish draught and perhaps pony as well. Regardless of pedigree, it is the horses that shine. Their owners seem to acknowledge that fact and make themselves less conspicuous in an effort to avoid comparison.

It was a fitting note on which to end our Irish trip . . . well, almost. The town of Wicklow was the dispatch point for many Irish convicts condemned to a life of punishment in Australia. The whole scene has been recreated in the gaol. When we think times are tough, it's worth thinking about our forebears. One of my ancestors left this port condemned to life on the other side of the world for stealing a cow! Nearby are the Powerstown Gardens, set in hundreds of acres of Wicklow countryside framed by mountains, and a vista well worth exploring on your last day in Ireland. There's plenty of walking to be done—the landscaped formal rose beds, fountains and sweeping lawns mean a lot of exercise.

Second Time Around

At the bottom of the whole gently sloping area is a Japanese garden. Totally different to the acres and acres of pristine grass, this garden is steeply sloping and rigidly terraced. Small conifers, azaleas and camellias, all neatly trimmed, present the familiar picture of Asiatic garden design. Grasses, gravel and rocks are interspersed with stunted and twisted trees. By now the going is really tough, the downward path narrowing with every faltering step. Finally, we're at the bottom; it will be a stiff haul back to the top again. Janine sees it first. There, on the guard rail built to prevent a fatal plunge into the valley below, is a simple sign: NOT SUITABLE FOR WHEELCHAIR ACCESS. Only the Irish would put it at the *bottom* of the path. There's a special something about the people and the place. That's why going back there is a must.

Dogs and Other Memories

16

Gone Fishin'

Many of my friends reckon I'm the luckiest guy on earth: Geez, mate, living in Tassie, that's the best trout fishing anywhere. Yep, but somehow the taste doesn't have much appeal, and to tell you the truth I've never had the time to learn fly-fishing. With spinners and lures there's never been a great deal of success. Perhaps it's just my technique. Anyhow, one day I'll have a few words with the bearded burbler—old Rex—and maybe he can point me in the right direction. But saltwater fishing, now that's different.

It all began one heck of a long time ago, before young Harry had even thought of becoming a vet. A family holiday down the east coast of Australia, leaving Sydney and driving to Melbourne via the coast road, meant an overnight stop at least somewhere near the sea. Victoria's Lakes Entrance, even back in those days, was a pretty place and for kids the need to wet a line was, so to speak, a thirst you just had to quench. But our dad didn't have the faintest idea about how to catch fish. Sure, they're in the water, but he reckoned the only way to get them was with a silver hook (money to you). Kids don't go for that sort of talk and Mum reckoned we should be given a chance anyhow.

So here's the story: two young boys about six and eight years old sitting on an old wooden bridge, dangling lines over the edge into the water flowing below. Dad was a very impatient man, and a young fella like me had no idea what a bite even felt like.

'C'mon, roll up, it's time to go,' he told us.

All we had were a couple of old corks, pretty big things really, six or seven inches long and about two inches in diameter—solid cork with the nylon line wound around it. They were bought at the local fish and chip shop, and only came with one hook and one sinker. None of your fancy brightly coloured casters back then. What did you use for bait? Hadn't a clue really, but the shopkeeper had given us a couple of chunks of mullet and we'd threaded it on our hooks, somehow managing not to thread the hooks through our fingers at the same time.

'C'mon, c'mon, we've got to get going,' Dad said again.

'Leave them a little longer, dear, they're enjoying themselves.' My mother was obviously enjoying herself as well, for reading was one of her favourite pastimes.

Eventually Dad won out and we had to roll up the lines. 'Gee, mine's heavy,' I said. 'I'm having trouble, Dad, could you help?' And you'll never guess, or perhaps you can by now, that on the end of the line was an enormous flathead. How we got it up on the bridge without it severing the line with those razor-sharp teeth I'll never know. How we got the hook out without getting spiked I can't imagine. We did, but it took an old guy sitting next to us to show Dad how to clean it and fillet it. Honestly, he couldn't kill an ant, let alone a fish.

We were hooked. Like all good fathers, even though deep inside he was against the whole thing, if the kids needed something badly enough he'd come across. So one afternoon there appeared on the front lawn a little dinghy. It was made of plywood and had three seats, one in the middle, one in the bow and one in the stern. There was a set of oars and rowlocks, an anchor, and that was it. No boat trailer, nothing like that, but all in all it was fairly light and with effort three or four of us kids could carry it around. We lived on a huge double block of land above the Lane Cove River. It was a fair way down over pretty steep rocky ground and then an almost vertical cliff face before you reached the water. So to get this little dinghy of ours into the briney proved more than difficult. Eventually it was launched at a local boat ramp, and under the guidance of one of the neighbours we were taught to row. It's a skill that once learnt you never forget, much like riding a bike, and it took no time at all for the pair of us to gain quite a bit of expertise in the art.

The Lane Cove River fifty years ago was a real mess. Pollution was its second name. It was nothing to see thousands of dead fish floating endlessly out towards the harbour at low tide. It'd make you sick—and it did because we'd often go around the rocks and get a good feed of oysters.

'Have you been eating oysters again?'

'No, Mum, no. No, honestly, we haven't.' But then a good bout of gastroenteritis some four hours later would convince her that we were lying through our teeth. The oysters tasted good but, in hindsight, they were probably so full of mercury that we must've looked like walking thermometers.

Dad had the reputation of being able to procure just about anything—from a doll's eye to a toothpick, he used to say—and that was pretty right. So, sure enough, guess what turned up in the garage one night: a little outboard motor. Boy oh boy, we were made now.

It was a British-made Seagull, I think; none of your fancy Japanese stuff here. It had a huge silver flywheel on top which you started spinning using a piece of old rope with a knot at one end and a wooden handle at the other. It would only go forwards but you could drive the boat in reverse by turning the motor around the other way. Steering and throttle control were on a little handle sticking out the front—that design feature certainly hasn't changed. The compression was so weak that you could actually start the motor by putting one hand on either side of the flywheel and giving it a good spin, but by golly, it beat the hell out of rowing.

Fishing in the river improved as the pollution levels began to drop. Oh, there were a few scares from time to time in the early days. We had a dog taken by a shark just off the big sandspit right in front of our house. A lot of the kids saw it happen. The water was only about two feet deep. It didn't frighten us, it just made fishing all the more exciting. Even Bob Dyer came up with his wife Dolly to try and catch the shark. There were plenty of sharks around; quite often you'd be out in the middle just drifting along with the tide, lines dangling over the back, and you'd feel something come up and bump the bottom of the boat and rub a little bit, making the boat rock. When they got that close you just sat pretty still and hoped they'd go away. We used to take plenty of chances, I s'pose. Kids do, don't they. No life jackets, nothing like that. There weren't too many rules and regulations, but then again there weren't too many hoons out there either, so we probably weren't going to get hurt.

There was a rock pool built by all of us kids and a few of the adults from around the area. It was right down on the waterfront, where we used to keep the dinghy. A shallow rock shelf stuck out at one end of the pool. It was well above the high tide mark and there was an overhang above, which helped to protect it from the weather. The dinghy would be pulled up there and turned over till we were ready to use it again. The motor—yeah, the motor we'd cart home, it was light enough. And the petrol tank sat right on top of it like a big blue devon sausage. The rock pool was good for swimming at high tide although the bottom was nothing but mud and oysters, and you had to be careful you didn't cut your feet. We could stand out in the deep water right against the wall and have small sharks nose into the rocks as if they were smelling us. They probably were; it would've been pretty easy to lean right over and touch them.

The little dinghy was the pride of our life and it got a ton of use. Our interest in fishing continued to increase, and books and journals appeared in our bedrooms as the quest for expertise increased. Boy, at high school I was the envy of quite a few of the kids. 'Could you take me out fishing?' said Kevin. 'Sure, mate, no worries.' So there we were one weekday in the school holidays, out on the Lane Cove River, with a bucket full of bait, three or four lines and heaps of enthusiasm. I'd read recently in a fishing journal about a flathead donger. This was a fairly primitive instrument, but it certainly seemed like a good idea. These days when you catch a flattie the ideal thing is to hold it at the back of the head with a pair of plier-like grabbers. That way you can get the hook out without getting spiked, 'cos by heck that hurts and those teeth in front can cut the line like a whisker. My donger was something special, a one-off copy of a model I'd seen in a fascinating article on fishing accessories. It was simple in design, just a long lump of wood, a little bit bigger than a hammer handle, and in one end I'd driven three nails—they were fairly long, about three inches, and protruded right through the timber to provide a triangular pronged tool. The idea was, I explained to Kevin, to just pull the fish up on the gunwale . . .

'What the heck's that?'

'This bit here, mate,' I said, pointing to the top rail along the side of the boat. 'And when you get him there, whack him with the old donger and drive those nails right into his head.'

Boy, we were real pros. Kevin had never been fishing before, in fact, I don't think he had ever been in a boat in his life. His sense of balance was equivalent to a drunk trying to do a high-wire act after a night on the town. 'For Pete's sake, sit down,' I had to tell him half a dozen times, 'or we'll end up in the soup.'

At last the fishing spot was reached. 'We'll just drift up here,' I said. 'Ever caught a fish before?' He nodded. I didn't believe him—even the way he held the line was wrong, wrapped around his hand. Ten minutes later, the poor sod was sorted out. Then, bingo, he hooked one. Beginner's luck, but it looked all right and he was going to need a hand. Talk about excited, he was jumping around all over the boat like he had ants crawling up both legs.

'I've got one! I've got one!'

'Yeah, yeah I know, sit down, sit down.'

Slowly but surely, the fish came into view, quite a nice flathead, somewhere around the one-pound mark, but good for kids, that's for sure.

'OK, remember what I said, pull the fish up onto the edge. When you get it there, whack it.' Cripes, now I've got one too! 'You're on your own.'

What a mistake that was!

The next twenty seconds went something like this. Kev's enthusiasm peaked and as it did he stood up to really drive the donger through the fish's head and send the poor creature into eternity. He'd heard all about getting spiked and it wasn't going to happen to him. The boat listed really badly to his side so I stood up and shifted my weight to the other in an effort to stabilise things. Arm raised, Kev prepared to deliver the fatal blow to the fish but the fish had other ideas and flipped neatly off the hook as Kev's downstroke descended on his piscatorial partner. At this very same instant, he lost his footing. The boat rocked precariously over to my side and Kev, being unable to arrest his downward thrust, drove the donger right into the side of the boat, some four inches below the waterline.

'Get it out,' I shouted. And with that he gave one mighty jerk and not only did the donger come out but so did twelve square inches of plywood. A geyser erupted as the boat stabilised.

'Do something!' screamed Kev.

'Bloody sit down,' I yelled at him. 'Shove something in the hole.' Water was now flowing through it like a fire hydrant.

'What'll I use?'

'Take your shirt off and use that.' So he did and shoved it straight through the hole! I'm rowing like billyo to the shore, Kev's bailing, now he's shoving his trousers in the hole. All he wants to do is talk about sharks, but I'm just too intent on rowing. In the end we made it and, funnily enough, some years later Kev took up rowing professionally. But this time he was in an 'eight' with seven other blokes, and I reckon it would take that number to keep this bloke stable in a boat.

17

Car Yards

Barking dogs have been a problem for as long as dogs have been with people in suburbia and, no risk, they're hard to keep under control. These days, with the more effective use of dog training and citronella collars, we seem to be making some inroads into the problem. Going back twenty-five years ago, this just wasn't the case. People often went to desperate ends to try and stop dogs barking. There was the inevitable bucket-of-water trick, blowing of a whistle, cracking of a stockwhip, etc., etc.—all of which tended to create as much noise as the actual barking itself and get everybody offside.

You could buy so-called anti-barking muzzles. These were either leather or nylon webbing and fitted firmly over the dog's foreface to prevent it from opening its jaws more than a fraction. Regrettably, these things were only designed for dogs whose head had a long tapering profile. Tough luck if the offender was a boxer or a rottie! Worse still, experience has taught some sad lessons. Leaving a muzzled dog unattended can have a deadly outcome and the muzzle should only be used when the dog's under supervision. What has happened on occasions has deeply upset both the owners and myself. With the muzzle in place, dogs have vomited or become distressed and salivated excessively. Being unable to open their mouths effectively to get rid of the material, they have choked. A pretty sad end to a problem, you'll agree.

The alternative in those days was surgery. We termed it de-barking.

There was always some question about the legality or, in fact, the efficacy of such an operation. After getting legal opinions, and consulting various authorities, it was almost universally decided that if euthanasia was the only other option then de-barking would be permissible. So what did it involve? Did it stop the dog barking totally? No, it didn't. It just modified the bark. I used to tell people in those days that it was the Neville Wran syndrome. In other words the dog's voice, or bark, became a lot softer and somewhat higher pitched, but muffled. Sure, the dog still barked, but rather than a fully fledged WOOF WOOF WOOF it sort of came out as errf, errf, errf. The dog was still able to lead a perfectly normal life, still interact with other dogs, still eat, breathe and react in every other way perfectly normally. Quite honestly, I've never been really opposed to this surgery, if it meant sparing the dog's life.

To explain to you simply what's done will take only a moment. Under a general anaesthetic, several cuts are made in the dog's vocal chords. This simply alters the pitch of the bark and the animal recovers extremely quickly. It's pretty painless, though some dogs do have a slight cough for a few days. But that's about it. The odd individual may need a second go because one side or the other may partially repair itself. It's no big deal. Over the years there have been quite a few patients whose lives have been turned around. One dog in particular stands out in my mind.

Brutus was a big dog, a hell of a big dog. He was a Doberman/Shepherd cross. Short-coated, short-tailed—someone thought he looked like a Doberman, so they cut it off. And very short-fused! Black and tan, a head like a brick, one ear with a great chunk bitten out of it and calluses all over his elbows from lying on concrete for the best part of his life. He belonged to a security organisation that specialised in looking after car yards. You know the sort of thing, used car lots with a fence around the back and the sides and those great steel fortress panels they'd pull across the front after closing. The company had quite a few dogs, at least a dozen or more, and all of these had been surrender cases: dogs that had become too big for their owners or whose owners had moved away; dogs that couldn't be handled and savage dogs. When nobody wanted them, they ended up here. The crazy thing about all these dogs was that in the clinic they were as good as gold. Very often we'd get one in with a problem, surgical or medical, which would necessitate a day or two in hospital. They loved the nurses. They were the greatest sooks you'd ever want to meet. They'd jump on you, lick your face, kiss and cuddle you—you'd never guess what they'd really been trained to do. Out on the job it was very different; set one foot inside the car yard and you're gone, mate. A real Jekyll and Hyde lot!

Brutus had a problem: he barked and he barked and he barked. The mongrel never shut up and this was becoming a real problem. Quite a few of these car yards were in suburban areas and the sound of a large dog barking from the time he went in at around 6.00 p.m. till the time he came out some twelve hours later was pretty darn annoying. The complaints started. Brutus had to be silenced, or he had to go. Now, he was a really good dog, a first-class guard dog. No one set foot in the Five Dock yard while Brutus was on guard. De-barking was the only viable alternative. He came through the surgery like a champion.

CAR YARDS

'Give him about a week off, Dave, will you, and then he can go back on the job,' I told the owner.

It was about a fortnight down the track and there sitting in the waiting room this fine Monday morning were Dave and Brutus.

'Problem, mate?' I asked Dave.

'No,' he said, 'I thought you'd like to hear about him, it'll be all over the papers tomorrow.'

And the story, my friends, goes something like this. Brutus was employed to guard this particular car yard on Parramatta Road for twelve hours each night during the week and from Saturday night through till Monday morning. They didn't open on Sundays. When Dave arrived on Monday morning to collect his charge, the dog couldn't be found. 'I called him and called him but the mongrel wouldn't come. He's always waiting at the side gate, but this time I had to go inside and have a look.' Dave started to laugh. 'You wouldn't believe it,' he said, 'I found him all right, around the back. There he is, sitting as meek as you like, staring at the office wall, and there's this bloke pinned to the damn wall. Every time he flinched, Brutus stood up, growled and took two steps forward. You're not going to believe this,' Dave went on, 'but this poor bugger had been standing propped against the wall ever since Saturday night. His left trouser leg was very wet and it hadn't been raining.' The cops then arrived and carted the man off. Dave said he was heard to say, 'I didn't think there was a dog in the yard. I mean, he always used to bark all the time. I couldn't hear any barking so I just jumped in.'

Ah yes, Brutus, you were a good lad. They changed his name to Whispering Death. Brutus didn't know that; he just gave me a great big lick, a wag of that stump of a tail and raced out and jumped in Dave's van. These dogs are great animals, trained to do a job. They know when to clock on, and they know how to clock off.

I've been to another car yard since then, with a television crew, but the problem was very different. Two dogs were more or less on permanent duty. In daylight hours they slept in a large kennel area at the back of the yard and at night they were on guard. The problem was that the dogs had taken a real liking to the little orange indicator lights on the side of some vehicles. They preferred Commodores and Magnas. This is going to be a challenge, I thought, as we stepped through the front gate of the yard. The dogs were still on the loose. They were big and they looked mean. Mallanois are a breed like a German Shepherd, a sandy orange in colour, but with a very short coat. I hadn't run into any of these before. Whoops a daisy, the bitch grabbed the leg of my trousers. She was quick; boy, was she quick. 'I think you'd better put her on a lead,' I said, 'before she grabs something else!' Our anxious sound recordist looked like he was dancing on tiptoe.

The second dog was a desexed male and didn't seem to pose anywhere near the threat that his mother did. Sure enough, in the last week these two dogs had consumed eight or more indicators. They had just plucked them off the mudguards, sat down and chewed them up. They would then go back for the globes and the wiring as dessert. The owners had tried lots of things—mustard, hot sauce, chilli and various dog repellents—with absolutely no success. If it rained overnight it all washed off. Dencorub did work, but it had major side effects. It stayed on OK but managed to fog the plastic on the indicators and leave blisters on the duco.

When you looked around the place, it was just wall-to-wall

concrete and the pair of dogs had very little entertainment. They just had to be bored, and the young male seemed the most likely offender. It was a little game they'd invented to pass the time away and the indicators on these particular vehicles were far easier to get to than those on most of the other models in the yard. No point in trying repellents, I thought, we'll keep these dogs amused. A couple of 'intelligent toys' like Kongs and Cubes, and some good beefy bones, should do the trick. Hell's bells, we introduced a couple of bones to the two dogs and there was a full-on blue! The bitch was the boss and she towelled that son of hers up in no time at all, in spite of the fact that he was the male. All the same, the solution worked, and worked very well, and I'm glad to report that the five dollars spent each week on some nice meaty bones more than outweighed the damages bill that the constant replacement of indicators served to accumulate.

18

Wyong Again

Ann had once been a receptionist at the old clinic down at Gladesville. The daughter of a wonderful Italian family, she was just so full of life that it fairly shone from her very person. She also had a great love of dogs, a terrific affinity with people, and was not just an employee but also a friend. Her dad had bred a litter of greyhounds about twenty months earlier. They were big rangy dogs, mostly red fawn in colour, and well suited to straight track racing. Ann's dad was intent on getting these dogs to the track and winning lots of dollar bills. As the vet on the scene, it was the job of yours truly to make sure these animals were always in the best of health and physically fit. Almost weekly, Ann would bring at least three of them to the surgery for a thorough going-over. From time to time there'd be the odd sore spot or minor injury, occasionally a low-grade illness or bowel infection, and once a bout of tonsillitis. But in the main, nothing really substantial—certainly nothing to explain why they weren't winning races.

These dogs could literally fly on the trial track. Let me interpret that last bit. As well as racetracks there were a number of privately owned racing circuits, both straight and circular in construction. Here trainers could take their dogs and teach them to chase. The tracks were valuable for assessment of a dog's performance since distances were accurately measured; and a stopwatch became the necessary accoutrement for anyone remotely connected with the sport. This is where you came to trial your dog. Cauchi's trial track had the necessary facilities.

'P'raps I should come and have a look at them trial,' I suggested to Ann.

'Dad would love that,' she said, and arrangements were made.

A cold and chilly early Sunday morning, with frost still on the grass, is the typical scenario. It can get pretty cold at Kellyville. I'm at the finish line, so's Ann's dad. She's down there with the dogs, three hundred metres away. Each one will come up separately. She waves the red scarf. The first dog goes into the starting boxes. The lure moves. The lids fly. The dog's away.

It's a fantastic sight to watch one dog charging up the hill after a drag lure. You can see every muscle rippling, straining and flexing, feet hitting the ground with amazing speed. Dew flies from the lure, like the bow wave of a boat. The dog charges into the catching pen. Sawdust explodes around the dog as he plunges to a halt, panting heavily in the cold morning air. Clouds of steam arise not just from his mouth but from his body as well. They try, by golly they try!

The watch says 16.2 . . . that's flying, really flying, on a dewy morning. Up comes the next one. Just 0.1 behind. Still terrific; and the third one the same. Ann's dad and I get the same time. But why don't these dogs win? The times they run here would win anything. By now I've got hold of two of them. Her dad has the other. Ann drives back up, walks over to check on the time; she's happy, but like me can't understand why they don't reproduce this sort of speed on the racetrack. The dogs jump all over her. She gives them a hug, a kiss and a cuddle. Who says you're not supposed to do this sort of thing with greyhounds? They love her, that's patently obvious.

Ann and her father went off home, but another client had asked if I could stay and look at his two dogs as well. Not a problem. Home was only fifteen minutes away and the rest of the family was probably still sound asleep.

His wife was clocking times with me. 'What did you get on that one?' she asked on the way back from the catching pen with a big white dog.

'Oh, about 17.1,' I replied.

'Gee,' she said, 'I've got 16.8.'

Fair enough, I thought, she might've missed it a bit. But it was always best to clock fairly hard. That way you didn't fool yourself that the dogs were going faster than they really were. Up came the next. I clocked more carefully.

'What did you get?' I asked, before she disappeared to get the dog.

'16.6,' she said.

I'd got 17 dead. Something funny was going on here. It would take at least another ten minutes for her hubby to come up from where the boxes were. 'Let's clock another trial,' I suggested, 'while we wait for your old man.' Up came a big brindle dog belonging to another owner.

'16.6,' she said. I had 17 again.

'Perhaps your watch is out,' I said.

To test this you reset both watches on zero and then, holding one in each hand with the two buttons firmly pressed against one another, you push hard, both watches together. And you stop the clock the same way. Times should be identical. They were. 'Show me what you do,' I asked, as the next trial got ready to leave. The lids of the boxes moved just a fraction.

Click went my watch, but it was another moment or two before hers went off. Perhaps her reflexes were a bit slow; still, I was getting a time a good three to four tenths worse than hers. 'Could we try that once more?' Same result.

'Just when do you press the button?' I asked.

'Oh, when I see the dogs.'

'You've got to press it the moment the lids move.'

'Oh no,' she said, 'you've got to give them a chance to get out of the boxes first.'

Should I tell him, or should she?

Two or three weekends came and went and still Ann's dogs only managed to fill minor placings at Wyong. Things were no better at Appin either. Just what was going wrong with these dogs?

One Thursday night Ann was in for her regular visit, but on her own with just two dogs. 'How's your dad?' I asked.

'Oh, he's not real well, the doctor said he's got a touch of pneumonia.'

He was a pretty tough old geezer, only a little bloke but wiry and he never really seemed to get crook, so this must be bad. 'He reckons we'll have to scratch on Saturday if he's not better by then.'

That'd be tough, because the whole family really enjoyed the racing. The dogs were in fine order, as happy and bouncy as I'd ever seen. The way in which Ann handled the pair of them was totally different to her dad's way and they seemed to respond. They really, really loved her.

Today, animal behaviour problems form a major part of so many veterinary practices and a major part of 'Harry's Practice' as well. But back then I was about to learn a very important lesson on animal behaviour. 'Tell me something, Ann, who does most of the work with the dogs?'

'Oh, Dad does a lot of the walking and feeding.'

'Yes, but at the trial track, who handles the dogs?'

'I always handle them at the trials because Dad doesn't trust my clocking. But at the races he handles them because I have to put the money on.'

Very interesting, I thought, very interesting indeed.

Saturday morning. 'Ann's on the phone,' called out Helen, my receptionist.

'How's your dad?'

'He's no good. He wants you to scratch the dogs and I'll come up and get a certificate.'

This was all a bit unfortunate. P'raps there's an answer, I thought—and when Ann got to the clinic I had one.

'How would your dad feel about you taking the dogs there on your own?'

'No, he said if he couldn't be there, the dogs should be scratched.'

'What if I went . . . what if I went with you?'

'Yeah, Dad might think that was OK.'

A call to her home and the deal was stitched up. Let's hope no one there knew I was telling a whopper. Ann and her fiancé went to Wyong without her dad *and* without me. There's no way I could've gone, but something told me that she could handle things in her own way. By five-thirty that afternoon she had a treble, three out of three. One of them ran the best time of the day.

How do you tell a client like Ann's dad that these three dogs are males, not females—they like Ann better than they like you and they'll do things for her better than they'll do them for you. It was hard, and I honestly don't think he believed me. But from time to time when Ann did have a chance to fly solo the results were always sensational.

19

In the Good Old Days

There were lots of country racetracks in New South Wales. No TAB, just a couple of bookies fielding on the local dogs and the interstate gallops if they wanted to make a quid. Very much more relaxed all round. A couple were straight tracks. No bends, no corners, just a straight line. One was a good, steep pull up a hill. The dogs jumped as a bunch and flew over the three or four hundred metre journey. It was built just for greyhounds. The other track was actually part of the thoroughbred racecourse. Saturday afternoon saw the lure and starting boxes installed on what was actually the finishing straight for the gallops. The lure ran right up the very centre of the track. It sat like a miniature sled on two steel runners following a guide wire which ran through its centre. No hill here, just a flat surface with a very slight dip in the middle. Journeys were the same, three and four hundred metres.

Both of these venues attracted the regular attendance of local trainers and a real camaraderie built up around the race meeting. Everybody knew what everyone else was doing and if anyone was getting up to any tricks, take it from me, it didn't take long for the rest of the mob to find out. Every trainer or strapper was full of advice—there was never a greyhound that wouldn't go better if he had it. In the opinion of the trackside experts everyone did everything wrong, excepting, of course, themselves.

'Harry, you know that black dog of mine?' asked Pam.

'Yeah, which one?' I inquired, as there were at least three or four I knew of in her kennels.

'The big fella, Fred.'

I remembered him. The dog was a notoriously bad beginner. He'd leave the boxes a good two or three lengths behind the rest of the field, and yet on examination there was never very much wrong with him in the physical sense. In other words, I didn't believe injury was the cause of the problem and, frankly, neither did anybody else. The dog was a first-class maniac, which didn't surprise anyone—his father was too. Approaching the boxes Fred would start turning cartwheels, leaping in the air and throwing himself from side to side. When he was finally locked away in the starting box you could literally hear him banging and clanging inside. As a result, when the lids went up the dog was generally far too preoccupied to get away with the rest of the field.

'Well, Harry, someone said I should give him some Valium,' Pam told me.

As a veterinary surgeon one tries to have a certain amount of ethics, particularly when it comes to the use of drugs in the racing industry. How do you, therefore, comment on a request for information such as this? 'Well, Pam,' I said, 'I guess if I don't tell you about it and you don't tell me about it, then we'll probably be OK.'

Valium was used quite frequently, in the days before swabbing became a regular occurrence, to overcome episodes of cramping. The dose used was very small, and while the average person might think the effect of this drug would be to greatly slow down the dog to which it had been given, quite the opposite was, in fact, the case, as another client found out to his substantial cost.

'How much Valium do you think we'd need to pull up a dog?' his familiar voice asked on the telephone.

'I can't tell you things like that,' I replied. It's hard enough to win races, let alone lose them.

'Yeah, but I need to lose this one.'

Oh dear, a little bit of hanky-panky. It went on then and there's a fair bet it still goes on today, otherwise the stewards would be out of a job. Where money's concerned you need to be careful. Today it's probably a lot more subtle.

'I'm gonna put him in the bag,' the client went on. And for those of you who don't know what that phrase means, it simply says that this particular animal was going to be a red-hot favourite with the bookmakers. He'd pull the dog up so it couldn't win, the bookmakers would take heaps of money at odds well above what they should've been, and they would keep it in the bag when the dog lost. He, of course, would get a percentage for his trouble. 'Do you think one of the yellow tablets would stop him?' he asked.

'I don't know, but one would slow me,' I said.

It was a very sad and sorry client that fronted the desk in the surgery on Monday morning.

'Geez, mate, what happened?' I asked.

'Harry, you don't want to know.' Oh yes, I did. 'I gave him a tablet,' he said.

'The full tablet?'

'Yes, mate, the full tablet.'

'What happened?'

'Well, the mongrel was sound asleep when I went to get him out of the kennels and rug him up for the race—had to fair dinkum shake the bastard to wake him up. The bludger was just walking around with his eyes half shut, yawning. Had to keep tugging on his lead so the stewards didn't give me the once-over. Even walking down to the start, the dog had his head practically dragging on the ground.'

Now, for this dog, who was also by the aforementioned ratbag sire, this behaviour was totally out of character and that, my friends, is the understatement of the century. He was about ten times worse than Pam's dog Fred, if that were physically possible. He was always such a bad dog at the boxes that he would be declared as a 'bad box dog' and put in before the rest of the field.

'Well, Harry, when we got to the bloody boxes I knew something was wrong. It was like some mongrel had flicked a bloody switch on him. I declared him like usual and in he goes like a lamb, gets straight down, eyes the lure and never damn well moves. The ship was sinking and there was no way off. The rest went in and the lids went up. The bastard landed three in front. He only ran a tenth outside the track record—won by seven lengths!'

Ah, the best laid plans of mice and men, or should I say, greyhound trainers and bookies.

Pam got the story secondhand. 'It's your decision,' I said. 'Don't tell me, I don't want to know about it, but it's obvious you don't need that much.'

'Geez, Harry, I've never done anything like this before in me life.'

'Well, whatever you don't give the dog I'd take yourself,' I told her in a sort of throwaway fashion.

By Monday morning all of the racetrack mafia were having a good laugh after Saturday's meeting. The story told to me goes something like this. Pam's husband Steven had been in a bit of strife with the stewards at the club. He normally handled the dogs on race days and probably did a good part of the training at home as well. But his affinity with the amber fluid often led to an overdose and he was banned from handling dogs on the course through being, on several occasions, more than slightly intoxicated. Pam had to handle them. The behaviour of her husband on numerous prior occasions had caused her severe embarrassment and she, too, was insistent that he leave the dog handling to her.

Anyhow, Fred bolted in, at very substantial odds. Everybody was happy except, of course, the bookies, but then they're seldom happy. After the dog was kennelled, it was down to the bar to celebrate the win. Pam was absolutely ecstatic—it was obvious that this sort of therapy was exactly what the dog had needed. She shouted for the bar, not once but twice, and while all and sundry were consuming their drinks, she herself guzzled down three double whiskys. My dear friends, a cocktail of three-quarters of a five milligram Valium tablet plus three double whiskys taken in rapid succession is a dangerous one. Pam rocked, she swooned, she fell across the bar and collapsed on the floor. The mafia came to the rescue. One strong man on each arm, one strong man on each leg, and they manhandled the poor anaesthetised trainer right through the middle of the betting ring, which by now was crowded with punters. There seemed little in the way of a place to put her to recover, but the back of an HQ station wagon isn't just a good way to transport dogs. It was obviously a good spot to sleep off a hangover as well.

'Harry, I've never been so embarrassed in all my life!' she said later. And that was really something coming from Pam, because she was, my friends, a real lady.

20

Out of the Box

The greyhound industry has attracted, like most racing industries, some great characters over the years. Old Bob was one of these. He lived in a little, well, perhaps not so little, terrace house in Leichhardt in Sydney. It was one of a number. You know the things I mean. Side by side, two storeys with a balcony up top, front door to one side, beautiful wrought iron lacework and thick heavy steel front fence. There was always access via the rear lane and the whole backyard was pretty minuscule and surrounded by a high picket fence. Very often the loo and/or the laundry were halfway down the backyard.

Bob became a great friend and from him I was to learn the basics of greyhound training. How this man ever managed to survive was beyond me, but Bob loved his dogs and the dogs loved Bob. There was nothing else in his life. Everything he earnt he spent on the dogs. A couple of women had been part of his life for a while, but they made the mistake of delivering that fatal ultimatum: it's me or the dogs. It was always the dogs.

In this tiny backyard were a whole gaggle of wooden kennels, at least eight or ten of them. For certain, council regulations would never have permitted this number of dogs in any backyard. Didn't worry Bob; in fact, very little worried him. The dogs would kick up a terrible din, barking at all hours of the day and night. There'd be pups, brood bitches and race dogs all kennelled there or racing round the backyard, which was totally covered in concrete and almost continuously wet, for one thing Bob was scrupulous at was keeping the place clean. The hose was never far away. The din must have been amazing. It was bad enough when you were in there and I've been there at the craziest of hours. You could hear them at the end of the street. Never worried Bob.

'How do you put up with all this racket, Bob?' I yelled over the yodelling pups demanding their morning feed.

'Whaaat?' he said in a high-pitched sort of yodel matched only by the continual buzzing and whistling of his constantly overtuned hearing aid. Bob was about as deaf as a beetle. You had to walk right up to him and yell in the other ear just to get his attention. Convince him to turn the darn thing down a bit and you still had to yell to get over the constant 'zzzsssiing' it made. For Bob everything was easy—all the dogs were called Boy and all the bitches were called Girl. If only everything in life could be this simple! The reason why the neighbours never complained was explained one evening. Bob used to work on the waterfront, bulk loading wheat. One particular shift he was standing on the edge of the hold, guiding the massive loader into position, when a pulley slipped and the loader swung backwards, sending him spinning into the hold where the driver, unaware of Bob's predicament, dropped some fifteen tonnes of wheat on top of him.

They made them tough in those days. Bob got out all right but with almost total loss of hearing in both ears. Compo was forthcoming and he got a fair swag. With that the old fella managed to buy a whole block of terrace houses, so whenever the neighbours complained about the dogs Bob would throw them out. After all, he was their landlord. It's a case of put up and shut up, isn't it.

Just occasionally I'd walk with Bob and the dogs. He was great to talk to and had some fantastic yarns about places he'd been and things he'd done. Just to be able to stroll along in the afternoon sun, with a few dogs gently pulling away at the end of a lead, felt good anyhow. The biggest problem with this wonderful old gentleman was his propensity for wearing gumboots. It probably came from the fact that the backyard was continuously wet—it was definitely the best form of footwear. There we are, out walking this particular day, when he runs into a mate. We get yarning. Now, some dogs are definitely stupid. This big brindle and white pup that Bob had was a classic example. Every time you'd stop, the dog had to cock his leg on something. You'd swear he was a diabetic. So here we are, stopped in the middle of the road, and the dog cocks its leg on Bob's gumboot. This would probably have been fine if the dog had weighed around twenty-five kilos, but he was a forty-kilo monster and he proceeded to fill Bob's gumboot with more than a cupful of warm yellow liquid. I'd never heard Bob swear before but that was a time to add a whole lot of new words to the vocabulary.

Many of the laneways in and around Leichhardt are pretty narrow and it's difficult for delivery trucks to negotiate a lot of them—and it was particularly difficult this afternoon. Bob and I were walking side by side, eight dogs in front of us, down this little cobbled lane. 'Toot, toot' came the sound, and behind was quite a large van with a rather angry-looking driver yelling and gesticulating out the side window.

'Bob, we'll have to get out of the way,' I said.

'What's that, boy?' he said through the continuing whistle of the damn hearing aid. 'What's that?'

'We'll have to get out of the way,' I yelled in his good ear.

'Whose way?'

'The damn truck!' The horn blared again.

'What luck?'

'The truck, Bob, the truck!'

By now the driver was out of the truck and marching towards us. He was a fair lump of a bloke, tattoos poking out between the vestiges of a pretty tattered dark blue singlet. 'Get off the XYZ road, you XYZ people and your XYZ dogs.'

'What did he say?' asked Bob.

'He wants us to move.'

'Move? Who wants to move? I'm stayin' right here.' Bob was a pretty determined old bugger. 'We've got as much right to be on this road as he has.' The driver was on us now. Bob swung around to confront him as a torrent of abuse spewed from the man's mouth. 'What did he say?' asked Bob. I don't think he really wanted to know—the intent of the driver was pretty obvious. Frankly, the best option to me seemed a peaceful retreat, out of the laneway and into the park. Basically that's where we were headed anyhow. But you don't threaten Bob, not unless you can back it up. 'Hold these dogs, boy,' he says to me. I've now got eight of them. Bob was no spring chicken, around mid-fifties at a guess, but fit, very very fit. A man who was never frightened of hard physical work. He walks right up to this big bloke. Must've given him at least twenty kilos in weight, but nothing in height or reach. 'Well,' he says, through the screeching of the wretched hearing aid. 'Either you're gonna teach me a lesson, boy, or I'm gonna teach you one.' Now, what this truckie didn't know was that Bob could handle himself pretty well. As a kid he was a first-class boxer and went on to fight semi-professionally for a lot of his younger years.

Bob rolled up his sleeves. The driver shaped up. It was on. The big ugly truckie lumbered towards his older and leaner opponent, muttering obscenities and flailing the air with his huge hairy fists. Bob just stood his ground. The old fella never moved, patiently waiting for this bloke to come to him. And he did, swinging both arms like a rotary clothesline in a howling westerly. Bob just ducked and weaved, never lifting his hands. The big fella must've kept swinging for a good twenty seconds. Never got anywhere near the target; Bob handled himself like a pro.

Then, in an instant, it was over. Like lightning, Bob's left went out, catching the great ox fair on the side of the nose. A right to the soft, bulging stomach. The bloke doubled over. An upper cut smashed into his chin on the way down. And that was it.

'Should we turn off the motor, Bob?' I asked.

'What rotor?'

Ah, stuff it.

'Give me the dogs, boy,' Bob said, and off we shuffled into the afternoon light. Heaven knows how long it took the bloke to get up, but he obviously did or I'd have read about it in the papers the next day.

21

Life on the Farm

'I think we should have a pet pig. I've read all about them, they're really great pets and we could teach it to do lots of things. It'd be great on TV.' My wife is always full of good ideas.

'They're huge,' I said.

'No, no, no, not a normal one. I've seen these miniature things.'

It doesn't take very long to realise you're on the losing end of an argument. That's where you usually end up in our house, and try as I might to explain that we don't possess the genetic material to breed miniature pigs in Australia, it was a total waste of time.

'I've seen them, I've seen them in Melbourne, I saw them at the show. I've organised to get one.'

Told you it wouldn't have mattered what I said. A pig was going to get here anyhow—but would it stop at one, that was the burning question.

Everything had been arranged, totally behind my back. The pig, or rather piglet, was to be collected on my next trip home from Melbourne. I'd be met at the airport and the piglet transferred into a carry cage for the trip home. 'Everything is under control, she'll ring you just before the airport. You won't have to pay anything, I've already done it.' Yes, and probably from my cheque book. In fact, what it cost for this so-called miniature pig would've bought two or three litters of the normal ones.

So it's Friday afternoon, and as busy as it usually is on the last day of the week at any airport. Bags already checked in. Sitting waiting in the luggage collection area of the Ansett terminal. Plastic transport cage in hand. No pig. It's getting late. Perhaps she's gone to the Qantas terminal. Out the door, run down the road, race into the baggage area there. No one with a cage. No pigs. No person who looks like a pig person. No message. Nothing.

'She hasn't turned up,' my mobile relayed.

'I'm sure she's coming, she rang to say she's on the way.'

'I've tried her, but she doesn't answer the phone.'

Better get back to Ansett, that's where we're supposed to meet. By now the guy in special baggage knows exactly what's going on. 'A pig, Dr Harry! What do you want with a damn pig?'

'Don't blame me, blame the wife.'

He's on red alert. As soon as the pig arrives it'll be whipped into my carry basket, passed over the counter to him and sent on its way to Tassie. But time's running out, they're calling the flight. 'You'll have to hurry up, Dr Harry.' That's stating the obvious. Suddenly she bursts into the foyer looking like something from a Lismore hippy commune. Bare feet, tattered cotton dress, hair in dreadlocks and one or two snotty-nosed children at her feet. In her right hand, a large plastic carry cage with the precious cargo. 'Make sure you pick a pretty one,' were my final instructions from Janine.

'Tip the box on its end,' I say. Things have to be done at a million miles an hour. Open the door, peer inside. A black one, a tan one and a white and tan one. 'This one will do,' I yell, grabbing hold of the party-coloured piglet by the nearest hind leg I could find and lifting it holus-bolus from the cage. The one thing you learn about pigs from a very early age is that they scream, and boy, do they scream. If they haven't got all four legs firmly planted on a solid surface they squeal. It's high pitched, it's loud and it's continuous, and this piglet has the best set of lungs money can buy. Everyone's watching—must be fifty or sixty people milling around, waiting for luggage, looking incredulously at this piglet dangling from my right fist.

I quickly dropped it into the transport cage, slammed the door closed, checked the lock, and failed to notice that one of the snotty-nosed kids was more intent on playing with the two piglets I'd left inside their cage than with anything else. He upended the box and with that both piglets flew from the cage like pigeons from a basket. They were off and running and so was I, by cripes. Squealing piglets and jumping passengers were going in every direction. It was a riot and, fair dinkum, there was no way yours truly was gonna get caught up in the melee. I literally threw the box at the baggage master and bolted up the stairs out of the pandemonium and down the corridor to my departure gate.

No doubt about it—never has been—the piglet got a far warmer welcome at home than yours truly.

'Where is she? Is she pretty? Let her out. Let's see.'

'Go on, Dad, let her out.' Wasn't anyone happy to see me?

Out she flew. Our kitchen had a lino floor and to a little piglet that's pretty slippery stuff. She tore around the kitchen and the sunroom, skittering rugs and furniture in all directions, squealing in absolute and unabated fear.

'This is no pet pig,' I said, 'this is just some razorback piglet from out west that I think's been half starved!'

'No, it's definitely a miniature pig. I've got all the instructions and we mustn't overfeed it.'

Dead right, I thought, anybody who feeds this thing properly is going to end up with two hundred kilograms of bacon running around the place. At this stage the poor little waif was somewhere about the size of a fully grown cat, but weighed a lot more. It took probably four or five days before the new arrival settled down to life in the Cooper household, which is probably pretty good because life in this household is far from normal. Wasn't too much longer before Daisy, as she came to be known, would actually lie down and sleep with the cats and the dogs, and Janine on the lounge if she felt so inclined. There are plenty of photos to prove it. Then disaster struck, not at once but slowly. She started to grow.

'We need to teach her to walk on a harness, because I'm taking her down to the school next week.'

'You must be mad, walking a pig on a lead, you'll never do it. Besides, how do you think we're going to get the harness on her?'

Problem was, any time you started manhandling Daisy she would squeal. It was deafening, and with the nearest neighbours only a kilometre away it seemed certain we'd be reported for murder.

'Let's slip it on while she's asleep.' Seemed like a good idea to me, except that I was the one chosen to do it. 'Don't wake her up, be careful.'

I tried and eventually after three or four goes managed to get the whole harness on. Normal training practice would have seen the harness left in place each day for several hours until Daisy got used to the contraption, but we were in a hurry, or rather Janine was. I clipped on the lead. That was the signal for

Daisy to wake up from what by all accounts was a pretty torrid nightmare. Janine had made the mistake of wrapping the end of the lead several times around her wrist. Daisy bolted straight out of the kitchen and into the sunroom and right under the table. My darling wife was sort of aquaplaning on her abdomen behind her and could no doubt provide us with a glowing description of the underside of our sunroom table, because that's where the pig finally came to a halt, wrapped around one of the legs. Janine was saying plenty, but Daisy was saying more! One little pig has a lot of pulling power.

Several more nights of training didn't really do much to improve things. But by the time the school visit rolled around, I'll admit, there was an element of control. Just about all the available animals had been talked about. Grade 6 was fascinated. There were pigeons and puppies, guinea pigs and kittens, and the piece de resistance was saved for last. She was so good—she stood there, letting all the kids pat her and play with her curly tail. But everything was going far too well. Suddenly, from the back of the room, one of many party balloons exploded. So did the pig. She was off, squealing and running, diving under desks, around chairs, stuff going in all directions. The kids were screaming too, even the teacher went for cover, sitting up on the desk. How could one pig make such a fool out of two adults? She did. Ten minutes down the track, Daisy just ran out of grunt.

At around eighty kilos, it was time to move Daisy out of the house and for Janine to admit there was no such thing as a miniature pig. By now Daisy had become extremely tame and also extremely destructive—that snout could create so much damage to the backyard that something just had to be done. 'We'll ring her,' I suggested. The family wasn't too happy about the idea but it seemed the only way to halt her cultivation of the property. After all, that famous children's poem referred to the wood where a Piggy-wig stood with a ring at the end of its nose—so why not ours? Getting it there was the difficult part. If you slip a noose around the top jaw of a pig they pull back with quite a deal of force and just simply stay there, enabling you to do just about whatever you want. Rather than use a general anaesthetic I thought a local would do the trick. Getting the needle into that nose proved to be a job and a half. It was so tough and so firm, just like solid rubber. The next step was to introduce the ring itself, a brass implement about four centimetres in diameter. Once inserted, it locks together. Ah, but getting it in, that's the job, and it took nearly twenty minutes.

The ring sits very differently to those you see in a bull. In a pig, it's vertical. For the first fortnight or so, every time Daisy touched anything with that ring she would squeal. Everyone, myself included, probably regretted having done it, but in time it all settled down and, had the job been done at an earlier age, there's no doubt she would have handled it better.

'I think she's lonely.' My wife had now become a porcine psychologist as well.

'How do you know she's lonely?'

'It's the way she looks.'

You can't argue with that sort of logic, can you. But somehow in life, providence always seems to lend a hand. Not too long before, Katrina and I had handled a couple of piglets as part of the opening sequence of 'Harry's Practice'.

'One of those would be ideal,' suggested my darling.

'Oh yes, which one?'

'The black and white one, it's the prettiest.'
'But it's a male.'
'Yes, I know,' she said with a smile on her face.

Fellas, you're beaten before you start! Donald joined the farmyard and he and Daisy grew up together until finally they both became what I've previously referred to as two hundred kilograms of walking, grunting bacon. They outgrew their stable, they outgrew the yard and, finally, they moved on to greener pastures out near Scottsdale. Sure, we miss them, but until the advent of genuine miniature pigs in this country we'll have to be content with something just a tad smaller . . . guinea pigs!

22

Flossie Remembered

The farm at Annangrove was big enough and fertile enough to support at least one cow, and if you live in the country, then a house cow is surely a must. First you start with the cow. The best place to get one seemed to be McGrath's Hill. Every Saturday a huge auction took place. There were two totally different auctioneers. One was Jerry by name, an Irish man who sold household belongings and general junk in the morning and poultry in the afternoon. The other, a man forever wringing his hands, sold cattle and horses after lunch. It was a thoroughly social day. There were more tyre kickers than there were buyers. Stuff was often cheap and this was surely the time to buy, as grass was scarce and the local dairy farmers were inclined to cull anything they thought might not go through another lactation.

It was a dry and dusty yard. There were a good number of cattle on offer, mainly Friesians and quite a few Hereford crosses too. Calves, weaners and poddies bellowed and called from their pens undercover. Steers and cows milled around in the yards while skinny youths dobbed painted numbers on their rumps for identification. Over in one corner were two Jerseys. No way you could estimate their age, but they certainly seemed quiet. It was near the end when they finally came up for sale. Bidding was slow. 'What am I offered, buyers, what am I offered?' The auctioneer always called everyone 'buyers'.

'Fifty dollars,' came the call. 'Fifty dollars, fifty dollars, buyers, I'm only offered fifty dollars for the pair. They're worth more than that. C'mon, buyers, c'mon. Wringing his hands a little more furiously as the bidding slowed to a trickle, he called, 'Sixty-five, sixty-five, buyers, any advance on sixty-five?' I waved the Akubra. 'Seventy dollars, seventy dollars, buyers, it's with the man with the hat, against you over there. Are you all done? Are you all done, buyers?' The hand wringing was now in a frenzy. 'Are you all done? Once, twice . . .' Not a movement. 'Sold, sold to the man in the hat. What's your name, sir?' 'Cooper.' 'Thanks, Mr Cooper.' And so the wringing and the sale went on.

The cattle would be drafted along a race into a small yard for collection by the carrier and delivery to home. This was an opportunity too good to miss. The money was paid and the long plastic glove pulled on to the right arm for the first time in a long, long while. 'Mind holding these two girls in the race for a minute?' I asked the skinny youth with the paintbrush. 'Whatcha gonna do, mister?' he asked. 'Just you watch and see,' I said. With both cows in the race it was easy to do a quick rectal examination and a pregnancy diagnosis. Jackpot, one was in calf! The other was empty. They'd both been sold as empty.

Back at Annangrove, both cows gained weight. There was plenty of feed and once they got the worms out of their system they fairly rocketed ahead. By the time the barren cow had really built up, the market had lifted considerably. She went back to the sale ring and brought more on her own than we'd paid for the two together. The other one, Flossie, as she came to be known, was our first house cow. She became a real pet, had something like five calves for us but every one was a bull. What rotten luck. The artificial insemination man would call on a regular basis and he'd get her in calf first time just about every season. We paid top dollar for the best bulls. How disappointing.

Hand milking is good for the soul. It's something you can't rush. Standing there in the head-bail I'd constructed, with the wood clamped loosely around her neck, she'd munch away on the bucketful of feed in front of her while I stripped the milk from that warm udder. Milking once every second day was more than enough to keep us going. The calf got the rest. We'd simply lock him up the night before and she'd fairly fly up the driveway the next morning to get to him and the tucker. Some days you're in a hurry, some days you're in a bad mood. It doesn't pay to be in either state of mind when you're going to milk a cow. They can read you like a book, kick over the bucket, manure everywhere. It would invariably splatter all over you and, to top it all off, she'd empty her bladder as well. Take it easy, take it slowly and that way everyone winds up with what they want. Flossie has taught me more patience than any other animal I've owned.

My mentor, Roley, from up at Raleigh, happened to catch a glimpse of her one day when he was visiting. 'Do you know,' he said, pointing out the brand on her hip, 'she's from one of the best herds in the Windsor district. But she must be getting on now, that place was dispersed six or seven years ago.' She *was* an old girl and as the years progressed you could hear her joints groaning even as she got to her feet. One morning she didn't get up, she couldn't get up, and no drugs in my medicine chest could get her to stand. Dignity in death is as important to animals as it is to us. The family hugged her as I took her life away and she lies where she often used to lie in the shade of the willows by the little stream.

But that was not the end of our having cows.

Up on Roley's place years before, there'd been a family of cows with a most peculiar colour pattern. His herd was mainly Friesian but there were always a few Jerseys in the mob, just to lift the quality of the milk. They were different cows, smaller, quieter and with the most beautiful eyes of any animal. He called the foundation cow Buttercup, not very original but it stuck. She was party-coloured—white with patches of light and dark fawn—so distinctive that you could pick her in an instant. Every calf she had was marked the same.

'You'd better take this young lady home,' Roley said, carrying out a small poddy calf in his arms. And take her home we did, all the way from near Coffs Harbour back down to Annangrove. The spitting image of her mum, Lucille grew up to be a beautiful cow, but like so many animals raised as pets, the bigger they get, the more of a problem they become.

Because she was so quiet, Janine had taught her to be tied up along the chainwire fence that encircled most of the farm. It was just a question of moving her along and controlling the grazing.

'Lucille's really becoming quite a handful,' my wife shouted down the phone one day.

'What's wrong now?' I asked.

'Well, I was trying to move her this morning along the fence and when I bent down to undo the shackle she jumped on top of me.'

By this stage Lucille was well over twelve months old and quite a big heifer. She'd not been mated as yet.

'Doesn't it mean she's in season when she jumps on top of you?' Janine went on.

'No, darling, it doesn't normally mean that,' I said. 'It's the one that's being jumped on that's in season! How does that make you feel?'

'Ha, ha, ha,' was the sarcastic reply.

Lucille was just being friendly. Cattle play like this all the time, but my darling was pregnant, and being outwrestled by a far larger opponent. Commonsense prevailed, and Lucille moved to greener pastures with Kerry and Tim up around Gosford way. They tell me she still got up to her old tricks there.

23

Blondie

'Did you see the new Welsh foal down in the paddock?' Janine asked. I had. It was the first foal of the season and there's always excitement when it arrives. Down in the most sheltered paddock at Relbia, Cinderella had produced for us a most stunning Palomino-like filly. Perhaps it was even a little too light to be Palomino. But how do you tell your wife that you think a foal is blind? 'It couldn't be . . . it couldn't be,' she said. Disbelief is hard to pacify.

'Let's get them into a stable and then we can all have a good look,' I suggested.

Poor little thing, its eyes were closed and streaming tears. It was bumping into everything—mum, us, the fences, everything. Gee, I was upset. Finally, after what seemed forever, we got them both into a stable where it was dark—and deliberately so. Every time light seemed to get anywhere near the foal it would race off and crash into something. At least in the darkened stable it stood still. 'Nothing wrong with its appetite,' said Heidi, as it sucked strongly from its mum. No, there was nothing wrong with this, but how do you handle a blind foal? Time for some expert advice and thankfully, as vets, we are able to access that whenever we need to. 'Harry,' said Andrew in Melbourne, 'blind cats, blind dogs, no problem—they can learn to live with things. But a blind horse, mate, there's no hope.' That's not what I wanted to hear. He said he'd be down in

Tassie in about three weeks, and if I could keep the little girl going till then, he'd love to come and have a look.

Chris, my colleague, a horse vet from down the road, called in a few days later. We both examined the precious foal and both came to the same conclusions. All the tests and all the examinations convinced us that she couldn't see. Sure, there was nothing wrong with either eye itself except that it was totally pink. The lids were similar, no colouration at all in the eye or the skin around it. The problem had to be within the brain. Chris's book detailed two conditions in particular that seemed to fit this problem. One of these was common to horses with Sabino markings (patterns of white that extend irregularly high up one or more legs). She was too light in colour to see that clearly but her dad and her grandsire both had the same pattern. And the breeding was close—the same grandsire on both sides of the pedigree. That didn't help.

Fourteen days down the track and madam is growing like there's nothing wrong. Getting around in the stable she seemed to be able to find things without difficulty. Perhaps it's just her sense of smell and touch, we all thought. Come Saturday, Janine was off to a show, which left me to do the feeding. 'Try and put the pair of them out in the round yard for a bit of exercise,' she suggested.

'Aren't you worried that she'll do some sort of damage?'

'No, she sticks pretty close to the mare, I think they'll be fine. Besides, the yard is pretty shaded from now on.'

Cinderella was easy to lead, a real pet. I walked her out the door and the foal trotted right along behind. Hang on a minute! This foal just dodged around that verandah post as if she knew it was there. Perhaps she isn't as blind as we all think. 'Come back in, old lady,' I said to the mare. The foal followed.

Let's set up a bit of an obstacle course, I thought. So, using the farm bike and a wheelbarrow, I did just that. Walked the mare through the middle and got her to call the foal. Standing on the other side, she whinnied to her baby. It charged across the yard as if to join her, then stopped dead. Another thirty centimetres and it would have hit the bike. Perhaps the youngster *can* see? Try it again. 'C'mon, old girl, call your baby.' I didn't have to tell her to do that. She did, away the foal came again, this time it was the wheelbarrow she stopped centimetres from. You don't smell a wheelbarrow, you might smell a farm bike, but how do you know exactly where they are? She can see. She can see!

Over the days and nights before this, I'd thought about ways of housing a blind foal—perhaps fences that emitted sound; perhaps the whole paddock should be padded. I don't know, somehow putting down a foal seems to be just the hardest thing. But by now we'd all but made up our minds. 'I know we can't keep her,' Janine had whimpered, adding immediately, 'Isn't there anything we can do?'

Boy, I couldn't get on the mobile quickly enough now. Answer your bloody phone, I thought. I willed my wife to pick it up. She did. 'She can see,' I yelled, 'she can see. I tell you, she can see.' If tears could flow down a phone line, I'd have had a pretty wet ear at the end of the conversation.

True to his word, Andrew turned up just as he said he would. 'Sure she can see, mate, sure she can,' he said with authority. 'Let me explain what's happened here. See how the eyes are totally pink, there is absolutely no filter left for her to screen the full rays of the sun. Every time she steps outside it's like being hit with a million candle-power light. She simply closes her eyes.'

If an animal (or, for that matter, a human being) doesn't open its eyes in the first three or four weeks of life, then those parts of the brain that actually detect the images from the eye never develop, and although the eye is normal the animal's totally blind. By putting the foal in the stable we'd put her in the dark, we'd let her open her eyes, we'd let her brain centres develop, and now she could see.

Blondie, well, you wouldn't know her today. She shares a paddock with another little Welsh pony and one of our mare Michelle's foals. Her colour is Cremello, a sort of very light cream colour, and her eyes have now turned a vivid blue. Of course, she is so tame that she follows you around the paddock like a dog. Come to think of it, she's starting to behave like one. Only this morning she took to rounding up the sheep when they got anywhere near her biscuit of hay. Imagine that, a little white pony chasing thirteen sheep around a paddock!

Sometimes you do things deliberately, sometimes you do them by accident, sometimes you don't know why you do them, you just do. We'd done the right thing here and by God I'm glad we did.

24

A Long Time with Long Tails

'If you really need to know something about an animal, then go out and get one.' It was a piece of advice once tendered by an old-timer when a young vet first started in this game. Pretty right, too. To know about dogs, you need to own a dog. To know about birds, you need to breed birds. To judge cattle, you need to breed cattle. It's no good reading about things in books. A look is worth a thousand words, a demonstration is worth a thousand looks. But having a go is worth a thousand demonstrations. Greyhounds were going to be my thing, they were easier to handle than horses. You could spend two hours in a stable grooming and brushing and sprucing up a horse and then you might get a kick in the bum for your trouble as you walked out the door. A dog is different. It can be barking its head off at two o'clock in the morning, you can yell and scream and throw something at it or over it, and then at breakfast all it wants to do is lick you to death. Yeah, I like horses, but I probably prefer dogs.

It really only took twelve months to get the first one. He was a big white and brindle dog, with the kennel name of Lefty. He came from Newcastle—Wallsend, actually. Reared on a farm, he was a good-looking specimen of a dog who showed promise when he was young but never really amounted to anything. Like so many of his mates before him, he never won a race. Neither did the next two. They were so slow that a geriatric in a pair of galoshes could've beaten them, but that's the way it is.

In the meantime a couple of the vets at our clinic had a good one. She was quick, her name was Ellen's Lightning and she went on to run third in the Futurity, a fantastic effort for a pretty little black and white bitch.

You got to meet so many interesting people around greyhounds, you learnt the language: a slip, the fly, a three-dogger, cauchi's, scicluan's, wenty, trackleg, cockroach. There are hundreds of terms and you need to know the meaning of them all if you're going to succeed in the business. And then there were, and still are, the muscle men—those seemingly miraculous lay personnel capable of extracting at least an extra two-tenths from that dog of yours, taking it from an also-ran to a champion. You learn plenty, you listen a lot, you digest and eventually you come out with an interpretation of the whole scene that suits your particular way of looking at things. Weekends spent at trial tracks, on cold Sunday mornings with hot dogs and steel muzzles rubbing against your frozen ears, threatening to snap them right off. In little rowboats at Botany, fending off four panting hounds more intent on climbing into the boat with you than swimming to improve their fitness. And of course, the race tracks, the punters, the bookies and the atmosphere are really something special and something unique.

In partnership with a couple of young trainers we bought two really well-bred dogs: a bitch, white and brindle, a pretty-looking thing who could really run; and the dog, a big blue fella with long legs and a little white star right on his chest. But alas, vets shouldn't own race dogs. The bitch contracted a severe respiratory infection, when vaccination was not as good as it is today, and in spite of all my medication slipped off the face of the planet. The dog injured himself so badly at his first start that the rest of his career was never anything more than average, though he did run a couple of placings.

All this buying of other people's dogs hadn't really produced much of note. We'd even gone all the way up the coast to buy one at Wauchope. It, too, was hopeless. Better breed our own, I reckoned.

The dog's name was Mogal Khan. She was a very quick bitch and I borrowed her from a client to breed a litter of pups. She was mated with an Irish import, Come On Clopook was his name, a huge black dog with a very good record back in the Emerald Isle. Needless to say, all the pups were black, they were reared locally in the Sydney area and educated at around fifteen months of age. None of them had shown much ability early on. Perhaps they needed a bit more time, I mused, and perhaps a longer distance. Wrong again. They were the slowest greyhounds I've ever owned. At Harold Park one night, two of them were in the last trial of the night. 'Jim', Jim Beatty, was the starter and the electrician at the track. 'Don't turn the damn lights off, mate,' I said to him, 'my two are still coming. I know they're black, and we'll never find them in the dark.' They were one and a half seconds slow! Ah, well. I'd borrowed the sister to Mogal Khan as well; her name, wait for it, was Sweet Peach. God knows who chose it. She was mated with a dog from the Mudgee district. He was a big black fellow who'd done most of his racing in Victoria. (Time to give up on all the imports.) His name was Bandar Prince, a full brother to an outstanding racer called The Stripper. Sweet Peach had a litter of only three pups, two bitches and a dog. Once again, they were black.

Marriage interrupted things just a bit and my first wife and I jetted off to the UK to work and enjoy our honeymoon. We ended up staying almost two years. The pups were born almost as we left and good old Dad came to the rescue again. He managed to find a guy up the bush, an itinerant sort of shearer who travelled around from place to place doing a bit of this and that, and he'd be happy enough to rear the pups on a one-for-one basis. We'd lease him one of the others for twelve months anyhow, just for his trouble. There was a condition. We would draw straws as to who got what. There was to be no trying out beforehand. No risk, these pups got a great start in life. They spent most of their days running free over thousands of acres and only came home when he banged their feed dishes together. Then he locked them up for the night.

'G'day, Dad, what's up?' The phone crackled and hissed as it did during most long distance calls some thirty years ago.

'Got a bit of a problem, son.'

'What's happened?'

'That bloke with your pups, he's dead.'

'He's what?'

'He's dead. Seems he was on some track somewhere, getting the pups started, and the hare came round the inside rail and hit him on the leg. Broke his leg. Poor bugger got a clot. Went to his brain and killed him.'

'Geez, that's tough. What was he doing with them on a track?'

'Trying to sort out the best one, I reckon.' Dad was probably right.

He organised to collect the pups and put them in training in Sydney. And payment—he was good enough to organise that too, because the shearer's family wasn't interested in the dogs. 'Back in my day it used to be five bob a week to rear a dog,' Dad said. He had been everywhere and done everything before we kids ever came along. 'S'pose it's gone up a bit since then. How does a dollar a week sound?' And that's what he paid, $150 to rear three pups for nearly twelve months.

Over in the UK I'd bought Ginger Lashes and two other bitches, all of whom we'd hoped to bring home by ship on our return but rabies struck and that was that. They all had to stay behind. Ginger kept racing, one of the others was sold, and Margie and Ginge finally came home eighteen months later. I've written of them and of the fire in my previous book, so I'll scout around that now and get on with what happened when we got home.

The three black pups all showed plenty of ability. There was a small black dog, Bobby, an even smaller black bitch, Princess, and a tall racy, rather shy, black bitch, Suzi. It was a cold Saturday afternoon in Lithgow and, boy, it can get cold up there. The dog track is set in a sort of a gully and gets very little sun. On this day, the grass was still frozen in the shadow alongside the starting boxes. We were in the last race of the day and reckoned my little bloke had a good chance of winning. It's a long wait walking around the betting ring talking to this one and that. Six people, all clients from Gladesville, came up and tipped me their dog in the same race. Well, I thought, that's six I don't have to worry about. My feeling was that none of them had much ability at all. That only left one and the breeding read like 'out of bed by breakfast time'. So there's the proud owner just before the start of the race, walking round, lead in hand, to the catching pen (this is where the dogs finish and, obviously, where you catch them, if you can).

'What are you doing here?' asked one of the clients.

'I've got a dog in this race,' I said, pulling the racebook from my back pocket and running a grubby finger down the page to box 8. 'There you go, owner H. Cooper.' They were flabbergasted. Well, if you're a good punter you keep your mouth shut and we'd just averaged six to one for our money. We'll win it, we thought, and we did, by six lengths. You have no idea how good it feels to lead in your first winner. There had been nine dogs before this one. How sweet it is. The litter went on to win over thirty races between them. Don't get the wrong idea, though; you don't win all the time. Eventually there is another dog faster than yours.

Cowra was a great place, about four hours drive from Sydney. It was worth the trip. As I learnt from one of my more successful clients many years earlier, the great thing about Australia is that it doesn't matter where you go, the money's the same. At Cowra they had the same money but the competition was probably a little bit weaker. Bobby was really quick, but he could only go for about three hundred metres. I should tell you at this stage that greyhounds, like racehorses, have two names—the one you read in the racebook and the one that's used at home. The two are usually totally different. That way the animal doesn't get confused when the crowd calls out its name.

So there we are, first time at this little country track. It's tight. Boy, is it tight. Sharp bends and short straights, just the sort of thing that will suit these little black dogs.

When you get to a track, first up the dogs need a bit of a walk just to stretch their legs and empty out. I won't bother to describe what that means, I'm sure you get the picture. Then they're marched in, identified according to their racing papers, ear tattoos etc. and weighed, and they must conform to a certain weight each time they're raced. Finally, they're kennelled ready for racing. Bobby was first up, he'd won at Lithgow in pretty smart time and was graded against a fairly ordinary field, so we thought. The lids flew. Bobby had the 1, the red box. It's closest to the rails. It makes good dogs champions and he went like one. The official margin was eight lengths. I'd have said twice that far. And the bookies had bet us six to four, pretty good odds. Now it was Princess's turn. She was over the five hundred. Drew the 7, the black. The race started on a corner, she'd never seen the place and they never saw her either. Four lengths winner; how good is this, a double on our first visit! We'll wait a week or two, we thought, and we'll be back. Sure enough, we were, this time with the three of them.

'Hello, Bobby,' said the kennel steward over the top of those little half glasses that people wear for reading. 'How's Bobby?' he asked.

'Pretty good.'

'On the job?'

'Always is.'

How in God's name this bloke managed to know the name of the dog then is beyond me, but by the time we'd been there on the fourth or fifth occasion he knew all of them! Race Two on the programme. Princess draws the 4, the squeeze. Right in the middle—4, 5 and 6 are the worst boxes. As the field jumps, the dogs from the outside come across, squash those in the middle and put them out of action. You need to begin like a blur from the 4. She did and that was that. Even money they bet us and we had plenty on, and they took it, the bookies, because there were always enough of the locals willing to support their own dogs; they reckoned they were unbeatable. By the middle of the programme, we were feeling pretty cocky. But Suzi was a worry. She was a nervy little girl, really frightened of people and never greatly experienced in a race. In fact, this was to be her first start. She drew the 8, pink rug, right on the outside, probably where she should've been. The lids flew, she came out slowly, dropped across to the fence (the inside), gradually hunted up, but didn't look a chance as they turned into the straight. The three leaders moved off the rails, the little black lady saw daylight, and exploded past them. She won running away. Knowing her temperament, that may very well have been what she was doing. She was terrified. Six to four they bet us and our pockets were bulging. One more race to go. Bobby's turn.

It's pretty tough grading when you've only run two races and suddenly you're in the free for all, racing against the track record holder and two visitors that you're sure were deliberately assembled from other tracks in the area. A four-dog field. They only made one mistake, they gave Bobby the red. Six to four, the two bookies put up. Six to four? Out of the red? In a four-dog field? He was only one tenth behind the track record holder and he'd only seen the track once? In my left hand was four hundred, the bookie took it, handed back the ticket, never touched the price. 'Want it again?' he asked me.

'Sure do,' I said. 'That the price?' They were confident, but then so were we.

'Absolutely, for all you've got.' And I had plenty—by now close to two thousand dollars, which nearly thirty years ago was a lot of money. 'I'll take the lot,' he said, and did. And Bobby took theirs. The track record holder finished six lengths behind Bobby. That little dog could only get three hundred but, boy, could he fly. Cowra was good to us and Cowra bookies probably helped pay for my first house.

Not everything goes according to plan. It's fine to win races in the country but winning races in the city is a different matter altogether. Bulli was a speed track with very long straights and a wide U-turn. But Bulli had a reputation for being, shall we say, just a little dodgy from time to time. You needed to be in the know to get well looked after at Bulli. We weren't; in fact, it took three nominations before Princess would even be considered as a reserve. Fourth time round, we nominated Bobby as well. He'd won five on end. And guess what! They drew Bobby, not Princess. Ridiculous, really. Bobby could only get three hundred—no chance for him in this race. But there he was, sitting up there and about to wear the red rug all over again. The bookies' board had a pretty good idea of how things were going to finish. Bobby was fifteen to one, the dogs in 2 and 3 were even money and six to four, the rest were name your price. The 2 and the 3 were the peas (another little doggy expression, for a dodgy bit of grading). Well, we mused, things could be worse, they could all fall over and break their legs; at least Bobby will be in front on the first turn. By starting time, Bobby was quoted at twenty-five to one. You don't need a lot on them at twenty-five to one and you should always have something on them.

As always, Bobby flew the start and by the time they hit the first turn he was a good five lengths clear of the 2 and the 3 dogs. The rest of them were looking for a taxi. Then providence struck! The 2 dog rolled off the fence, straight into the 3 dog, and it was on. The pair of them just stood there fighting with one another while Bobby, totally oblivious to the melee behind him, continued on down the straight to win by some seven lengths in what was to be the slowest time recorded at the track for about six months.

It was customary at some tracks to leave the prize money behind. You do that in the hope that you might get a start next time round. No chance here. I collected every cent, smiled at the secretary and thought, as I walked through the door, we'll never be back. And we never were.

But it's racing in the country that's really good fun, particularly in outback New South Wales and up the coast. Things can sometimes get a bit dodgy, particularly when you're not well known, and in those days HLC was just your ordinary vet. The track was Mudgee; our first appearance at the joint, with a little white dog called Roger. He was quite a character. He had a chronic injury to his left wrist, but with a bit of this and that and the appropriate strapping had managed to find all his old form again. He had this crazy habit of howling in the boxes as the hare approached but he seldom missed the start and always gave a good account of himself. He'd been off the scene for about eight weeks and his form prior to that was fairly ordinary. The injury simply hadn't responded to treatment, but now things were good and confidence was brimming over in the camp.

The bookies bet six to four on about their favourite, nicely positioned in the 1 box, and on Roger's old form he could've given this bloke a start and a beating. But his form of late meant his chances of that were considered remote. We knew better. Roger drew the 2, right alongside their local champion, the bunny rolled, Roger howled, the lids flew and this little white dog absolutely exploded out of the boxes. The further they went, the further he ran away. It was only four hundred metres, or thereabouts, and as they turned into the straight he was a good six lengths clear. The favourite was a distant second. Then calamity struck. The hare stopped, well, almost stopped, Roger dived in to grab it and as he did so the favourite caught up. Well, almost. The hare started again. So did Roger, still maintaining a good length or two's lead over the favourite. In fact, the hare slowed again twice—all of this in a distance of a hundred metres—and still Roger put his head over the line a full length in front of the favourite.

It was of interest to read the programme some time later. The surname of the second dog's trainer and the hare driver were the same. But you just smile, take their money and make a mental note never to come back.

Lots of things have changed since those days—there was the fire and all those dead pups. It goes without saying that this sort of thing kind of takes the wind out of your sails. Some of Ginger's pups reared up at Orange went on to win races in the city; in fact, one of them was a very successful hurdler, but that fire and the disaster it brought really did finish things up. There was the odd dog from time to time, but it's been nigh on twenty years since I've even thought about owning another greyhound. Yet, everything goes the full circle. There are six beautiful babies galloping in a two acre paddock behind the house; perhaps these will be the champions that everyone looks for. Janine and Pam, our trainer's wife, between them raced a bitch called Dashing Rainbow, a brilliant dog in Tasmania, who went on to win nine races at Wentworth Park in Sydney— three in the best of the night. Injury once again cruelly curtailed her career, that's the way it goes. The six babies are Rainbow's pups, and if they have half the go and half the speed that she had they'll still be damn good dogs. You breed the best, feed the best and hope for the best! Stay tuned.

25

Steve was Special

Steve was a very special dog, a dog you never really forget. We first met on a New Year's Day in circumstances both of us *would* really rather forget. It was an urgent call, back to the surgery at Gladesville. What a pathetic sight the poor dog made. In a total state of collapse, he was bleeding from nearly every orifice. Blood drained from his mouth, his nose, his sheath and his anus. Urine leaked away, looking more like stout than anything else. The dog's temperature was in excess of 40°C. The very fact that he was alive had to be a miracle. The poor animal was massively dehydrated and as close to death as any creature could possibly be. This was a real emergency, heat stroke is a shocking experience. Down to the hospital. Packed in ice. Intravenous drip. Fans. Everything possible to lower his temperature and as quickly as possible. Frankly, I didn't give Steve much chance.

To catch up with the people responsible for this dog's present state would have been really worthwhile. You see, Steve was a greyhound, a male greyhound, a potential stud dog imported from Ireland and arriving in Australia around November time. He had spent two months in quarantine in Melbourne and was flown to Sydney on New Year's Day. He had been left in an open wire crate, sitting on the tarmac without any shelter and without any water, on a day when the temperature exceeded 35°C in the shade. Imagine what it would have been like on the tarmac! I couldn't. Heaven knows how long he was there. But a good guess would be around three or four hours.

He did make it, a testament to the dog more than to the treatment. Some animals' will to live is far greater than others. His was supreme. Three days later we considered his health good enough for him to leave hospital and travel to his new home in the Maitland district of New South Wales. It was sad to see him go, really. He was a pretty gaunt sort of dog. Long and thin and wiry—'the sort that won't say die', eh, Banjo. Red fawn in colour with a broken right hock (ankle) and a slightly Roman nose. There was a lick on the face and a good wag of the tail as a goodbye present. Really, you see so many animals in day-to-day practice that I thought that was the end of it.

Then one day, at the Gladesville clinic: 'Harry, I've got an old friend here to see you.' And there with Albert stood the old red dog, beside the familiar station wagon.

'What's doing?' I said.

'Oh,' he replied, 'I think the old fella's finished.'

'No, don't tell me that.'

'Can't get him to serve a bitch.' Stud dogs aren't of much value if they won't mate with a female, and Steve had neither the interest nor the ability to do that.

'So what's the go then?'

'I think we'll have to put him down.'

Seemed such a waste, all the way from Ireland, quarantine in Australia, a near-death experience at the airport. Got to be more to it than that.

'Can I take him?'

'Sure, if you want to.'

Why not, I thought, and I did. The dog seemed to remember. It'd been a good ten months but I swear he knew me and what

I had done all those months ago. His right hind leg was so badly damaged that he walked with a faint limp, but his long tail never stopped wagging and he wore an almost smiling expression on his face.

Steve walked into the backyard at Annangrove like he owned it. There were lots of other greyhounds there, not in the backyard but in kennels and runs at the rear of the property. Something told me this dog was going to be different. Kennel life was not his cup of tea; curling up on the back verandah with the whippet and the house cat were more to his liking. Somehow this old fella was just a really skinny and fairly fast Labrador. He loved children; in fact, there's every chance he taught Tiffany, my eldest daughter, to walk. There she'd be, crawling around on the lawn, and he'd come over and sort of nudge her a few times with his nose and then stand there. She would pull herself up using his front or back leg till she could stand with her arms wrapped around his neck. Then he'd walk forward very slowly as if to make sure she didn't fall over, till she could grasp that long thin tail of his. Away they'd go, just a short stroll two or three times around the clothesline and then back to the verandah. It was a routine they repeated half a dozen times or so each day.

He was an old dog by now—well, certainly old in greyhound terms—going on for eight years. Most don't live much past ten and though he'd managed to produce pups in Ireland he'd left nothing behind in Australia. It was worth a try at least, I thought. On the place there were three bitches from which we were breeding. It didn't take much organisation to have Steve's papers transferred to me, and that was it. We generally mate dogs on about the tenth to the fourteenth day of the bitch's season, but things can be a little bit unpredictable. The twelfth day came around and we introduced Molly and Steve to one another. He was quite interested and for a dog that had never mated anything in this country he sure wasn't gonna let me down. The initial idea was to just let them go and see what happened. Nature often has a way of working things out, and the two of them raced round and round the yard ducking here and there and playing with one another, a sort of courtship routine before they got down to business. She had produced two litters before. Now Steve, well, he knew how to do things the Irish way, but then the Australian way is a little bit different. The poor old dog had a great deal of difficulty actually getting himself on to the back of the bitch. He would try and jump up, fall off and try again. Finally, he gave up and just walked away and lay down.

It's at times like this you need to give a hand. Sure, we could've used artificial insemination, but Steve was keen enough and perhaps with a little bit of encouragement he could do the job. We'd try again at night.

Molly was ready, Steve was as keen as ever and I knelt beside them ready to render assistance if necessary. Very often things happen purely by luck. Over the years so many major discoveries have been made, just through a stroke of good fortune. My discovery wasn't too major, but it was lucky. As Steve attempted to hop on board for the third or fourth time, Molly got that little bit frustrated. She screwed her rear end sideways till it was pointing at my chest, and with that, Steve hopped around and used my thighs for a leg up, so to speak. Bingo! Molly thought it was good and Steve thought it was even better and that's the way it was from then on in. It was simply a matter of giving the old fella a leg up—much like swinging a jockey into the saddle. Steve'd catapult off my thigh, and

Bob's your uncle. A reasonable explanation seems that, with time, the old broken hock of his had become pretty sore and pretty stiff, not to mention all the old muscle injuries as well. He mated five bitches for me but, regrettably, his prodigy were not up to his potential.

Steve passed away quietly in his sleep just one month short of his tenth birthday. I think, of all of us, Tiffany missed him the most. A human had saved his life and in repayment he had taught a little girl to walk. That's why he's special.

26

Sally

Children have an amazingly high expectation of their parents. When your dad is a vet, let's face it, he can fix anything. Sally was a whippet, a gorgeous little dog, white and light tan in colour, just the sort of dog you'd expect a bloke like me to have as a pet. Most clients would know that greyhounds have been my interest for a long time. But it's difficult to have one as a pet when you live on a rural property. So Sally was a pretty good alternative. The clinic at Annangrove had been up and running for a year or two now. The place was nothing flash, just something I'd set up in what had been a large double garage. A waiting room, consulting room, lab, surgery, X-ray facilities and kennel block. But it did the job. The equipment was good, that's where the money was spent. It went on diagnosis and surgery. The theatre was equipped with the best anaesthetic and surgical instruments a one-man practice could afford. It worked well. Lots of segments for 'Burke's Backyard' were filmed in that surgery area, and the large circular burn mark on the ceiling is still there—a testament to the day an over-enthusiastic lighting technician pushed the 2K too close to the ceiling.

Little Sal was only about nine years old at the time, and the children used to attend the local public school. Each morning they would farewell her at the side gate and in the afternoon she'd be waiting for their return. It was a simple walk—they'd go along our drive, which I'd concreted (all four hundred metres of it), then turn right and walk another kilometre or so to the school. (Back in those days it was safe for children to walk to school. How sad it is that society has changed so that even such simple undertakings are now fraught with so much danger.) About 3.15 every afternoon Sally knew it was time. Perhaps she heard the bell. In they'd come and she would race and whirl around the backyard, excitedly barking and jumping all over the pair of them. Truly a delightful little dog.

The day to remember was a Tuesday morning in early winter. It was cold, and a slight frost had settled on the ground overnight. Getting up first and wandering into the kitchen, eyes half closed, I called to Sally from the window. No dog. Where was she? This was most peculiar, she was always there. 'Sally, Sally.' No reply. Time to go looking. We found her lying under a tree. She was barely breathing. Stone cold. Wrapping her in my shirt, I quickly carried her inside. There was no strength left in the tiny body, not even enough to shiver. Her gums were white, white as a sheet. My God, I thought, she's had a massive haemorrhage. Or maybe a snakebite. These things raced through my mind as I tried to inject some warmth into her wilting body. Too cold for snakes, haemorrhage was the most likely. Rat bait? Maybe, don't think so. No, what she needs is blood. And quickly! Calling for help. Hurry! Get here. Hold her. Wrap her up. Get a blanket. Keep her still. Put her on the table. Let me listen. Her heart was barely audible through the diaphragm of the stethoscope. Impossible to even feel a pulse. You couldn't tell where her teeth finished and the gums started.

'Will she be all right, Daddy? Will she be all right?' Children are crying. Wife's crying.

Gotta think straight. Down to the kennels. Grab one of the greyhounds. Lead it up. They're good dogs. Lay her on the table. Good girl, good girl. Someone come and hold her.

'What are you going to do, Daddy?' asks a shaking, tearful child.

'I'm going to take some blood from Brindy and give it to Sally.'

'Can you do that, Daddy?'

'Yes, I can, and you must help me. You hold this bag and you gently rock it just like this, that's it. You can see the blood flowing in, good, good.'

And the eyes of an eight-year-old child watch as the blood drains from the jugular vein of my faithful brood bitch into the plastic collection sack. 'It won't clot as long as you keep gently mixing it.'

'All right, Daddy,' she says through the tears.

We collected almost half a litre. Sally just lay there, a still, deathlike figure, hardly breathing, on the heated pad. It was hard to find any sort of vein into which you could insert a catheter. Success at last. 'Pass me the tape, please . . . yeah, that stuff, that's the roll. Yep, cut this off here please. OK, have you got that bag? Bring that in here, Tiff.' And Tiffany walked shakily through the door, still mixing the blood in the plastic bag. Blood hitched to transfusion stand, lines in place, away we go. And the blood dripped slowly down the infusor and into the still and frozen body of Sally.

Half an hour later, calm had returned. Brindy was back in her kennel eating a bigger than usual breakfast as if nothing had happened. Well, she wouldn't miss half a litre anyhow. And Sally was sitting on the lounge, somewhat shakily, but at least now she had some colour back in those gums. It was hard sending the kids off down the drive that morning. By the time they got back in the afternoon, Sally was so much better. Smiles mixed with tears as they hugged their dog. Dad got this one right. But Dad knew it wasn't over yet. There was no evidence of any external bleeding on Sally's body. All the blood that she'd lost had to be internal. Her abdomen was swollen and a simple puncture with a needle withdrew pure blood. This sort of internal blood loss reflects maybe half a dozen things—tumours on livers or on spleens, ruptures of major veins, damage to other internal organs from traumas like kicks or car accidents. Every one of them a potential disaster. Just what Sally's problem was I'd find out sooner than any of us wanted.

Next day everything seemed normal and the kids appeared to have totally forgotten what had happened to their little dog the previous day. She was bouncing around, licking and jumping as these timid animals often will. But to me she was still far from well. Before the week was over I would again find her in her previous state. Collapsed on the back lawn, white as a sheet, she'd had another bleed. Deep inside, Dad, the vet, had hoped that she'd have been strong enough for surgery, after the transfusion. It was Friday, my day off. There would be no other pressures, and as much time as was needed and every care could be devoted to her surgery. What a pity she'd bled again! Things in veterinary medicine often don't go the way in which we plan them.

More tears, more trauma. 'You'll fix her, Daddy, won't you?'

'I'll do my best.' I've always done my best.

Same procedure as before. Transfusion, a gain in strength, and then by lunchtime she had to be well enough and strong enough for the surgery that lay ahead of her. But we were out of time. X-rays had shown a large mass in the front section of her abdomen, just on or behind the line of her last rib. It was a tumour. There was no doubt about that. Hopefully, it would be on the spleen. Tumours on this organ can easily be resolved by removing the whole spleen and they are rarely malignant. Over the years we've pulled out some whoppers. One, from an Afghan of only seven years, weighed well over five kilos and was bigger than a rugby football. The dog never looked back, went on to win in shows and sire litters of pups. I prayed Sally's would be the same. It wasn't.

Sally had a massive malignant tumour on the surface of the liver. It had ruptured and bled. Exploration showed that it extended far beyond this initial area. The tumour involved nearly two-thirds of the organ. I sweated and toiled for two hours and seventeen minutes over that little dog. It's your kids' dog. You see their faces, remember their voices. 'You'll save her, Daddy? You'll fix her?' I couldn't save her. I couldn't fix her. I'd let my kids down, I felt so inadequate. In all my years as a vet I have never felt so inadequate. Your own children's dog and you can't save her. Nobody could've saved her. I know that. I knew it then and I know it now. With all the skill in the world, nothing could have removed that tumour and given life back to our little dog. I put Sally to sleep. I closed the wound with tears in my eyes and cleaned her little body so that no trace of blood remained. She lay so still and cold, her eyes dull and lifeless. Now she was at last at peace. How do you tell your children that you've failed them? How do you tell them that you, their idol, the vet they believed could fix everything, couldn't fix their dog?

I walked halfway down the drive to meet them on their way home from school. We sat under the willow tree and we cried. I hugged them, told them how I felt. I've always tried to be

Sally

honest. They cried again, but somehow my feelings of inadequacy were swept away with four little words: 'We love you, Daddy.' It was a very long, slow walk up to the house. We went to the grave and cried some more. Then it was over. We talked of heaven and where dogs go. Children have a faith far greater than ours—they don't question, they just believe. Sally was in a better place, and one day they'd see her again.

27

A Fishy Story

After the loss of Sally, the children really missed the company of their own dog. The coal fields of the Hunter Valley were home to plenty of whippets as well as greyhounds. The kids couldn't agree on which pup to take home from Daryl's place, so we ended up with *two* more whippets. In those days, part of my practice extended up into the Hunter area. On a Wednesday morning I'd be up pretty early and on the road by five-thirty, aiming to reach Branxton (near Cessnock) by eight o'clock. The back of the red XD Falcon wagon was chock-full of veterinary gear—couple of surgical kits, plenty of medicines, portable X-ray machine and an acupuncture laser. You had to be ready for just about anything a damaged greyhound could throw at a bloke. Driving up the Putty Road could be a bit hairy in the middle of winter. A lot of the little wooden bridges were covered with a thick layer of frost and on more than one occasion I found the wagon travelling sideways rather than the way in which it was being steered.

Noel Pickett had a greyhound stud which was used as my base. He would book in appointments over the course of the day. I'd look over dog after dog until nearly seven o'clock when we'd adjourn for a quick beer and a bite to eat. His wife was a great cook. I'd sleep overnight in the spare room and be gone by seven the next morning. The run home was down through Wyong and Calga then Hornsby and home. Stopping on the way at various training establishments, homecoming could be anything between seven o'clock that night and two o'clock the next morning. It was hard work, but enjoyable. These clients were good friends and I loved working with the dogs.

The travelling stopped when I got divorced. Somehow, lots of things in your life change when you meet that sort of challenge.

Janine had moved into Annangrove as if she'd lived there all her life. The clients loved her, I loved her and, of course, my children loved her. She wasn't their mother, she was their sister. She'd brought with her Kushla the German Shepherd and Louie the cat, a blue point Siamese, and would later acquire Shandy the diminutive blue cattle dog, another German Shepherd who's best forgotten, and a whole gaggle of cats. She was adamant that the kids should have as much animal contact as possible. 'C'mon,' I said, 'they're surrounded by animals. They come and go through the surgery all the time, the kids are always out there talking with the clients every afternoon.' I always reckoned it was a good idea. The practice was only a small one when you talk about the size of the building, but in numbers of clients it was one of the biggest one-man practices around. Most clients knew the children and enjoyed the interaction.

'You've got the best waiting room in the world, you know.'

'Don't be so damn silly, it's only tiny.'

'No,' he said. 'Out here, I mean. This is the waiting room.'

The client was a good friend, his gesture was towards my orchard. Extending out in front of the surgery, which was attached to the side of the house, was a collection of some thirty different fruit trees. Plums, apples, pears, peaches and nectarines, even a few citrus fruits. If things were busy, and they usually were, regular clients who had to travel a long distance invariably turned up with a picnic basket, and enjoyed a cup of coffee and some nibblies underneath the trees. Problems did arise around Christmas; it was a race between us and the clients as to who would get the fruit. The trick was to put up a sign saying, 'Danger, Fruit Sprayed', but that didn't work for long. At the end of the orchard were the horse paddocks, and clients would often feed the mares and foals a few treats over the fence. It was indeed the best waiting room in the world!

If Janine thought something needed doing she just did it. So one afternoon the goldfish arrived. And the tank and the rocks and the gravel and the filter and the plants and the feed and the light and the bill! 'Oh, they'll get a lot of enjoyment out of these,' she said. Yes, I thought, they probably will—until the novelty wears off.

'Who's gonna feed them? And who's gonna look after them?' Father enquired.

'Don't worry, I'll make sure the kids do the right thing.' And she did. The fish grew like stink. I began to wonder whether some of my anabolic steroids weren't slipping into the tank. There were three fish, two comets and one fantail.

As with all animals, if they're owned by a vet then something is sure to go wrong and of course it did.

'Dad, this fish has got a lump on it,' I was told.

'OK, I'll look at it later.'

That's the sort of standard reply any busy parent gives to an inquiring child. But this child was persistent. Every day it was the same story until finally I did look. No kidding, one of the comets had quite a big growth on the left side of its body, almost exactly in the middle. Well, something would have to be done about this, after all. The great thing about being a vet is that you've got a lot of mates who are also vets, and some of them know something about fish.

Anaesthetising fish isn't easy. You've got to get them out of the tank, dissolve this chemical and another chemical and slowly add it to the small bowl in which you've put the fish, until the fish starts swimming more and more slowly, and finally stops—swimming, that is, not breathing. Then you scoop it out onto the table, keep it wet by spraying a fine mist of water, and do whatever you've got to do as quickly as possible before popping it back into clean water. Sounds easy and it is, but you've got to buy the chemical in such large quantities that there's enough to anaesthetise half the fish population of your average harbour. Hang it, I thought, it's not a big lump; I've caught a lot of fish, they flap around on the deck for a fair while before they die, and I reckon the job will only take two minutes. Won't worry about the anaesthetic!

Bleeding was of some concern, though. No one seemed quite sure how badly fish bled, to tell you the truth, or how quickly the blood clotted. Just to be on the safe side I decided I'd use the Hyfrecator, a little instrument that effectively burnt things off using a very high frequency electrical spark. You just plugged it in to the 240, turned up the dial, picked up the little tool—something like a Biro—and went to work on whatever lump you wished to cauterise (burn off). Yeah, I'd use that, no bleeding with that gizmo.

Out came the fish, onto the stainless steel table. 'Keep spraying it, darl.' Janine was pumping water over it from a little squeeze bottle. Darn fish wouldn't keep still, jumping about all over the place. It was quite big actually, almost ten centimetres long. 'OK, OK, I'll hold it still.' And the would-be fish surgeon put a thumb and finger over the head and tail respectively. The fish stopped jumping, the whole thing was now swamped in water. Fish seemed happy. Janine was happy. Surgeon was happy. 'We'll zap it now.' Held the probe on the lump, depressed the foot pedal. 'AAAH!' Bloody hell, I'd just got the best zap of all time. The spark had earthed itself through my fingers into the table. There was a great white burn on both my thumb and my finger. The fish was still happily jumping about on the table, not a mark on it. What is it your parents teach you about not mixing electricity and water? My mother wouldn't use a steam iron for years because of that. I'd been a first-class idiot.

'Oh, yeah, sorry, darl. Let's get the fish back into the tank for a moment,' Janine said, more concerned for the welfare of the fish than her poor husband.

'My fingers are really hurting—you want to see to them?' I moaned.

A short lecture followed about the idiocy of my intended surgery and how she wasn't going to be a party to this anymore. And she was off!

But the lump's still there and the fish looks fine. OK, throw caution to the winds. A Band-Aid for each finger, grab a nice fine scalpel and seize the fish. Flop the patient onto the table. Hang the water! Hang anything, just get on with it! Get hold of the scalpel, get hold of the fish and scoop the lump off in one filleting action. It doesn't bleed. It doesn't even look like bleeding. Is the fish OK? Well, it's still jumping about. Just swab it with a bit of iodine and throw it back in the tank.

You know, the darn thing never looked back, truly. The wound on the fish healed quicker than the burns on my fingers.

'Good on ya, Dad,' the kids said, 'the fish looks great.'

28

Rosie

'Harry's Practice' was in Darwin. It was only a year or so ago. 'Harry, Janine needs you to ring her urgently,' Andre said as we strolled out to get into the van for the day's shooting.

'Hi, darling, what's the problem?'

'It's Rosie.'

'What's wrong with Rosie?'

'Well, she came back from her walk this morning and now she can't get up.'

'Are you with her now? What's the colour of her gums like?'

'Oh, they're really white.'

'OK,' I said, 'she's had a big bleed. Are you sure she hasn't been kicked by one of the horses?'

Every morning all our dogs spend a good hour or so free-running on the creek paddock. It's a big flat area of about twenty-five acres, it cuts the best hay, and there are rabbits and hares everywhere. The dogs simply enjoy being dogs, racing here and racing there in futile attempts to catch a bit of game. The exercise is just the best. But Rosie always had a bit of a fear of horses; it stemmed from the time she'd strayed into a stallion's paddock when she was just a pup. Hussar had picked her up by the scruff of the neck, and flung her yelling and screaming over the fence. She never forgot it and sometimes, if she got her ginger up, she'd race in and try and nip the odd horse on the heels.

'No way, the horses aren't on the flat,' Janine said.

'OK then, it's got to be something else. Could be a snake. I think you'd better take her into town and let one of the boys have a look at her.'

It's incredible how many times things go wrong as soon as you walk out the door. Gee, the whole day was spent worrying about what was going on back home. There was a time difference of a couple of hours and in a way that helped. Still, here we were, on a beach in Darwin, doing a story about a little Staffy that was more interested in swimming to Indonesia than in coming in when she was called. Top little dog. We actually surprised the owner having a cup of coffee in a local restaurant. We trained the dog using heavy-duty fishing line and food rewards, reeling her in on command and rewarding her when she came. The only problem was, first time she took off I'd tried to brake the line using my finger. Damn near cut the thing off. Burnt a groove about five millimetres deep right through the skin, and boy, it really hurt. Didn't do that again, I can tell you. Learnt to hold the caster against my chest.

'They reckon she's got a tumour on her spleen,' Janine told me later that day.

'That'll be OK, they'll get that out all right.'

'I wish you were here. Why do these things always happen when you're away?' Janine's a very capable woman. She can do most things with most animals—treat wounds, administer drugs, even pass a nasal tube in a horse when necessary—but something like this was beyond even her abilities. 'Could you give the vet a ring in the morning? Rob would like to talk to you,' she added.

'Yeah, no worries,' I said, and the feeling was one of relief.

'Harry, I reckon it's on the spleen, mate. She's pretty stable now and, uh, I reckon in another twenty-four hours we could operate and pull the thing out.' Rob sounded confident. Twenty-four hours later I'd be in Alice Springs, still a day or two away from getting home. Australia is such a big place, isn't it.

It was the local Alice Springs school, its carpark. We were getting ready to surprise one of the pupils. Everything had been teed up. We would all go into the principal's office, set things up, and wait. My young client was to be summoned to the office, where she'd find me. Surprise! We'd then go to her home and look at her Rotty and the trampoline. It's a bit of a thing when you're out working, that if the mobile rings during part of the shoot you're up for a slab! Leaving the phone on can be a very expensive undertaking, so invariably mine's turned off.

'Harry, the vet wants you to ring him, mate.' Andre sounded very calm and very quiet. His phone had made no noise, it had a vibrating battery.

'Thanks, mate,' I said and called the Launceston surgery.

'Harry, she's on the table, and it's not good.'

'What is it, Rob?' I knew what it was, he didn't have to tell me. Something in your gut, in the pit of your stomach, screams out NO! But thirty-five years of experience tells you Yes.

'Harry, it's on her liver. There's no way we'll ever get it and there's other bits scattered around the place too.'

These tumours are usually malignant. They have a habit of bleeding. Nothing was going to save our dog.

'Is she still on the table, mate?'

'Yes, Harry, she is.'

'Don't let her wake up, mate, don't let her wake up.'

And with that I condemned Rosie to death. From the other

side of Australia, I sent our dog away. I turned to the van. The boys looked away. After a moment, Andre and Steve put their arms around me.

'Give me half an hour,' I said, and walked away.

Ah, dear. So many memories . . . so many good times. You forget the bad ones. She was a great dog, a great sheepdog and the mother of many great sheepdogs, but more than all of that, she was our dog and her dad wasn't there when she needed him. Sally and Rosie, two dogs, same problem. So sad. Something inside you says 'You should have done more'—perhaps if you'd tried this or perhaps if you'd tried that, but you know that you're not God. Just a bloke with special training, special skills and perhaps a real affinity with animals. I let my dogs down, my family down and myself down. Dogs come and dogs go. There will never be another Sally and there will never be another Rosie, but the memories remain. Our families loved them both, and we love and remember them still.

We surprised my little friend, fixed the problem with her Rotty and went back to our hotel. Tomorrow it would be camels. But tonight would be the time to write and the writing went on until two o'clock in the morning, until it was right, and eventually happiness replaced sorrow. You've read the poem perhaps; and so many have told me what it meant to them. Well, it meant that much more to me. You see, Rosie was our dog.

29

Ebony, 'The Light of Our Life'

The last few pages of *Anecdotes & Antidotes* were given over to Rosie's poem. From your letters and from speaking to you in person, we know as a family that so many of you, our friends, have suffered the same loss. As viewers of 'Harry's Practice', no doubt you know that we have many dogs but that only two of them live in the house. Today Isobel and Tabbatha, two little Italian greyhounds, share our home, along with a Siamese, Tinkerbelle, and a moggy cat, Gretel. Not long ago it was Tabbatha's sister that lived with us. This is her story.

Right from the very start of our marriage there had always been an agreement that we would not have a dog actually living in the home. Even back at Annangrove the dogs were not allowed into the house proper, but of a Sunday evening they would find their way into the 'pub', as we called it. This rather large room, furnished in the fashion of an old English pub, was built on the side of the house and connected to it only via an outside walkway. There was a huge fireplace, and after dinner the whole family, dogs and cats included, would stretch out in front of the blaze. Invariably all would fall fast asleep, only to awaken at some crazy hour in the morning, shivering because the fire had burnt out.

That's the way things remained for something like fourteen years of our marriage. Then I relented. 'OK, but it has to be a short-coated dog. Remember all the problems with that Birman and then the Chinchilla? (These were two long-haired cats that never stopped moulting because our heating was built into the concrete slab that formed the floor.)

'I'd like a poodle, or a schnauzer.'

'You're joking, who's going to do all the grooming? They need a haircut every six weeks.'

'I'll manage that.'

There was no way my darling wife, with all the good intentions under the sun, was going to fit canine hairdressing in with everything else she had to do.

'But they're smart!'

'Too right they are,' I agreed, 'but just too much work for us . . . what about a whippet?' After all, we'd had them before.

'What about the cats?' Yes, she had a point. The cats, two Siamese back then, might not be a match for a whippet.

'Would you consider an Italian?'

By this I meant an Italian greyhound, which is only about two-thirds the size of a whippet and shouldn't be an unfair match for two very possessive felines. There was no reply, but one could sense the wheels turning. The breed does have a couple of problems. Some strains have a tendency to damage their front legs while growing, while others can be a bit sooky. Little more was said for the next few weeks, then the bombshell.

'I've organised to buy a puppy from Victoria. We have to pick it up at the airport in Melbourne. They're bringing it in to there.'

So it was that Roskyle Moonbeam Dancer, or Ebony as we called her, joined our family. She was as black as charcoal. Right from the very beginning, this dog was different. A real extrovert, wonderfully affectionate, extremely active; we christened her 'The Light of Our Life'. We even bought a second Italian to keep her company, and although Isobel was about six months younger, she and Ebony got on like no two dogs I'd seen before.

Every August Janine and I travel up to tropical Queensland. Mackay, Townsville and Rockhampton each host a 'Life Be In It' pet expo on successive weekends, and it is my job to talk and to sign the myriad autographs. In between, we enjoy a rest on Magnetic Island. Feeling very relaxed after a dose of winter sunshine, we stopped over in Sydney just long enough for me to do a day's television work and for her to do what women do so naturally—Janine went shopping.

It must have been just after three that Tuesday afternoon. Alone, back in the hotel room, my mobile rang. 'Hello.' There was a short silence. Then a voice I would hardly recognise as my wife's uttered just two words. 'Ebony's dead.' Ebony's dead? How could Ebony be dead? Just yesterday we'd rung the lady who was minding her and everything was fine. She couldn't be! Janine's cousin spoke into the phone. 'Harry, it's Julie here . . . Ebony *is* dead.' Janine was in a state of shock and they were on their way back to the hotel.

Ebony and Isobel had been staying with a lady who then worked for us. Ebony had come into season a few days after we'd left for Queensland. No one had told us. It was always a rule that any bitch in season must be walked on a lead! She wasn't. In an instant she had gone, and in another she would be gone forever.

After Rosie's death I had sat up for something like five hours, driven by who knows what sort of force to write. That's how her poem came to be. Ebony's was very different. The words would not flow. There were ideas and a line or two, but nothing like the motivation that Rosie's passing had been. Early April saw me back in Sydney, staying in that same hotel. It was not my usual venue. A light meal in the restaurant after a long day's filming seemed quite normal. 'A glass of wine with dinner?' asked the waiter. Sure, why not? 'Could I see the wine list, please?' Eyes following a finger down so many familiar labels. 'I'll have a glass of the sauvignon blanc, please.'

'Very good, sir, a glass of the Giesen?' A nod was enough.

The wine arrived . . . Giesen, Giesen, why was the name so familiar? Giesen was the wine we'd drunk the night Ebony died. I looked around. God, this was where we were that terrible night—the same table! Both of us just sitting, trying to eat something, but really not knowing what to do or say. Then awful memories hit me of the flight back home the next day, knowing we were going to bury another dog! So soon after Rosie! The clouds outside the window of the jet had looked so soft and gentle that morning. Suddenly it was that night again. Suddenly it all came rushing back.

'Excuse me, sir, are you all right?'

'Yes, thanks,' I replied. 'Just some very painful memories, I'm afraid.' There was a pause, merely a moment or two. The waiter seemed reluctant to go. I was sobbing. 'Please,' I asked in between breaths, 'please, could I have some paper and a pencil?'

That's how it was written. The restaurant was closed and all the staff had clocked off well before the words were complete. This is for you, our little dog. You deserved a longer life. In all of our combined years, and that makes over one hundred, Janine and I had never before lost a dog killed on the road. The Light of Our Life has gone out, yet it burns so strongly in our hearts. Ebony, it will burn forever.

For Ebony

A small town in Victoria
'T'was the setting for your birth
A little black canine angel
Sent from heaven to grace the earth.

Long legs of carbon fibre
Thin black tail to follow through
Dark brown eyes that glisten
Grace, and elegance too.

Your head was very different
Not like others of your breed
More like a racing greyhound
Broad, domed, and built for speed.

Infectious was her love of life
Her spirit free and bold
Once God made this little dynamo
He threw away the mould.

More go than most dogs twice her size
And tons of energy to burn
But at day's end she'd settle
On the lounge, so quick to learn.

The cats were bluffed, she had them beat
They could not work it out
How one black dog now ruled the roost
But believe it, there's no doubt.

You blame yourself, it's normal
But she'd had the dogs before
We needed that little time away
Though it cost us, that's for sure.

DOGS AND OTHER MEMORIES

The golden rule we here enforce
And the workers must take heed
Once a female comes on heat
It never walks off the lead.

It takes but just a moment
In a twinkling Eb was gone
Speeding car, a screech of brakes
The driver just drove on.

If only she'd been careful
If only she had not
'If only' are two simple words
But they mean an awful lot.

Such a short time with us
Why is it life seems so unfair?
You'd tear around the garden
Then sunbake in your chair.

With Isobel, your little friend
The time would fairly fly
On the pine bark 'neath the wattle trees
Was your favourite spot to lie.

Looking out the kitchen window
Somehow you are still there
For your friend here romps and races
While you romp and race up there.

We all miss you, little Ebony
No one will ever know how much
I even call Isobel by your name
There's the toy you used to clutch.

You had more brains than most dogs
I've met along the way
That heart of yours so full of love
How could we that love repay?

Ebony, 'The Light of Our Life'

A black and lifeless little form
Lying in an earthen grave so cold
With coat and toy, you'll need them
In that heavenly canine fold.

'Oh, Dad, I feel so angry'
'Heidi, we feel angry too
Let's yell and yell together
Keep on yelling till we're through.'

A family standing by the graveside
Screaming upwards to the sky
Just one thought within our heads
On our lips, just one word . . . Why?

Together in grief and anger
We stood a little while
Then walked away in silence
Tears caressed the little pile.

Now she lies there facing Rosie
As in life they'd often done
Rubbing noses through the garden gate
In the warmth of the morning sun.

Animals have no fear of death
When it comes they heed the call
For it isn't just God in heaven
Who sees each little sparrow fall.

'Where do dogs go when they die?'
Children ask me all the time
My answer is the same always
And y'know it suits them fine.

A child's beliefs are simple
Their trust so strong and true
'They go wherever you'd like them to go
But they'll always be with you.'

Dogs and Other Memories

Somehow this very simple answer
Always satisfies their mind
And dogs are so like children
Their love and faith are blind.

A dog's love for its master
A loyal canine never feigns
How great an animal's trust is
In a world where distrust reigns.

Now there are the three of them
And no doubt there will be more
Because nothing lives forever
Dog's heaven has an open door.

Our Pixie, Rose and Ebony
Do you hear us when we speak?
I'd give all the fame and fortune
For just a lick upon my cheek.

Dance on in total safety
Dance on beyond the stars
For I know in Ebony's heaven
There are no bloody motor cars.

Dance on little moonbeam dancer
Dance on in a starlit sky
Dance on our little Italian
For we can never say goodbye.

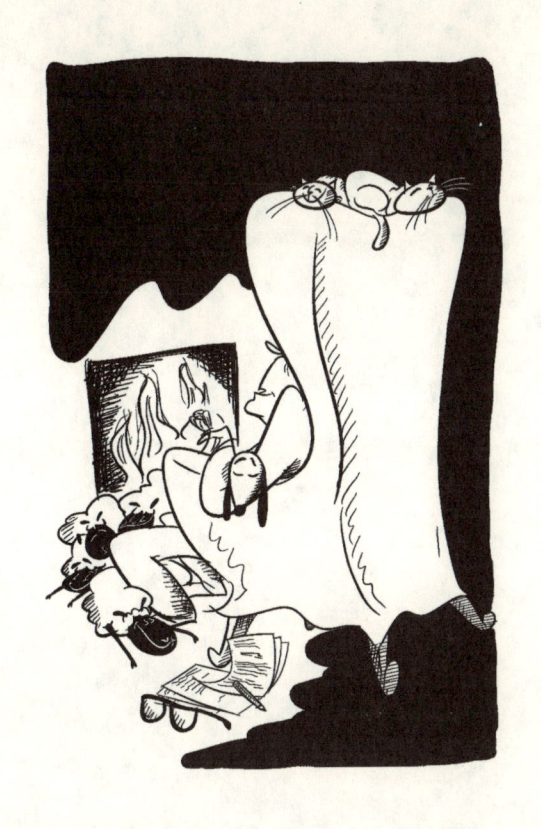

A Little Indulgence

Poems

The following is a collection of poems written over the last few years. In poetry it is often easier to express feelings than it is in prose. With your and my publisher's indulgence, they are included in this book. Some reflect a feeling I've held for some time that this country, which has nurtured my being for the last fifty-seven years, is changing—and changing in a way such that many of those things to which this nation owes its greatness are in danger of being lost. The best of the past will ensure a solid foundation for the future. Look after 'the bush'. *It* is what this country depends so much upon.

Where Have all the Farmers Gone?

He stood there, bronze and battered in a bus queue by the street
A grey suit hanging on his frame, ageing shoes upon his feet
A head now bowed with years of toil, shoulders stooped and bent
The lines of years etched deeply on those hands in toil well spent.

His gaze was always downward as he shuffled with the throng
But something in that ageing face cried out, 'I once was strong'
If only time could tell the tales, unlock a bygone year
Hesitation for a moment, ask him, there's nothing I should fear.

'S'cuse me' I blurted out, with a quaver in my voice
'What about a cuppa, up to you, y'know you've got the choice'
He turned around so slowly, and then his gaze met mine
His eyes still blue and youthful, his grey hair soft and fine.

'Yes, mate' he said, 'I'd love to join you for a while'
And y'know for just a moment there might have been a smile
We walked away together, his big frame almost dwarfing mine
Towards my favourite coffee shop, he said, 'Yeah, this'll do fine.'

The introductions took a moment, he knew he'd seen *my* face before
Said his name was Leonard, but then, 'Len would do for sure
I don't live round these parts, y'know, home's a long long way from here
Out west from Mudgee's grassy flats, well, I guess that's somewhere near.'

'Gulgong's such a thriving spot, I've been there a time or two'
'Ya know the place' his eyes lit up, 'there's very few that do.'
'Tell me, my friend' I said to him, 'of things you've seen and done
I'll write them down as best I can, while we sit here in the sun.'

Oh how he spoke of wondrous days, of men, and dogs and horses,
Of flooded plains, of droving stock, and dried-up water courses
Of times so hard that'd break most men and their women that stood beside
But something in their character made them take it in their stride.

My notes were writ in scribble on some scrappy bits of paper
I'd put them all together, and compile this story later
He drank his tea both black and sweet as most country people do
In his day the luxury of dairy foods was a gift to oh so few.

The more he talked the more I smiled and now he was smiling too
'Len, my friend' I said to him, 'there are very few left like you.'
He stopped and scratched his roughened chin, his mind was deep in thought
'Yer right, my son, the bush is dying, it's a trap, we've all been caught.

The banks gave us all this money, on the never never plan
They said spend it while you've got it, so we did the best we can
But no sooner had they lent it then, 'ullo, we want it back
With twenty four per cent interest, oh my God, they had the knack

Of sending people bankrupt, good people of the land
And then the bloody government steps in to lend a hand
Let's have a big recession, just like we have to have, it seems
Those stupid politicians—recession—must be in yer dreams

But it comes all right and, crikey, the damn thing took away me farm
A man had to sell everything, cattle, irrigation, and maybe my right arm
My wife she just couldn't take it, she said, "All those years of work
To see it signed away forever by some poxy banker's clerk."

She died last year, it killed her, I'm sure it broke her bloody heart
She felt that farm, the kids and us were such a real part
Of what used to be Australia, a land we thought we knew so well
But now it seems the country folk are all being wished to hell.'

What do you say to a man who's just exposed his very soul
How do you comfort a man in tears, how do you console
'I'm with you, mate, believe me I know just how you feel
Your words, your thoughts, your feelings are very, very real.'

And so it is in simple rhyme I hope to make my point with you,
The farmers of Australia are becoming far too few.
Without their daylong efforts, their daily, yearly grind,
The foodstuffs on our store shelves would be very hard to find.

A Little Indulgence

We've had it far too easy, we lot who live in town
Take a trip into the country and have a look around
Ask questions, talk to people, try to find a bloody bank,
A commonwealth employment scheme, go on, buy a stamp!

These things we take for granted have been taken from our friends
It's time the thing got turned around, it's time to make amends
Give them back the services and help this crazy nation
Stop teaching every one of us to worship rationalisation.

Len, my mate, I wish you well, they say you'll have to change
But old pal of mine, you never will, to you we must seem strange
My hope is simply this, in that time we shared and spoke
You will find in this busy city some other friendly bloke.

Take time to look around, my friends, next time you're in a city queue
There could be living history standing right next door to you
Do as I did, take a minute, learn, you may even shed a tear
For the foundations of our nation lie a long, long way from here.

A Winter's Morning

It's a foggy foggy morning, on a foggy foggy hill
Dew drops hang from branches and the trees are deathly still
Their blackened leafless skeletons salute the coming dawn
The quiet of the morning, a new day yet unborn.

Fences laced with spider webs that shimmer in the light
Their silver threads adorned with jewels like some celestial kite
The grass is wet and heavy and stoops as if to pray
All the creatures of the morning are silent on this day.

Every winter we feed horses for the frost is so unkind
From a four-wheeled motor bike with a trailer on behind
It's meadow hay and lucerne that keeps them nice and fat
And we check the whole place over, the hills and on the flat.

It was in the big creek paddock where the fog lay all around
In stillness and in silence it hugged the sleeping ground.
I was looking for the grey mare and her brand new chestnut foal
I called and called, yet nothing, had something taken toll?

I walked and walked the flat ground for what must have seemed like hours
Down along the creek now rising quickly from yesterday's heavy showers
Soon I began to worry, she'd always come before
'Minnie, come on, Minnie', my throat was getting sore.

I guess you always worry when things don't go as they should
It's part of human nature, sometimes poorly understood
For horses are a problem, they seem to find a way
Of getting into trouble, accidents can happen any day.

Was the foal stuck in the creek bed, or lying injured on the ground
Was the mare still standing by her side, just hoping they'd be found
Could they see the fences properly in the light so weak and thin?
Keep searching, go on looking, but where do I begin?

A Little Indulgence

Then standing by the trailer, with the fog still swirling round
I thought for just a moment I heard that gorgeous sound
When mares nicker to their foals to keep them so close by
It's such a sweet contented call, the volume's never high.

That's why I hadn't realised that all this time I'd been away
They were both there close behind, as if a game to play
And then you feel that wondrous feeling that sends shivers up your spine
The grey mare's breath upon my neck, I turned, her eyes met mine.

She put her muzzle in my hand, so soft and warm and gentle
And while we sat there talking and getting sentimental
The little foal was trotting round on legs both thin and long
How could such a scrawny animal grow up so big and strong?

I fed them as I have done to so many of their kind
A better pair of animals would be rather hard to find
We sat and talked the three of us, then walked and talked some more
You reckon they don't understand, I know they do for sure.

I love to talk to animals, in fact I do it all the time
And yes they all talk back to me but in voice of different kind
Their languages are all complex, but not difficult to learn
And you need to talk to horses if their respect you hope to earn.

The problem is for most of us we need to learn the key
That magical ingredient, but it's there for all to see
They may make sounds that we can hear, but that's not what I mean
It's their eyes, their ears, their tail, their legs, even the way they lean.

Talking is important, and not what you say, but how
The inflection in your voice, the pitch, the high and low
More important is the listening, they have just so much to say
But this world in which we live, leaves so little time each day.

Why not try it, you'll be thankful, for a real friend you will make
You don't need any wherewithal, it's just time that you must take
I promise you you'll learn so much, and a humbler soul you'll be
If you just listen to our animals, it's such a simple plea.

The motor coughed then sprang to life, in a moment I was gone
Into the fog and up the hill, there's more work to be done
The little foal cried out to me as if to say 'Good on yer mate
Thanks for worrying about us—oh yeah, shut the paddock gate.'

I'll be back tomorrow and we'll do it all again
It'll probably be different, no two days the same
It doesn't really matter, because you know I'll find the time
You see, talking with God's animals is a privilege of mine.

To Rain

Cracks in the ground,
Hope for the sound,
Of the rain.

Grass on the hill,
Feels the comforting chill,
Of the rain.

Floral frescoes awake,
To the life-giving slake,
Of the rain.

Trees in a stand,
Raise their leafy hand,
To the rain.

Fencing wires,
Lift their rusty choirs,
To the rain.

Cattle and sheep,
Their rumps do keep,
To the rain.

Rivers and creeks,
Waited days and weeks,
For the rain.

And the cocky gives thanks,
For the water in his tanks,
Rain.

In your terracotta boxes and glassy office towers,
How you hate the interruption of those 'intermittent showers',
But you folks in the city should not curse the next big wet,
Australia is a barren land and needs all it can get.

When hydrogen and oxygen combine to make a blend,
That we poor men call water, we can at least pretend,
To understand the science that creates such wondrous good,
So when it damps the waiting soil'll grow us wholesome food.

This water falls as rain drops, and in rivers to the sea
Sweeps in organised confusion, like some cyclic recipe,
To be sucked up again as vapour from the blue Pacific's foam,
And condense once more as rain clouds on some distant foreign home.

Stop next time it's raining. Do you smell the sweetest scent?
For nature is rejoicing, precious gifts from heaven sent,
And if you listen ever closely, you may hear the silent sound,
Whispered prayers of the pastures and the sighing of the ground.

A poem written by our daughter Heidi
My Wonderland

Donkeys would not bray, and the horses could not neigh,
For the language that they speak was foreign and not known.
It was my little secret and it wasn't hard to keep it,
For the gift bestowed upon me would die out and cease to flare.

The trees would sprout ears and would cry with real tears,
And the earth would tremble hurtfully with every trodden step.
But the sky in all its wonder would never dare to thunder,
For its only thought was pleasing the mighty hands of God.

And with every blooming flower, you could hear them on the hour,
With murmurs of the joy of life and whatever it may bring.
So let us come together, and not be sad in all our tether,
Just take the hand of dreaming and lend an ear to hear it sing.

A poem written by my wife Janine
Life

When you are young everything seems just great,
Why, every day, you are tempting of fate,
The smell of the air and the rain and the flowers,
The birds in the trees that sing on for hours.

Life seems everlasting with no fears at all,
Then suddenly one day you have grown tall,
For the things in your youth that you nurtured and treasured,
Don't even seem to weigh up these days and be measured.

But one thing's for certain, like perennial grass,
Life will go on even after we've passed
To another world somewhere and life will regress
To the beauty we saw in a childhood so fresh.

If wishes were horses then beggars would ride,
And I do hope my horse in the next world abides.

ALSO AVAILABLE FROM PAN MACMILLAN

Dr Harry Cooper
Anecdotes & Antidotes

Dr Harry Cooper, Australia's favourite vet and much-loved star of 'Harry's Practice', has a lifetime's worth of stories to tell about his experiences with animals and their owners.

From hilarious accounts of dysfunctional birds and cunning canines, to moving tales of the loss of childhood pets, *Anecdotes & Antidotes* is a collection of these very special stories, told with Dr Harry's trademark warmth and humour.

In the tradition of *All Creatures Great and Small*, *Anecdotes & Antidotes* will enthral not only animal lovers, but anyone who enjoys a good yarn.